IMAGES
of America

Champion, Great Bend, and Deferiet

I0807675

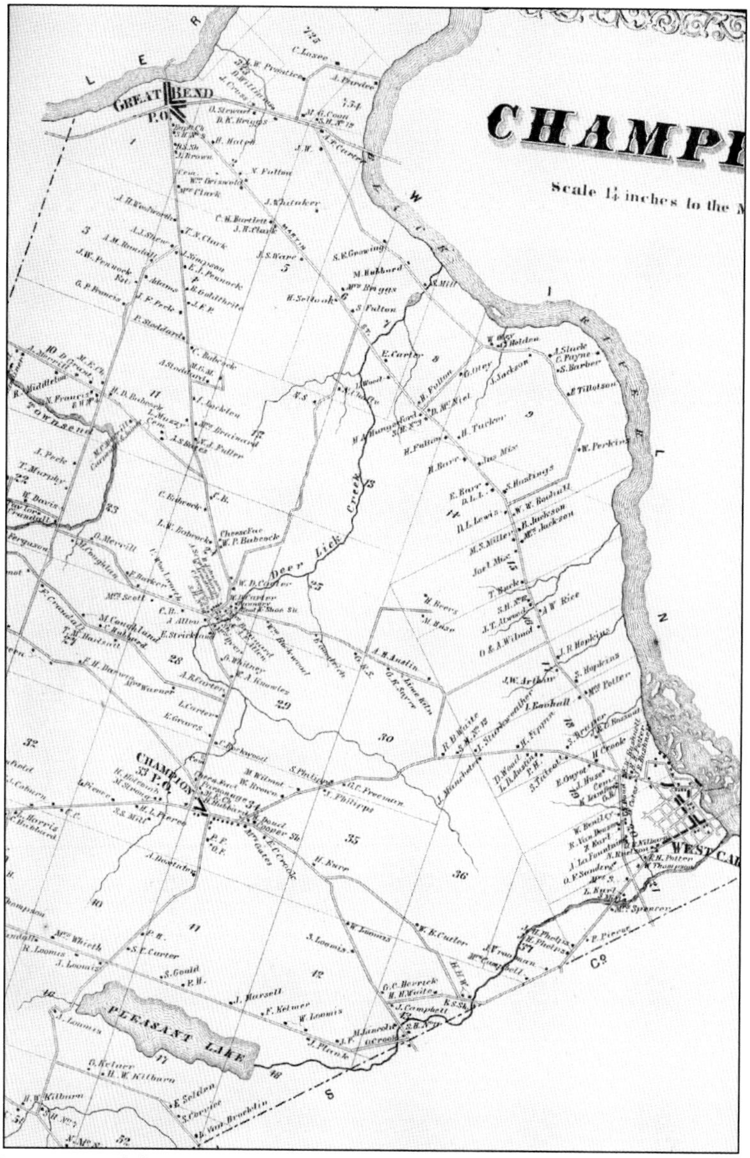

This 1864 Beers map of the town of Champion clearly shows Champion and Great Bend. The road going east from Great Bend crosses the Black River in the spot where Deferiet would soon be established. (Authors' collection.)

On the Cover: This photograph shows the 1952 Old Home Day Parade in Champion. Additional information can be found on page 38. (Brian Sech.)

IMAGES
of America

CHAMPION, GREAT BEND, AND DEFERIET

Lynn M. Thornton and Janet M. Zando

ARCADIA
PUBLISHING

Copyright © 2012 by Lynn M. Thornton and Janet M. Zando
ISBN 978-0-7385-7674-9

Published by Arcadia Publishing
Charleston, South Carolina

Printed in the United States of America

Library of Congress Control Number: 2011934177

For all general information, please contact Arcadia Publishing:
Telephone 843-853-2070
Fax 843-853-0044
E-mail sales@arcadiapublishing.com
For customer service and orders:
Toll-Free 1-888-313-2665

Visit us on the Internet at www.arcadiapublishing.com

To Jack, who made this possible
Thank you

—Lynn

To Marco and Guistina Zandomenego, who left their Italy for a better life, and to my family for their love and continued support
Thank you

—Janet

CONTENTS

Acknowledgments

The three villages that are profiled are different in many ways, but they are alike in the ways that count. People working, worshiping, relaxing, and having fun together make up the bulk of those we came across. We need to thank many people and organizations for their help with information and photographs; all have proven invaluable to research for this book. These include Laura Prievo and the records of the Heritage Room at the Carthage Free Library, and Suzanne Wiley for the wealth of materials she amassed during her tenure as Town of Champion and Village of Deferiet historian. Bonnie Schafer of the Jefferson County Historical Society provided information along the way, as have the archives of the *Carthage Republican Tribune*. Also providing help were Dr. Timothy Abel and his wife, Teal, who researched and gave editorial help, and James Powell, who provided indispensable technical help in scanning innumerable photographs. A number of individuals have generously loaned materials, especially photographs—among them Jim Redmond (who contributed the Helen Stott Collection), Joanna Sisson Emerson, Charles Clark of Adams, Mary Bach, the *Watertown Daily Times* (which allowed the use of David Lane photographs and the October 30, 1901, supplement), *Rats, Scabs and Robber Barons* by R. Joseph Gilbin, and 4 River Valleys Historical Society (which provided information and photographs), the John Peck families, John Sech and his son Brian, Carol Vargulick, Marcia Bears Bridge, Francis Burke, Barbara Monnat Burns, James Cassoni Jr., Angie Cassoni Cronk, Deferiet Fire Department, Deferiet Senior Citizens, Patricia Yuhas Kempney, Michael and Doreen Miterko, Edward and Norma Mullen, Margaret Murray, Edward Nabewaniec, Marie Adams Pais, Thomas Piche, Sonja Siedlecki Pierce, Stephen Powell, Stella Woycik Rigabar, Vincent Schneider, Dorrie Ward Snyder, Richard Staab, Dennis Turpin, Deferiet Archives, Monica Miterko Vincent, and the Zando family. To all the people in the community who offered suggestions, stories, and encouragement, thank you.

The following is a key to photograph credits: Charles Clark Collection (CCC), Jefferson County Historical Society (JCHS), Sisson Emerson Collection (SEC), Carthage Republican Tribune (CRT), and *History of Jefferson County* by L. H. Everts (Everts). All other photographs are credited as indicated or are courtesy of the authors.

INTRODUCTION

People move into new territories for a variety of reasons: land, a new life, adventure, space to grow, or material gain. One or more of these reasons motivated the men and women who settled Champion in the 18th and 19th centuries. Settlers traditionally follow water or other natural valleys into new regions, and for these reasons, many early communities in this area were founded on the banks of the Black River.

The Martin brothers chose to settle on the great bend of the Black River, and the town took its name from this natural feature. Deferiet, while also on the Black River, was named for the town's earliest and most famous landowner, Baroness Jenika de Feriet. It later became a paper-milling town and has always been populated by immigrants searching for a better life. Champion, while having adequate water for households and farming, never had the swift-flowing streams or rivers that are necessary for the success of a mill. Therefore, founding settler Noadiah Hubbard relied on other enterprises in the early days of the community.

While exploring the history of these three communities that lie within a 15-mile-perimeter triangle (a significant distance when shank's mare was the primary form of transportation), the factors that shaped their development and destiny will be touched upon.

In 1797, Noadiah Hubbard followed the Black River to Long Falls along with Lemuel Storrs of Middletown, who had acquired Howard, or Town No. 4 of the Macomb Purchase. While exploring the unbroken wilderness, they came to an area where the town of Champion would eventually be settled. Storrs offered Hubbard 2,000 acres of land in any part of the township, wherever he chose, for the price of $1.50 an acre along with the agency of all Storrs's lands.

Faced with an incredible deal, Noadiah Hubbard accepted the offer and returned the next spring with several family members and friends. They began clearing land in the center of what would become the village of Champion, planted potatoes, built a cabin, and then returned to Herkimer, New York, for the winter. The following spring, Hubbard, another group of friends, and 15 heads of cattle followed the Black River as far as Turin, trekked cross-country, traveled through Whetstone Gulf, and over the Tug Hill to Champion.

They arrived to find that an advance party sent to tap the area's maple trees had managed to burn down the cabin, and Indians had removed the potatoes left through the winter that were intended to be used for seed and fodder for the cattle. Even though Lemuel Storrs went bankrupt and Hubbard lost a large part of his investment, he decided to stay and help lead Champion into the 19th century by establishing a settlement with a church, school, tavern, and an economy that attracted doctors, lawyers, and other professional men along with their families.

Noadiah Hubbard is primarily responsible for the large number of stone buildings in the area, having commissioned many of them. Hubbard himself owned two stone homes, a stone distillery, a store, and several stone barns. Asa Eggleston was his mason of choice and responsible for many of the limestone buildings in the community. Hubbard also built the church that stood atop the hill on the edge of town, which is currently the Village Green Park, and oversaw the structures's removal and rebuilding in the village center when the hill proved too cold and windy in winter.

Champion had once been contemplated as the possible administrative center of the county. However, the selection of Watertown as the county seat instead prompted Champion's end as a center of culture and genteel living, as many of the village's lawyers, doctors, and scholars picked up and moved to Watertown.

Among the earliest settlers in Great Bend were the Martin brothers—Capt. Joseph Martin, Harry, Samuel, Timothy, Mason, and Enos. They were in Great Bend prior to 1803 and settled on present Route 26, the road from Great Bend to Carthage that still bears the family name, the Martin Street Road. Other early settlers included James Colwell and Samuel Fulton. Great Bend is a hamlet in the extreme northern part of Champion on the Black River, and was so named in reference to the somewhat unnatural course of the stream at that particular point. The first bridge across the river was built in 1804, carried away by spring floods in 1807, and replaced with the old covered bridge, which burned in 1840. The river and its bridges and dams figure largely in the history of the village.

Early settlers also included Egbert Ten Eyck and Olney Pearce, to whom credit is given for having made the first improvements here. They laid the foundation for the hamlet by constructing a dam across the river, the work being done in 1806 by a Mr. Tubbs, who was also an early resident. A sawmill was built the same year and carried away by high water within the month, but replaced a short time later. Henry G. Gardner built the second mill. In 1809, a distillery was erected, and between 1815 and 1824, Watson and Gates and Charles E. Clark built other improvements and milling enterprises, making Great Bend a place of considerable importance even in its early history. On March 5, 1840, the village suffered a destructive fire; however, the businesses that burned were soon replaced with others that were more substantial and modern.

Among the hamlet's several prominent industries, perhaps the most important was the pulp and paper mill, later owned by Watertown Capital but nevertheless a significant contributor to local prosperity. Other establishments were Chauncey Clark[e]'s feed store, H.H. Clark's general store, and Bignall and Reynolds, general dealers.

The history of the Great Bend paper mill dates back to September 1868, when the Great Bend Paper Company was incorporated with a capital stock of $25,000 to manufacture straw wrapping papers and board. The incorporators and officers were president George W. Clark, Herman Burr of New York City, Lewis H. Mills of Great Bend, and secretary James Sterling of Sterlingville, New York. Clark and Mills married sisters of James Sterling, whose father was James Sterling Sr., a wealthy and influential man known as the "Iron Master of the North."

The Sterling and Clark families were instrumental in the financial and spiritual growth of Great Bend. It was James "Big Jim" Sterling's daughter Mary Bradford Sterling Clark who established Trinity Chapel in Great Bend. In recognition of her relentless efforts to give strength and Christian teaching to the area, she was made the first Episcopal deaconess in central New York on December 31, 1873.

In 1820, Baroness Jenika de Feriet (de Ferriet) purchased the land that eventually became Deferiet. One of the hundreds of French nobility who fled France during the revolution, she acquired land from James LeRay de Chaumont. On that property, de Feriet built a $20,000 mansion, which was completed in 1824. She called it the Hermitage, where she entertained guests including Joseph Bonaparte, Napoleon's brother, as if she were still living in France. De Feriet's dream of thriving communities built in the surrounding areas did not materialize; and, due to her unhappiness, ill health, and financial problems, she sold her mansion and left for her homeland on July 15, 1841. De Feriet died on May 6, 1843, in Versailles, France. In 1871, the Hermitage burned to the ground.

In 1899, the St. Regis Paper Company was founded on land that had originally been part of de Feriet's property. This new development was the last big mill to be built on the Black River between Carthage and Dexter. The prime movers of this business venture were George C. Sherman and David M. Anderson of the Sherman Paper Company, with mills in both Felts Mills and Carthage. The factory was designed for mass production and had three Fourdrinier machines for the manufacturing of newsprint. The developers of the paper mill had great foresight, as they built a company-owned village for their workers in only two years.

With new endeavors also came labor struggles. In 1915, a conflict developed between the owners of the mill and the unions as they both clashed for control. This two-year strike brought national attention because it was a struggle for the survival of unionism in the papermaking industry.

Through two world wars, the Depression, and many other financial ups and downs, the St. Regis Paper Company remained a major player in the papermaking industry throughout the world.

Just like the many immigrants who came to America for economic reasons, the St. Regis Paper Company found itself in financial difficulty because of a change in the global market for newsprint and paper. St. Regis Paper was sold to Champion International in 1984. After numerous changeovers, the former St. Regis Paper Company, established in Deferiet, closed its doors in 2004.

The town's fertile soil yielded an abundant crop from the start, but there were hurdles in realizing any profit from selling produce since it was difficult to transport the farmer's bounty to market. Therefore, one of the first concerns of the settlers was the construction of a road. An 1801 letter to the New York State Legislature describes, in their own words, the transportation need for farmers "who have emigrated from Connecticut, Massachusetts, Vermont, New Hampshire, and the eastern parts of this state, [and] have not only been subjected to the inconvenience of excessively bad roads, but have been and are still obliged to go around by the way of Rome to Utica, and through Boon's settlements, and Steuben, a distance of at least forty miles further than it would be in a direct line." They ask the legislature "to take this case into your consideration, and to appoint commissioners to lay out a road from Johnstown, in the nearest direction to the High Falls on Black River, and to grant out of a future lottery, a sum of money which shall be necessary to open a road, and make it passable, or in some other way grant relief, and they as in duty bound will ever pray, etc."

Noadiah Hubbard, Benjamin Pike Jr., Eli Church, Harrison Mosely, Timothy Townsend, Joel Mix, Samuel Foster, Abner White, Mathew Kemp, Bela Hubbard Jr., Elisha Jones, William Davis, and William Crowell signed the petition. Their efforts were successful; within a few years, the roads were built, postal delivery became a daily occurrence, and commerce flourished. The road benefitted all three settlements, but Champion and Great Bend had much traffic pass through them, so stagecoach stops were built in both villages.

One

CHAMPION
THE FIRST SETTLEMENT

In 1797, a consortium sold Township No. 4 of the Black River tract to Gen. Henry Champion of Colchester, Connecticut, and Col. Lemuel Storrs of Middletown, Connecticut. Under their ownership, settlement began in 1798, although pioneer Noadiah Hubbard had visited the region during the preceding year in company with Col. Storrs and Silas Stow (soon to be Judge Stow) and made an examination of the land for the purpose of future settlement.

Some sources differ and maintain that Hubbard made the trip with Joel Mix and a surveyor, and that together they rafted down the Black River to Long Falls (later Carthage) and staked out their lands in Champion. In any event, an agreement was made by which Hubbard became the owner of a considerable tract of land and also became an agent for the sale of other parcels. Col. Storrs failed to keep faith with his promises, and as the result, Hubbard was holding land under an uncertain title and was only confirmed in his possessions after some time, much anxiety, and considerable expense.

On March 14, 1800, the legislature passed an act creating the town of Champion from the older town of Mexico, and included within its boundaries the part of Denmark lying north of Deer River. In 1803, a section was also set off to Harrisburg. In accordance with the creating act, the first town meeting was held at the home of Joel Mix on April 1, 1800, at which time officers were elected. Noadiah Hubbard was selected supervisor of the town. Settlement was rapid, and for a time it looked as though Champion would become the county seat. This was not to be, however, and the selection of Watertown halted some of Champion's development.

Notwithstanding, Champion became a thriving community, with a potash factory, distillery, cheese factories, two general stores, three churches, a school, and numerous homes. There was an active militia that served under Capt. Noadiah Hubbard and Capt. John McNitt, who began training new recruits as early as 1810.

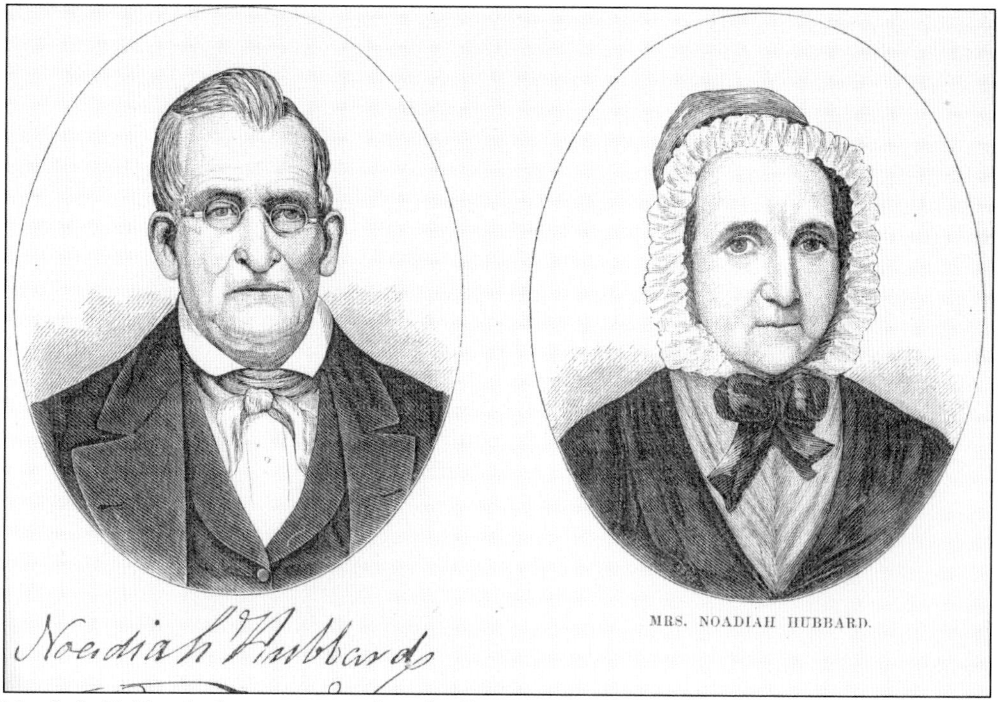

Noadiah Hubbard, the pioneer settler of Jefferson County, and his wife, Eunice, are pictured above. Hubbard first came to Champion in November 1797, and Eunice arrived in November 1799 with their three eldest sons. After traveling down the Black River from Steuben County, the family arrived at Long Falls, now Carthage, at noon on the second day. They unloaded the boat, assembled their wagon, and hitched up the oxen that had arrived by the overland route. Eunice then walked the four miles through the forest to Champion. They had 15 head of cattle that grazed in the woods and wintered well. The photograph below was taken looking up what is now Route 126. The general store is in the center of the photograph, and the building on the corner is the hotel. The ox is a typical animal that early settlers preferred to use in the fields, since oxen typically outworked horses. (Above, Everts; below, John Sech.)

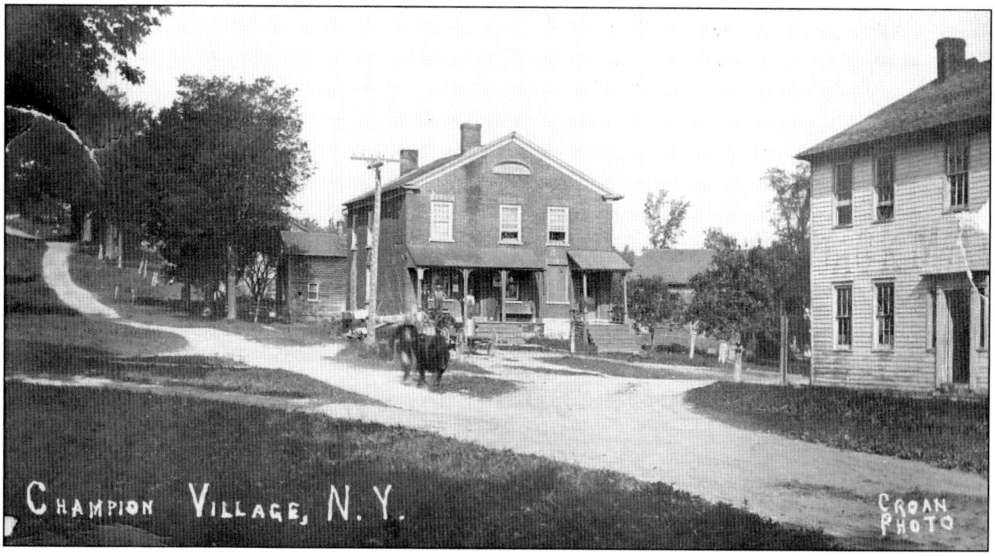

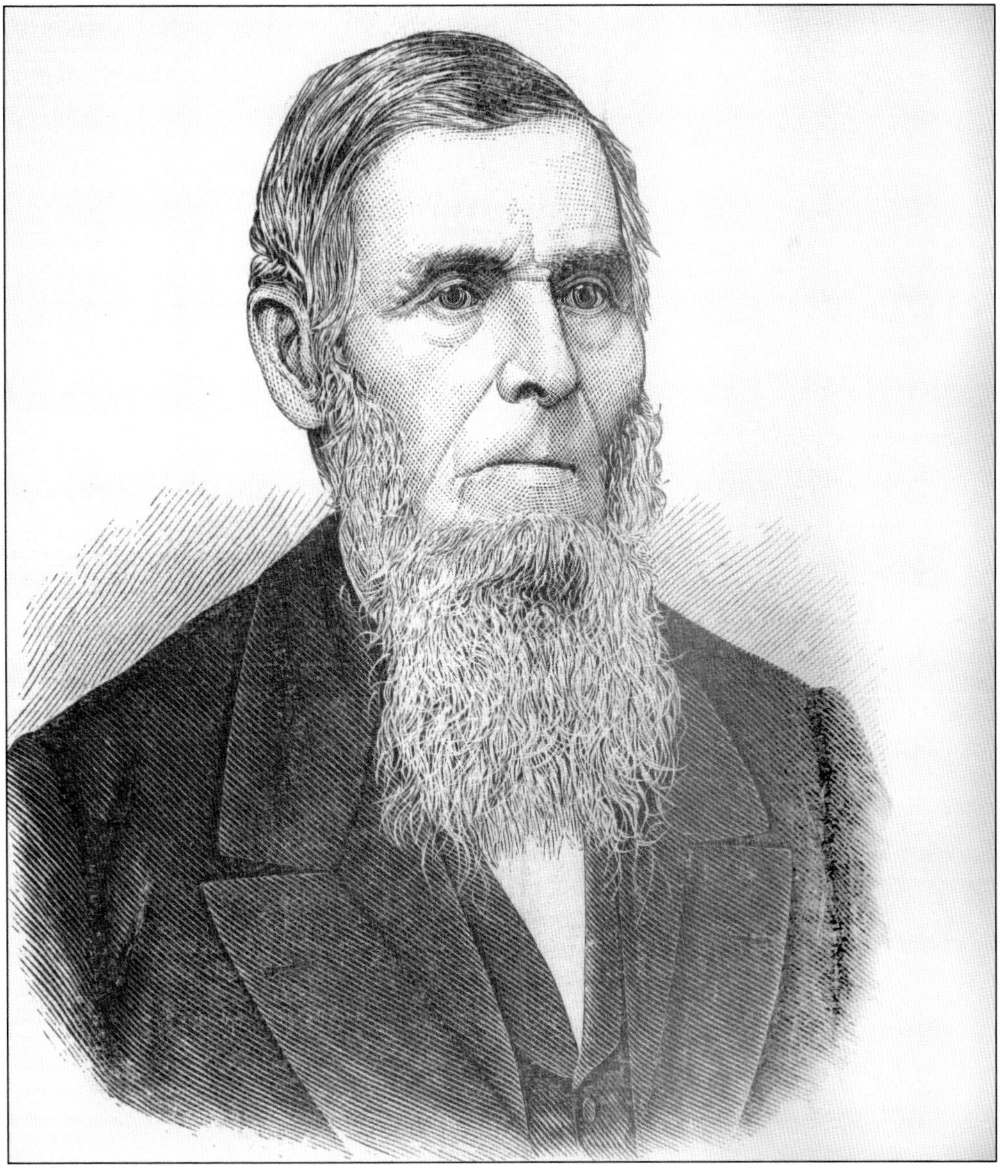

Hiram Hubbard, eldest son of Noadiah, was born in Steuben County in 1794. He was one of the three Hubbard sons to come on horseback to Champion in 1799. While still young, Hiram was sent to school in Herkimer. In 1812, a typhoid epidemic broke out in Champion and proved to be fatal. Many heads of families died, including Hiram's uncle Steven Hubbard, manager of the mercantile firm N&S Hubbard. Upon Steven's death, it became necessary for Noadiah to recruit Hiram, and at the age of 17, he took over the operation of the store. According to accounts, the firm conducted a large and successful business. Hiram and his father continued to run a distillery and potash factory in connection with a dry goods store. They also owned and operated a grist- and sawmill in Deer River and ran a dry goods store there as well. Hiram married Charille Matilda Sherwood, eldest daughter of Dr. Jonathan Sherwood of Champion, in 1823. In 1836, Hiram retired and lived in a stone mansion, where he brought his bride. They celebrated at least 54 years of marriage. (Everts.)

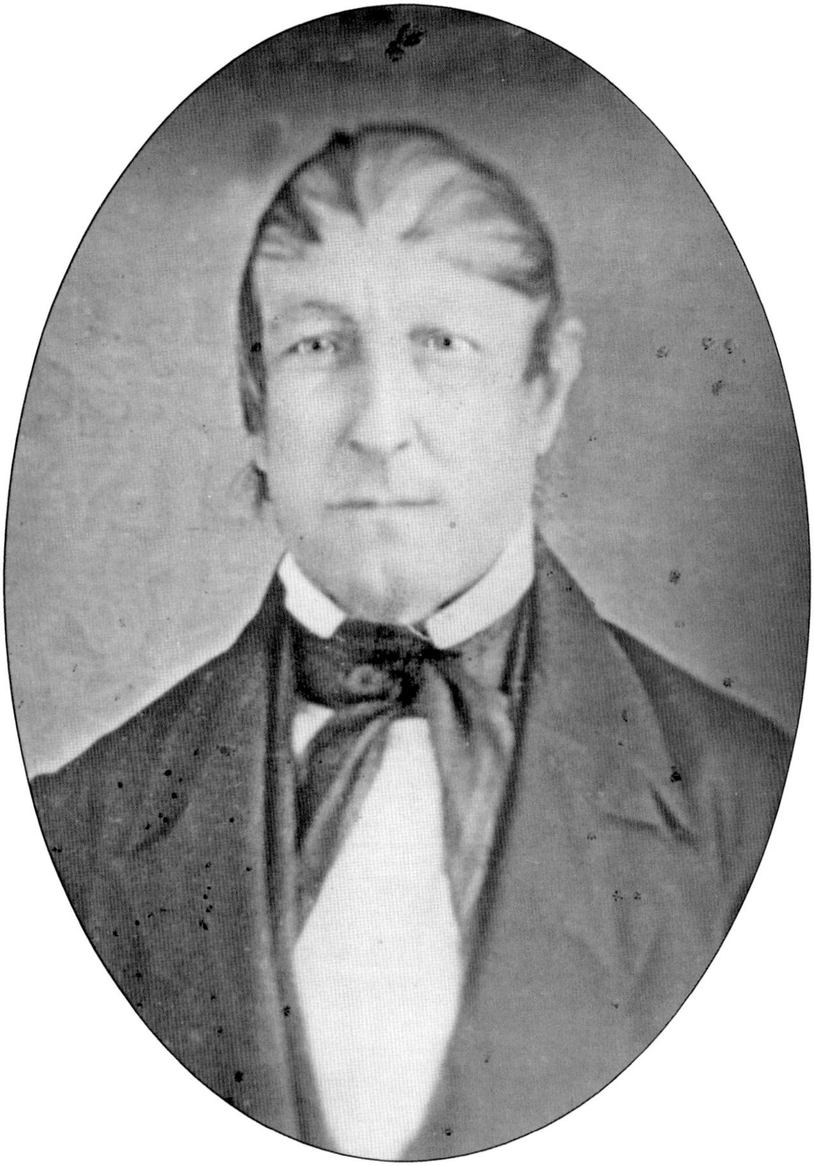

Nathaniel Dutton, Champion's first minister, was born in Hartford, Vermont, on September 28, 1779. In 1802, he graduated from Dartmouth College and was ordained in Westfield, Massachusetts, on March 5, 1805. Having been engaged by the Hampshire Missionary Society to make a tour of the Black River country, he started out on horseback on April 30, 1806. Averaging 30 miles a day over bad roads, Dutton reached Utica a week later. On May 21, 1807, he was installed in the church at Champion, where he preached with few intervals until his death on September 9, 1852. During his tenure, he assisted in forming churches in Denmark, Le Ray, Alexandria, West Carthage, Philadelphia, and other towns. On February 15, 1808, he married Sally Ward, Eunice Hubbard's sister, from Middletown, Connecticut. During his first 25 years in Champion, there seldom was a time when there were not students under his care, for formal education was not common at the time. During one winter, his pupils numbered 14, some of whom were boarders with the family. Grammar, Latin, Greek, and mathematics—such as algebra, geometry, and calculus—were taught. (JCHS.)

Two of Noadiah Hubbard's daughters became the wives of Hon. Robert Lansing of Watertown. Maria was his first wife; and Cornelia, Lansing's second wife, is credited with starting the Watertown Home for Destitute and Friendless Orphans and Children in 1859. Another daughter, Mary Ann, became the wife of Hon. George C. Sherman, a distinguished lawyer. Parnell Hubbard, a lady of considerable literary ability, resided in Watertown. The youngest of Hubbard's daughters, Parnell never married, but wrote extensive histories of the family and early settlement. These can be found in the archives of the Jefferson County Historical Society. Below, Hubbard women are pictured representing four generations: (1) Francis Hubbard Ives, mother of (2) Nellie Brower, mother of (3) Elsie Patterson, mother of (4) Dorothy Patterson Rogers. Dorothy was the mother of Peter and Linda Rogers, who donated the Hiram Hubbard Homestead to the 4 River Valleys Historical Society. (Right, JCHS.)

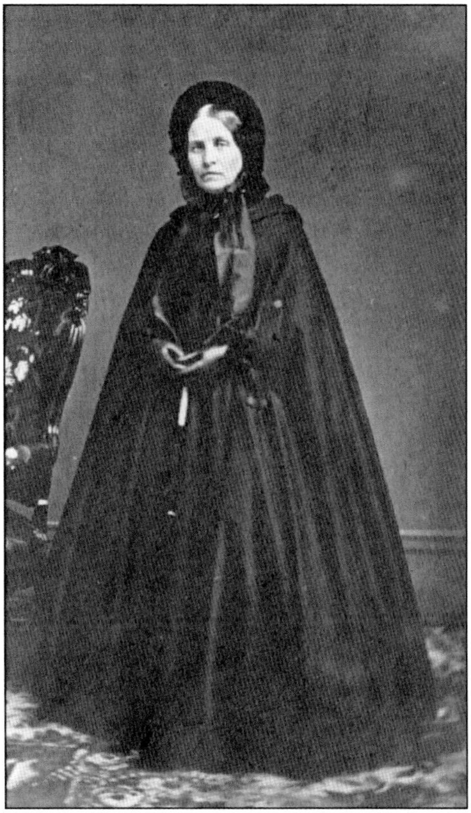

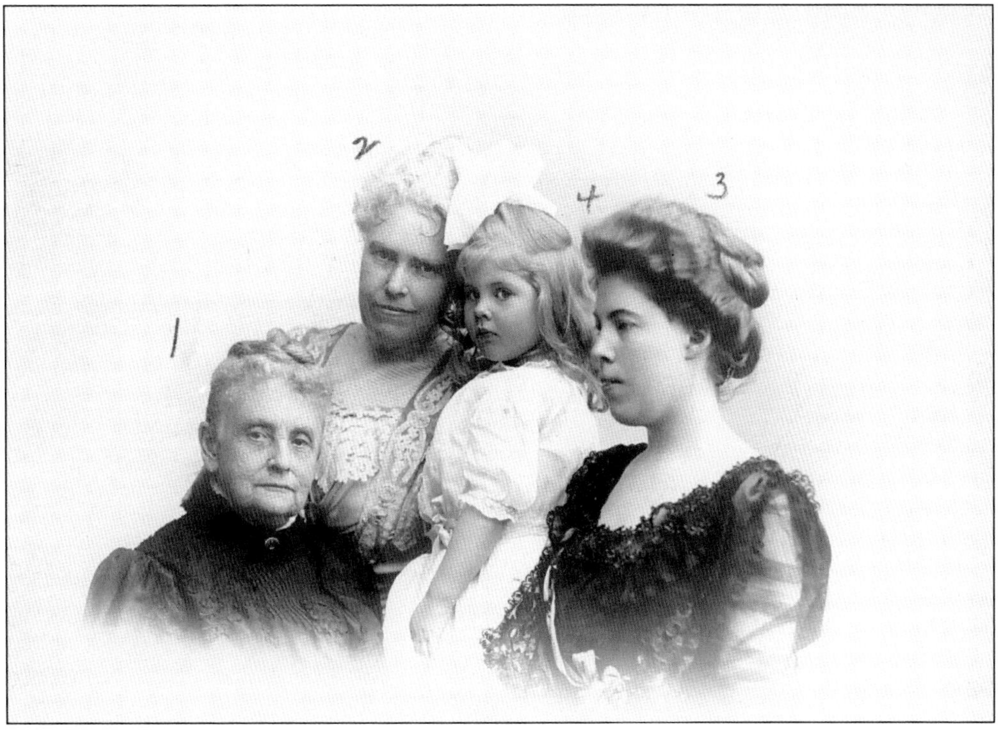

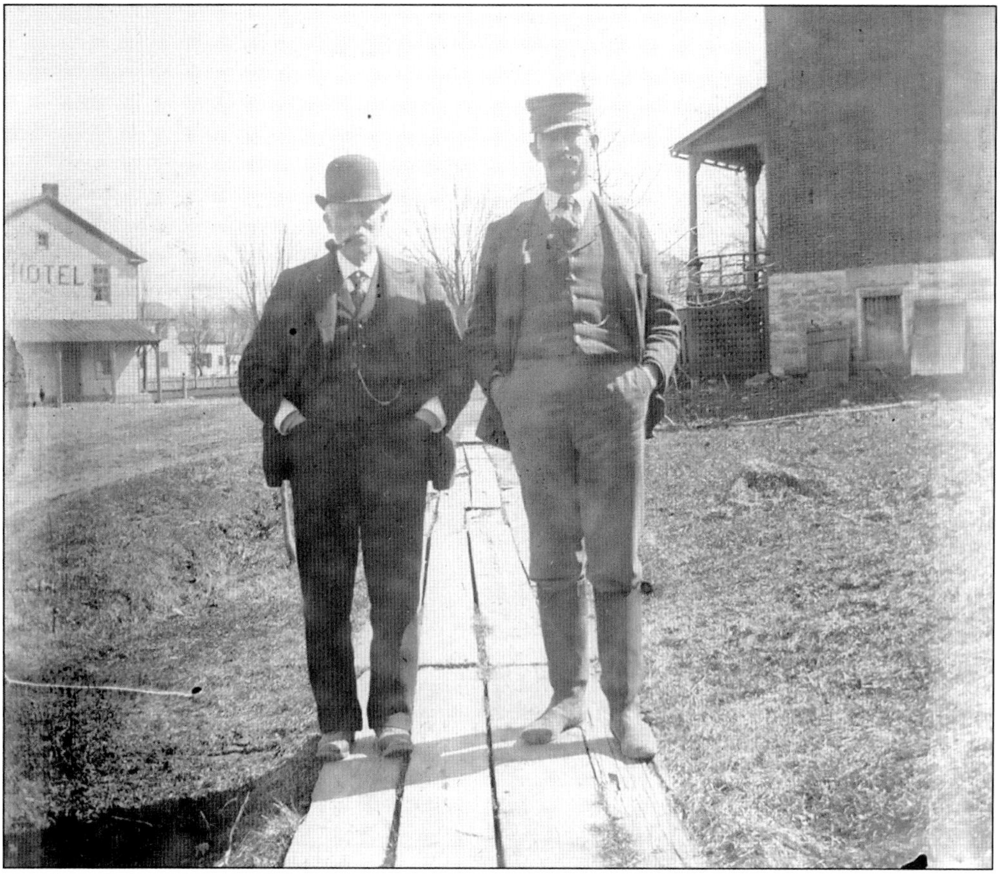

Unidentified gentlemen of the village, both obviously successful businessmen, are shown strolling on the plank walkway between the brick store and the Grange on Church Street. Behind them is the hotel run by Henry Ingram, pictured below.

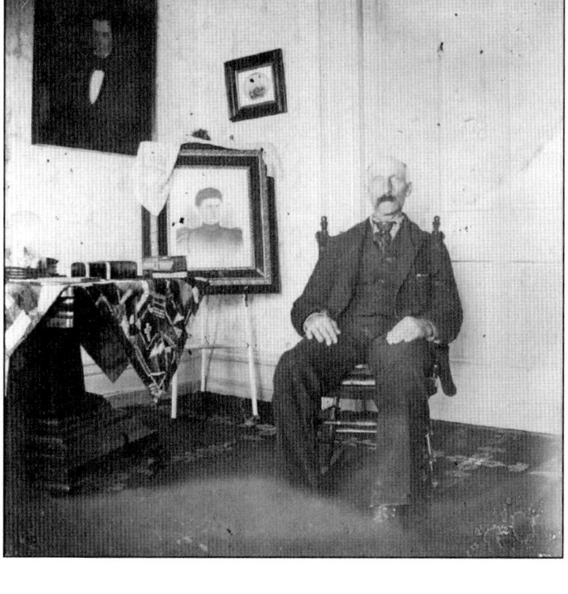

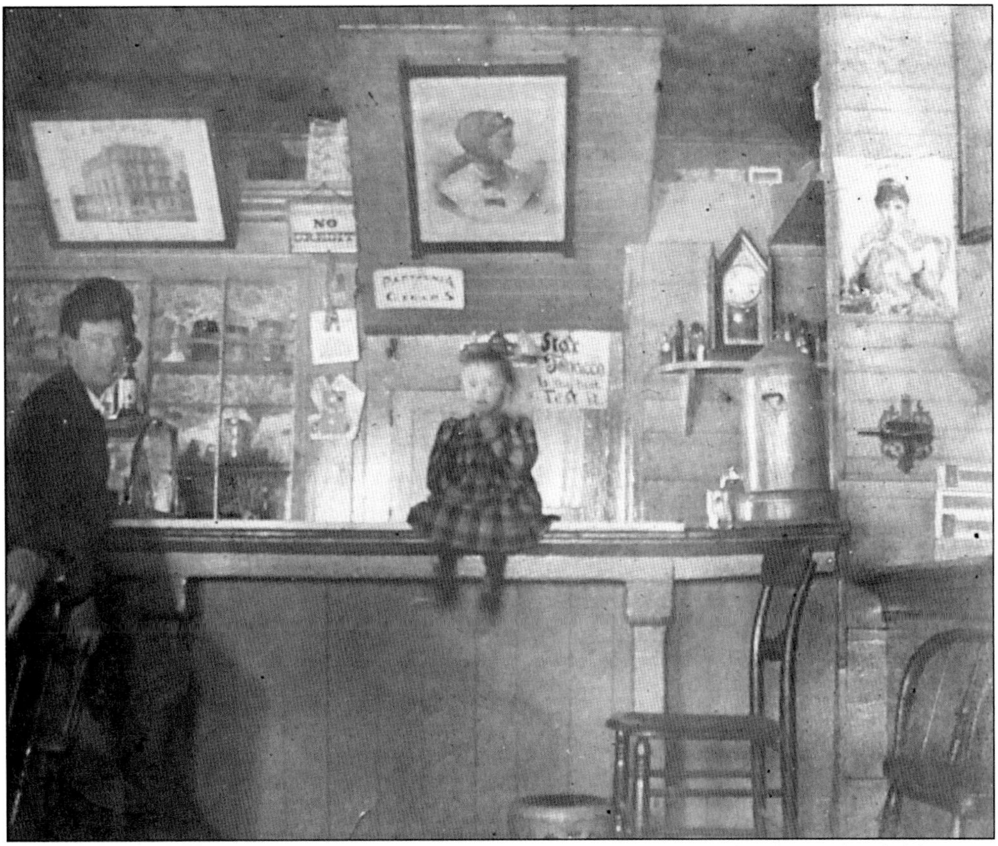

These two photographs show the interior of the Champion Hotel and its bar. The child sitting on the bar is identified as Maria Shedd, whose family ran the brick store across the street. The only two men identified in the photograph below are Charles Shedd (first row, center) and Henry Ingram (far left).

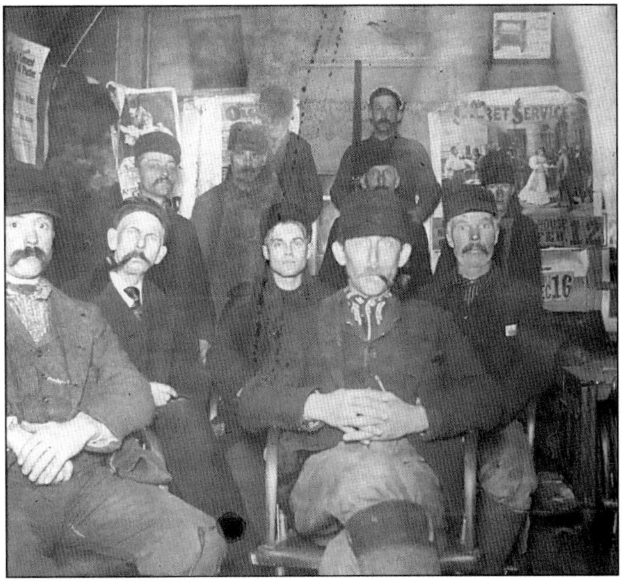

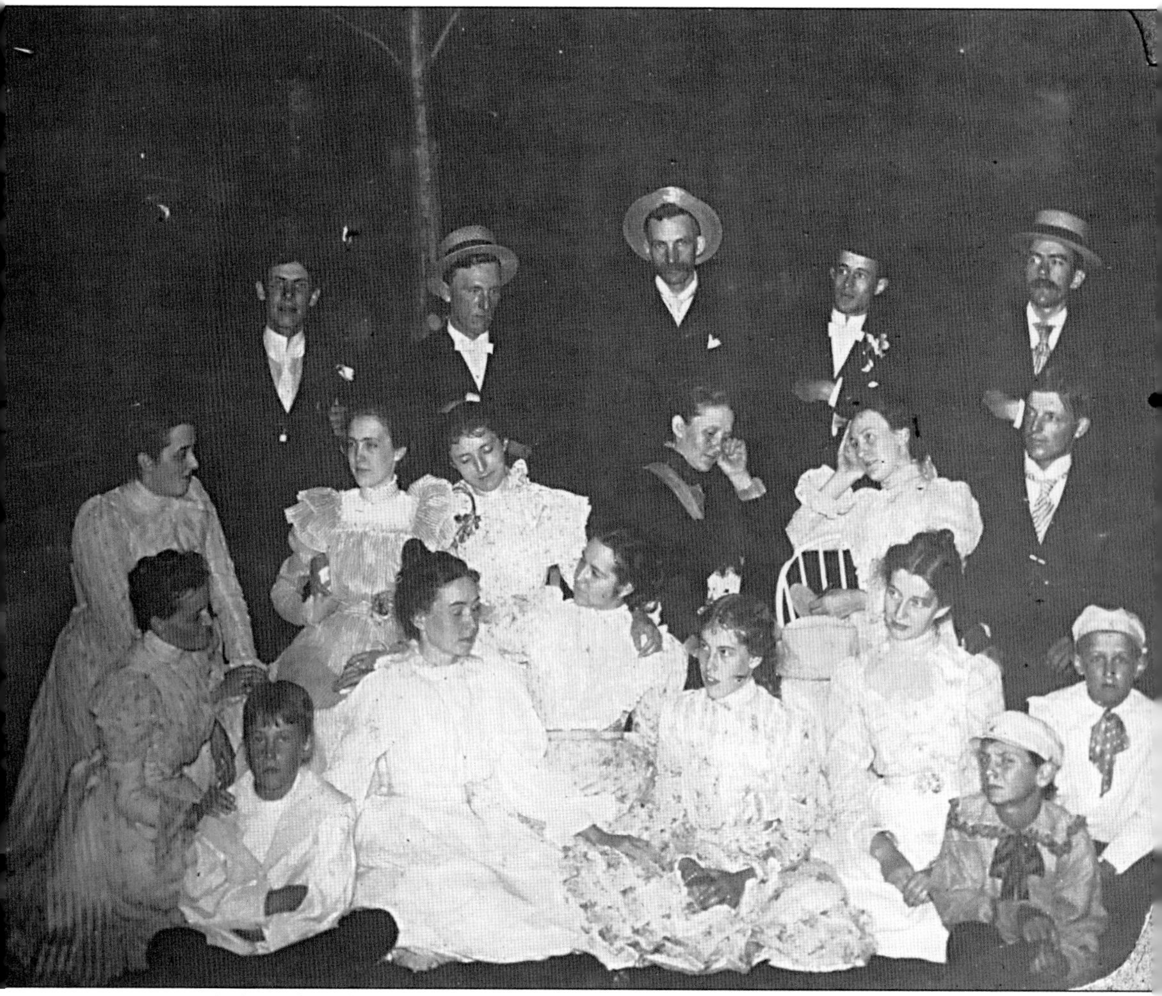

Young people from the Champion area have gathered for a group photograph around 1900. Some are related—like the Knowles, Brower, and Motts families, with Hubbard being the common connection. Others—like the Harris family from Bach Road, and the Graves family, who lived on present Route 47—reside on farms on the outskirts of the community. Some of the Hubbard relatives lived in New York City and Connecticut but returned to the homestead for summers. Pictured, from left to right, are (first row) Georgia Knowles, Cora Harris, Lina Pierce, Mert Knowles, and Earl Royal Crook; Front Row: Fritz Bower, Elsie Bower, and Townsend Raplee; (second row) Fanny Ives, Cora Holcomb, Libbie Hill, Carrie Babcock, and Grace Harris; (third row) Frank Graves, Will Harris, Jay Colvin, Rob Mott, and Charles Graves.

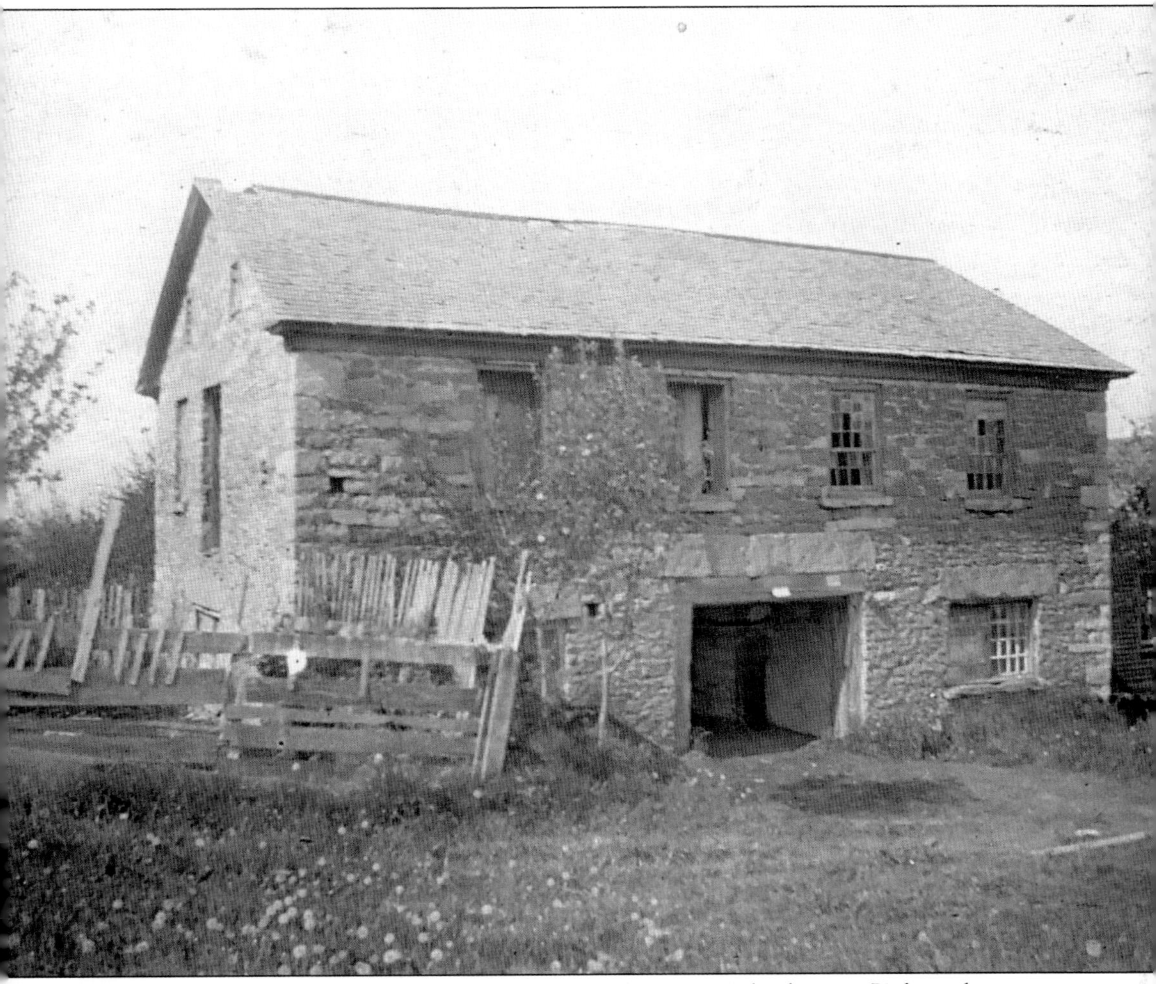

By 1810, the town of Champion contained 53 frame houses, 157 log houses, 79 frame barns, two distilleries, nine schoolhouses, one clothiers works, one carding machine, four gristmills, eight sawmills, one brewery, 210 families, and 1,471 inhabitants. This stone barn near Champion was built before 1820, possibly by Joel Hubbard. According to Solon Massey's *Links in the Chain*, Joel came with his brothers from Steuben to Champion in 1799 and soon took up a wilderness farm and erected a log hut. He married Mercy Austin in 1797. Joel and Mercy were the parents of 13 children, four of whom died in infancy. The remaining nine lived to an advanced age. Their names were Edward, Clement, Joel A., Charles, Wealthy, Phoebe, Julia Ann, Laura, and Cherille. With the exception of Cherille, all married early in life, settled in Champion, and raised families.

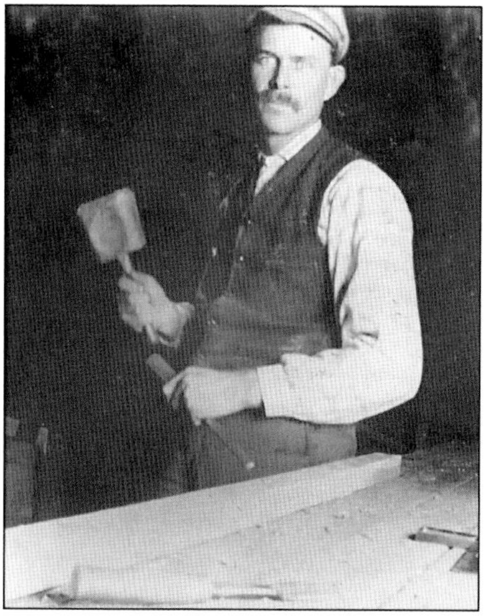

Charlie Russell (left) and his brother Savilion (below), sons of Allen and Lorinda Russell, were born in the mid-1800s and spent most of their lives in Champion. The family owned the Asa Gates stone house on Route 126 at the entrance to the village. Charlie, the younger brother, was a woodworker, and Savilion was a blacksmith; both had skilled jobs much in demand. With forge and anvil, hammer and tongs, a blacksmith made agricultural tools for farmers and iron rims for wheelwrights. He also repaired many iron objects used by residents. In an era when most structures were built from wood, few workmen were more useful than the carpenter and joiner. These men cut and joined timber and board into sturdy wooden homes and shops.

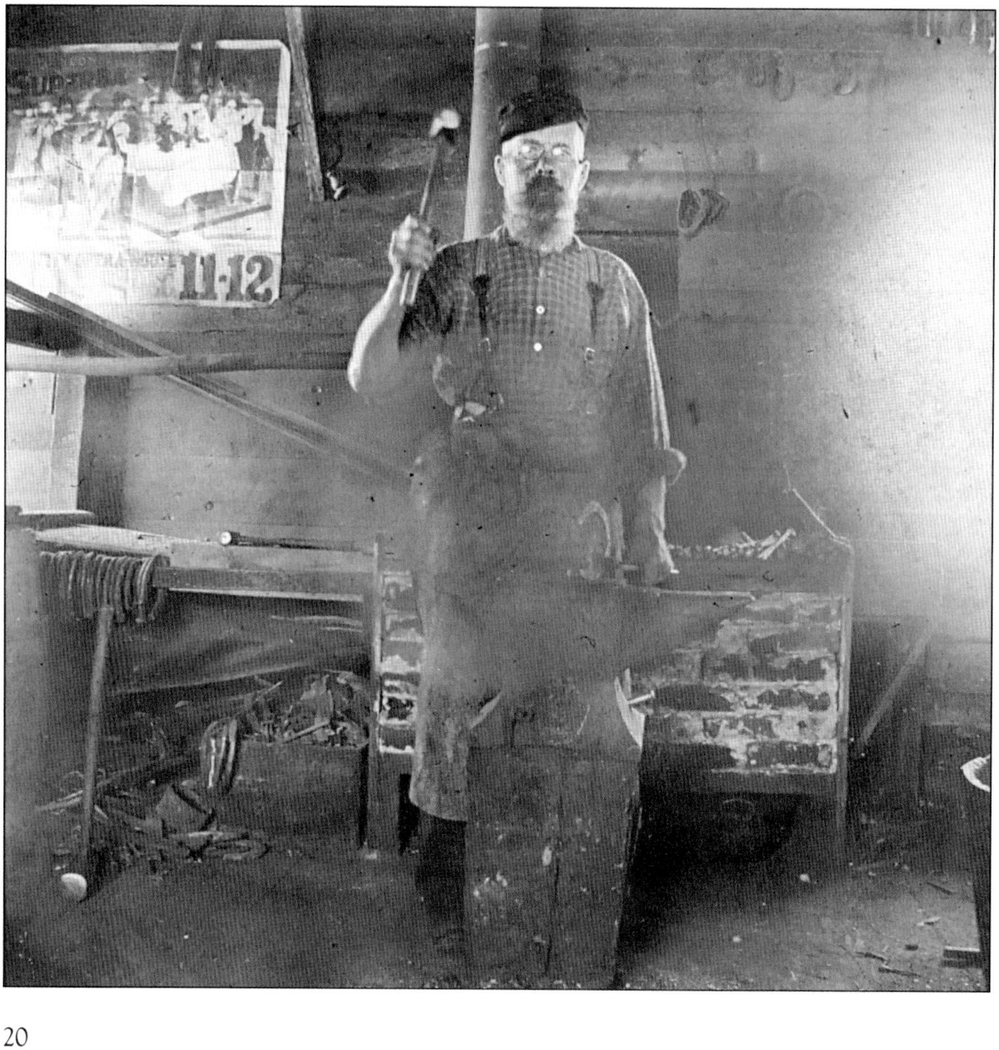

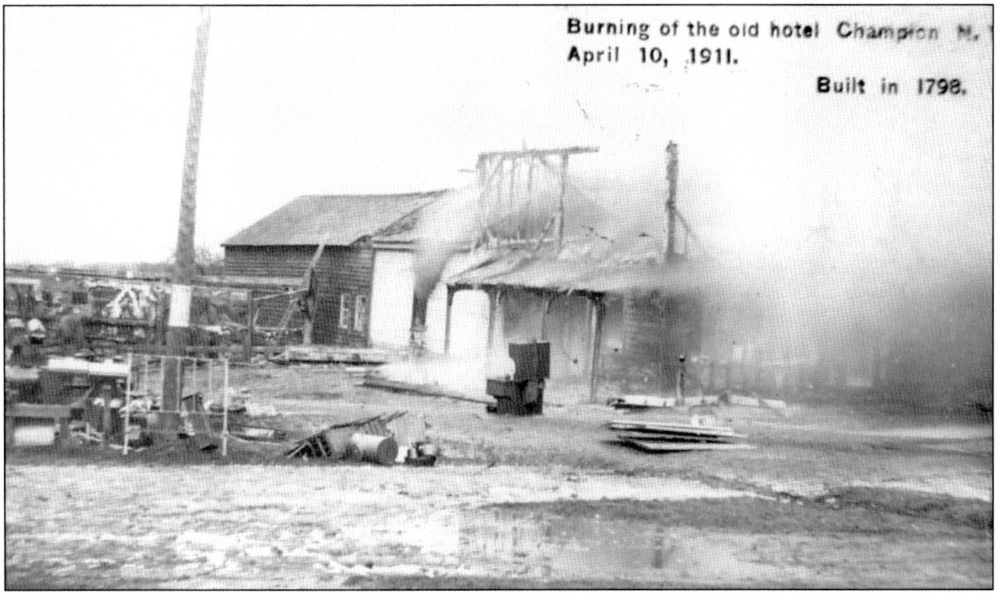

The old stage line from Utica to Sackets Harbor lay through Champion, and it was the only mode of public conveyance. Regular stage service by a two-horse coach began around 1812. The stage always stopped at Champion village to change its horses, probably at the tavern built by Noadiah Hubbard. He also built an inn and a general store; a stone doorstep dated August 1815 was used as one of the steps to his 1820 home. The hotel in this picture must have been constructed around 1803, as Noadiah Hubbard himself was living in a log cabin until 1801, when he built his first frame house (shown below). In his journals, he does describe giving shelter in his home (as required by frontier etiquette) to numerous travelers: "very often my floors were strewn with human beings as thick as they could lie."

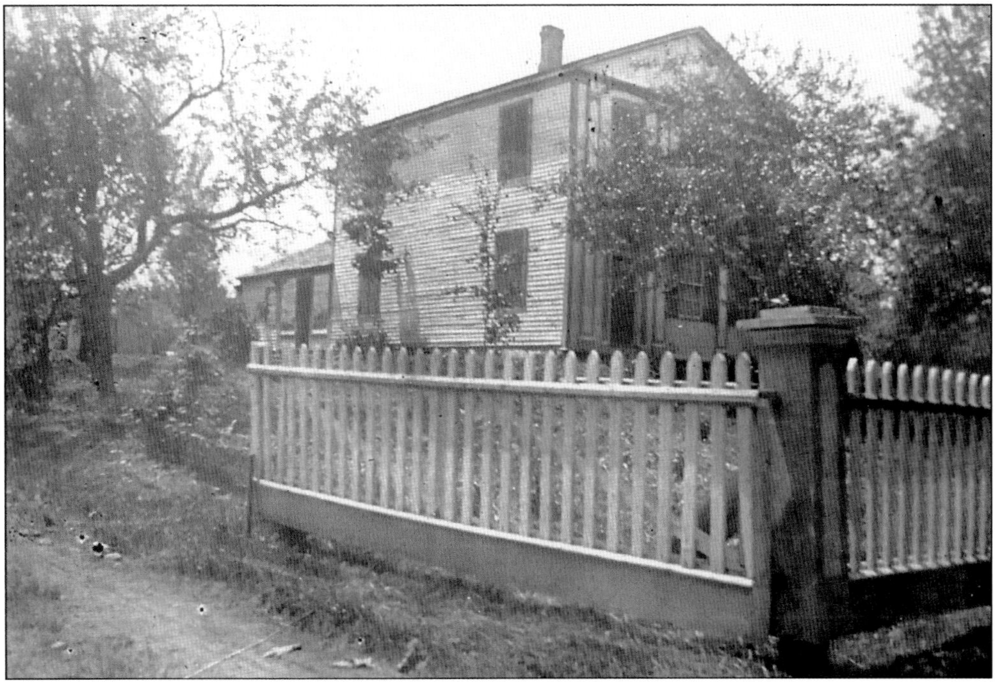

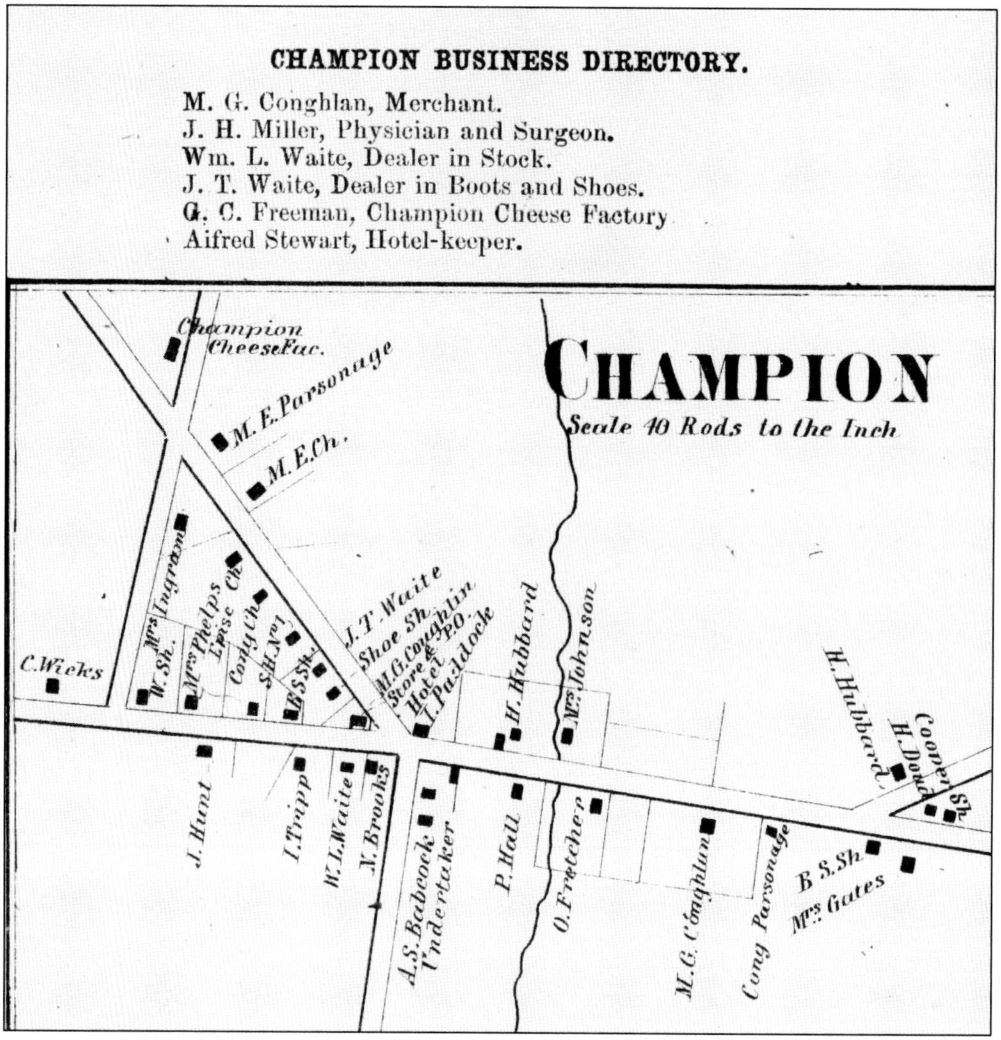

CHAMPION BUSINESS DIRECTORY.

M. G. Conghlan, Merchant.
J. H. Miller, Physician and Surgeon.
Wm. L. Waite, Dealer in Stock.
J. T. Waite, Dealer in Boots and Shoes.
G. C. Freeman, Champion Cheese Factory
Aifred Stewart, Hotel-keeper.

Stone's 1864 atlas shows the village of Champion, and also names the principal inhabitants and some of the businesses.

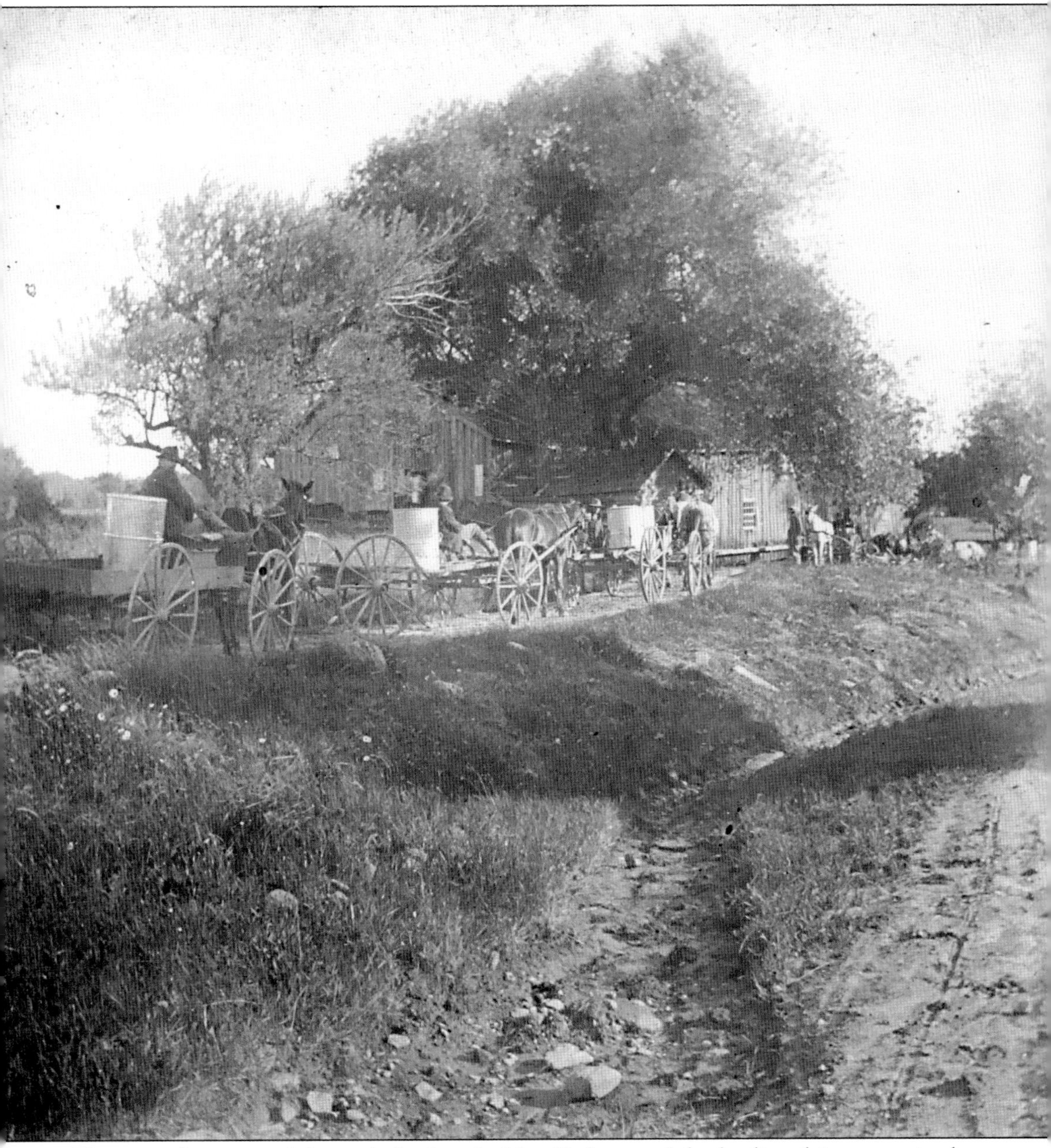

The manufacturing of cheese helped make New York one of the leading dairy states in the nation. Originally, all cheese was made on farms. The manufacturing of cheese was taken out of the home when, in 1851, Jesse Williams opened the first cheese factory in Oneida County, New York. The Champion Cheese Factory was one of three located in Champion village in 1864, the other two being the Babcock Factory and the Hadsall Factory. This photograph shows wagons on the way to the factory. The distance between factories was determined by the distance a man could drive a horse or milk wagon, which carried his milk in a large can, before breakfast. In this era, cheese factories, along with schools and churches, served as social institutions in the neighborhood. On the walls of the cheese factory, notices were posted for local sales, auctions, meetings, and social activities.

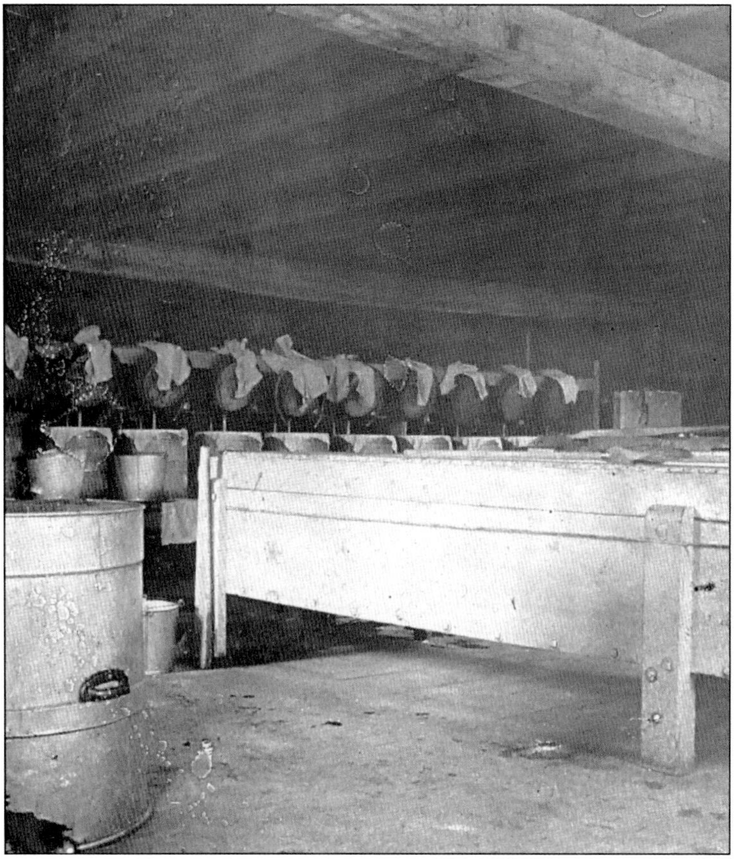

The photograph on the left shows the milk vats at the Champion Cheese Factory where lactic acid, color, and rennet or pepsin were added. The latter coagulated the milk into firm jelly-like curd in about 30 undisturbed minutes. The curd was then cut, stirred slowly at 100 degrees, the whey (liquid) removed, the curd then stirred, cooled, salted, hooped, and pressed. The cheese was then cleaned, re-hooped, re-pressed, and then cured. The quality of the cheese depended much upon the cheese maker's knowledge and expertise. The men pictured below are stirring curd.

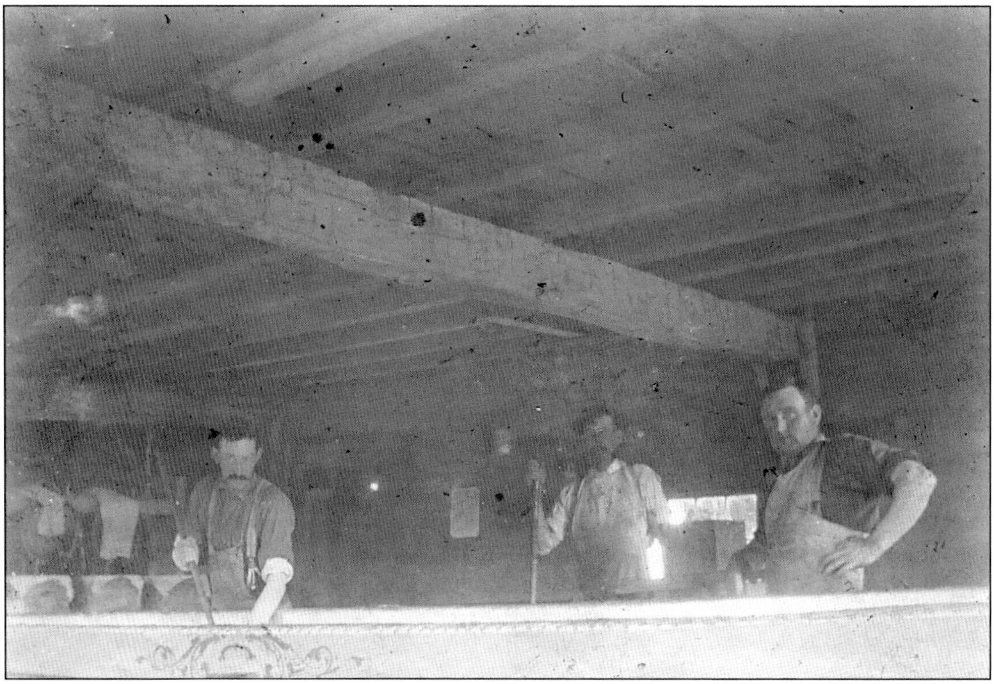

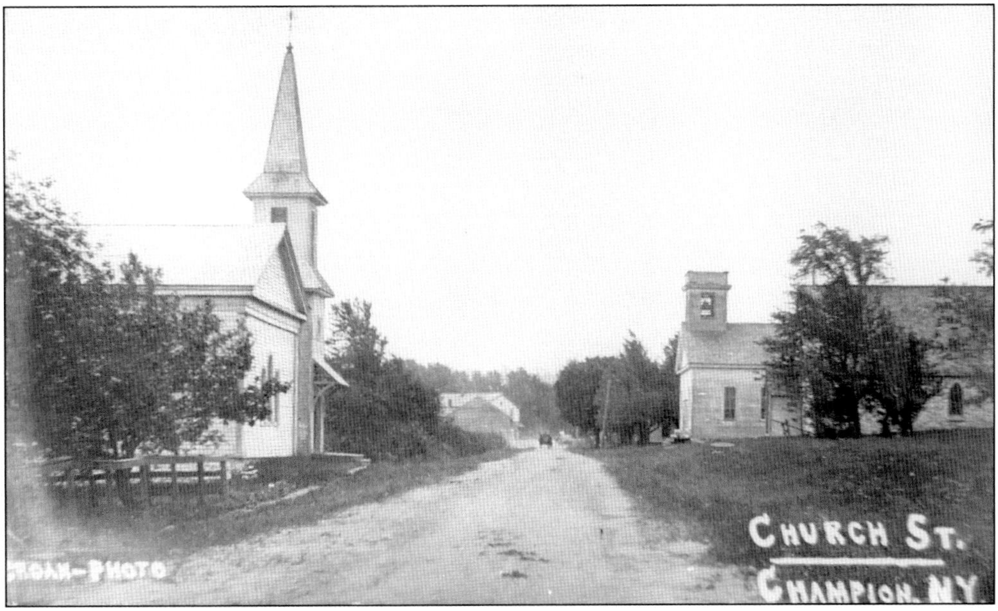

This view of Church Street looks toward the four corners intersection with Route 126, and the Methodist Episcopal church is seen on the left. The building on the right is the Congregational church, currently Grange No. 18. One can clearly see the bell in the steeple donated by Gen. Henry Champion. In the foreground is St. John's Episcopal Church. Below is a photograph of the Methodist Episcopal rectory, located just to the left of the church as it appears in the photograph above.

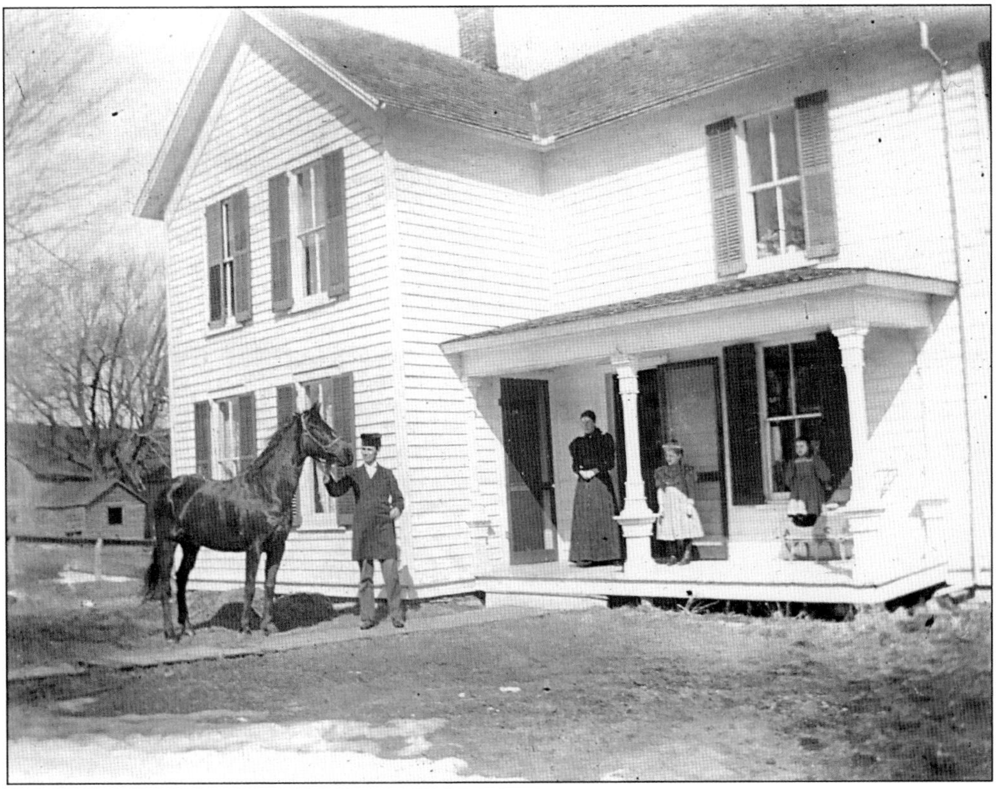

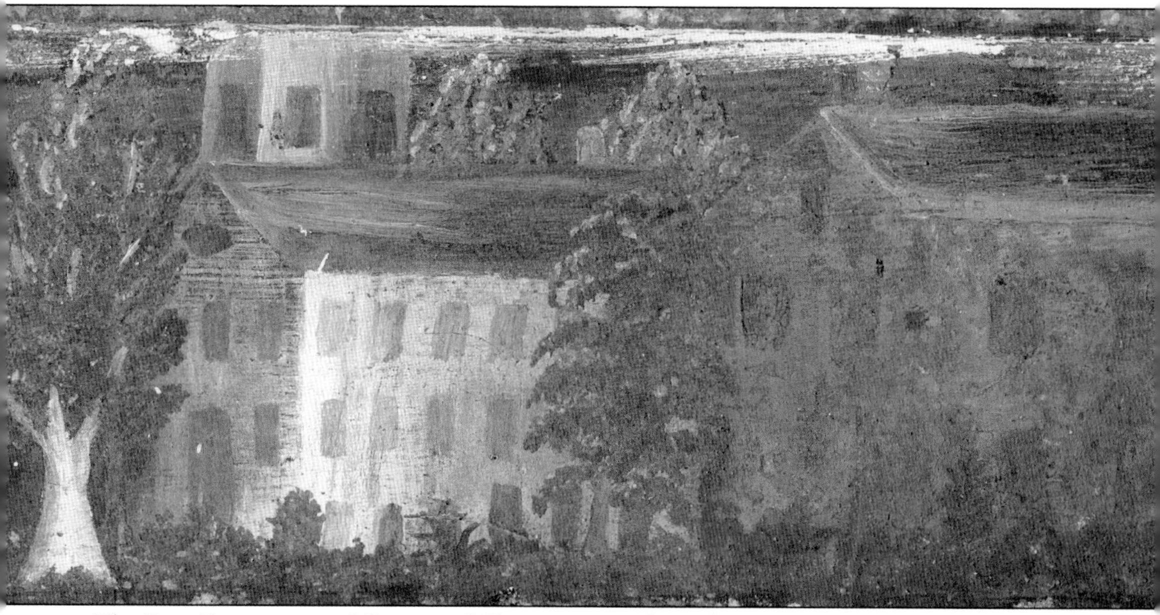

The First Congregational Society of Champion was formed on May 7, 1805. On the Fourth of July, 1807, landholders Gen. Henry Champion and Col. Lemuel Storrs gave the town two acres on the summit of a hill that overlooked the village for the site of a church and a public green. The location is currently Champion Village Green Park. Because of the War of 1812, which slowed building down, the church was not finished until 1816. It was the first church in Jefferson County, and Noadiah Hubbard was in charge of its construction. This church, with a bell donated by Gen. Champion, occupied the hilltop for many years. The wind in that spot, however, finally forced all of the buildings there to be relocated into the hamlet itself. The church was taken down, removed to the crossroads, rebuilt, and rededicated in 1841. Around 1910, the building became the property of the Champion Grange No. 18 and is still the home of an active local Grange. Pictured is a primitive painting of the church when it was still on the hilltop. (Bruce and Holly White Armstrong.)

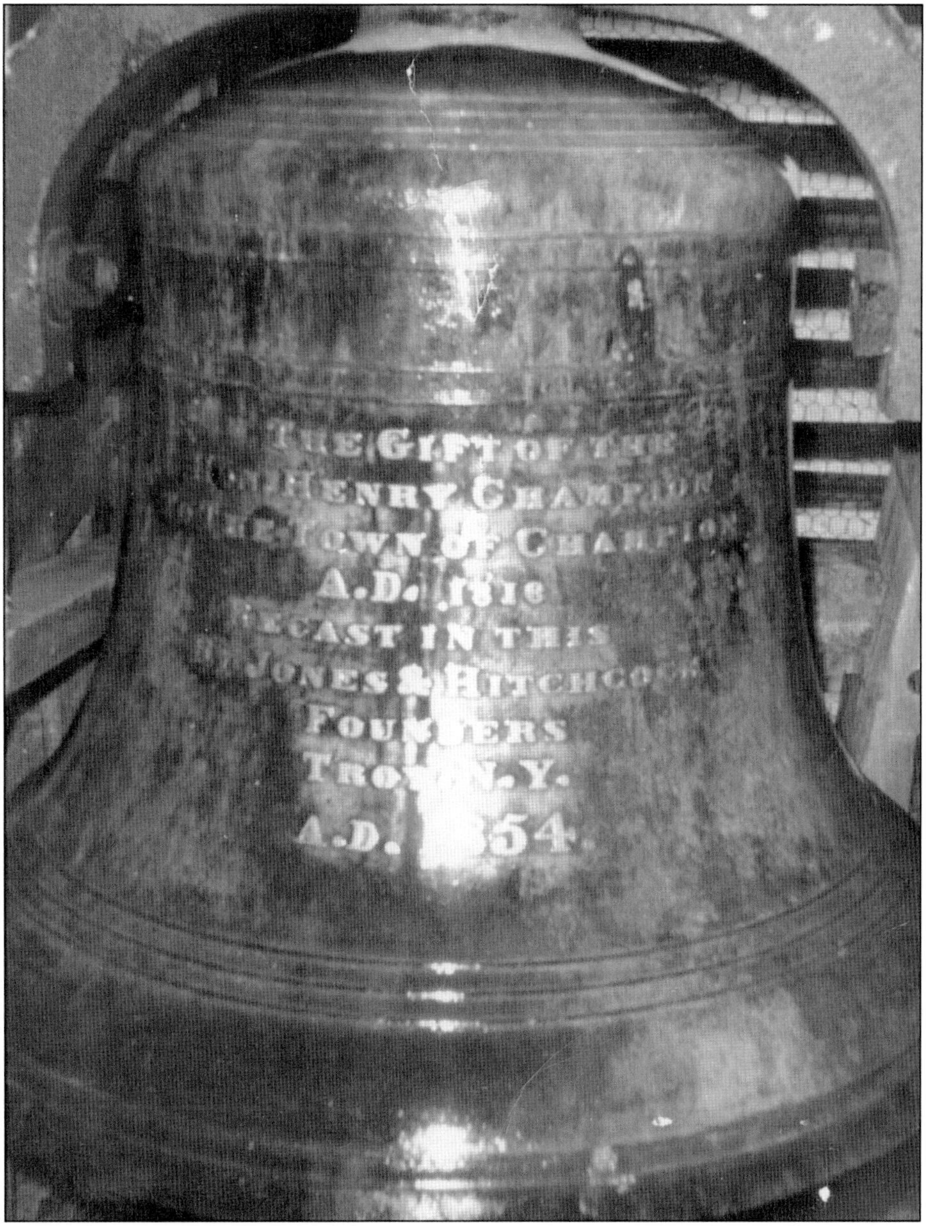

In the history of any community, bells have their own stories—whether it is calling the faithful to worship, the scholar to learn, or the community as a whole to fight danger. The bell in the Champion Grange Hall, which has pealed for nearly 200 years, is credited with being the oldest in Jefferson County. The bell was donated by Gen. Henry Champion, for whom the village was named, and was brought from Troy, New York, by oxcart. It was placed in a building, which also served as schoolhouse, meeting place, and Congregational church, at the top of the hill on Route 126. The bell later developed a crack and was transported back to Troy to be recast. Gen. Champion threw 100 silver dollars into the molten metal, which reportedly resulted in the vibrant, more melodious quality of its tone. When a villager died, it was customary to toll the bell the number of times equal to his or her age. The bell, which now resides in the relocated building, is still in place and is operational. (The 4 Rivers Historical Society.)

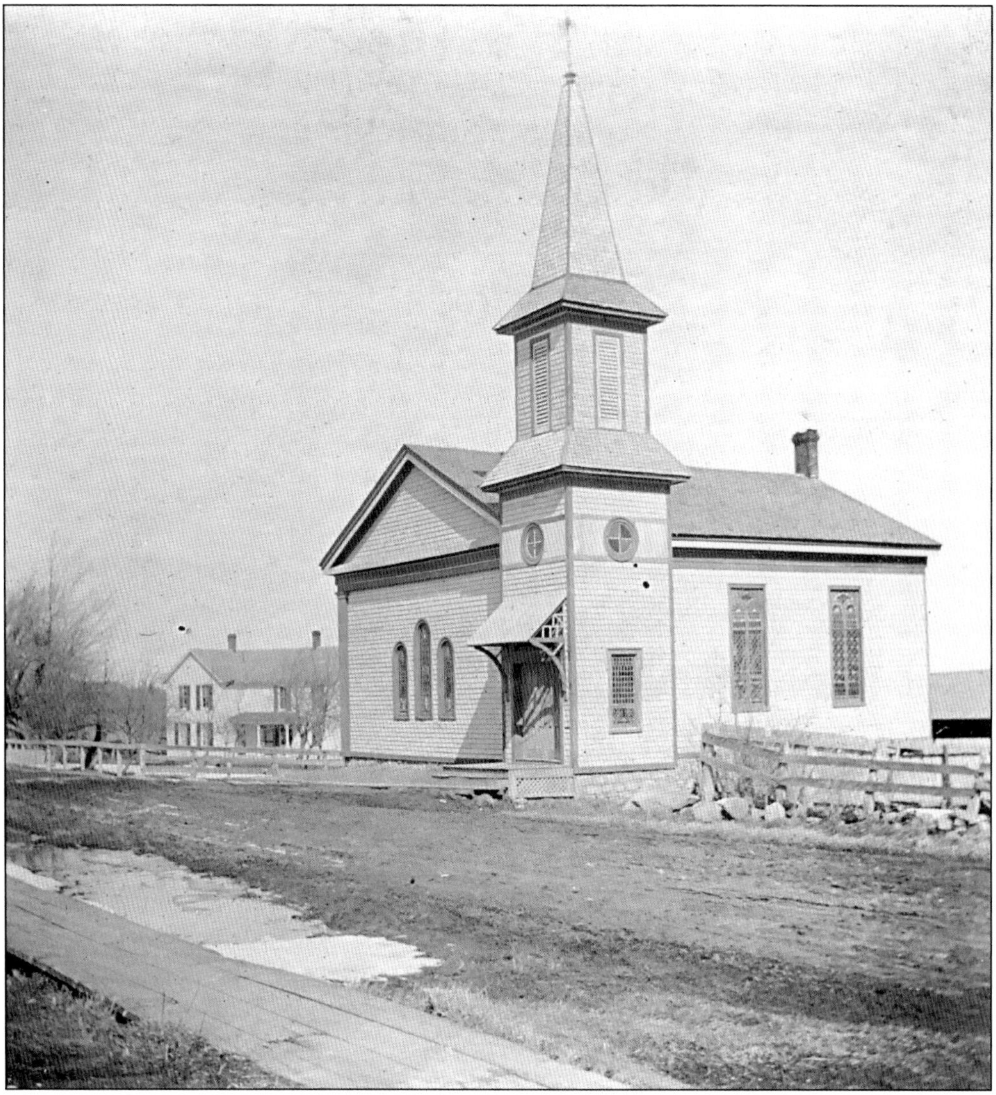

The Second Methodist Church, in Champion, was built in 1853 and dedicated in November of the same year. Hanna Bates, wife of Alden Bates, was a storekeeper in the village and instrumental in raising funds for the church building, which totaled over $80 for carpets and fixtures. In 1804, the Methodists formed the Black River Circuit, which included the whole Northern part of the state, west and north of the Adirondack wilderness. By 1820, Champion had a population of 2,080 and had grown to the point where more was needed than an occasional visit from the circuit's preachers. In 1825, the First Society of Methodists was organized. A church was built in 1825, and in April 1827, the Second Methodist Society was established. This second organization was the forerunner of the present church in Champion village, the First Society becoming the church in Great Bend. (SEC.)

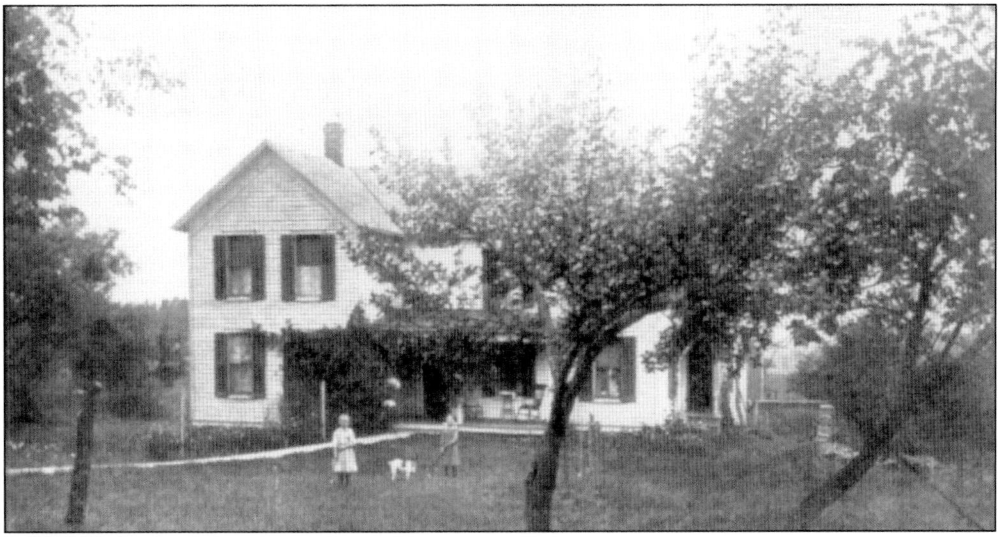

Pictured above is the Methodist parsonage, and below is the interior of Methodist church. This was the second church in Champion. (Both, SEC.)

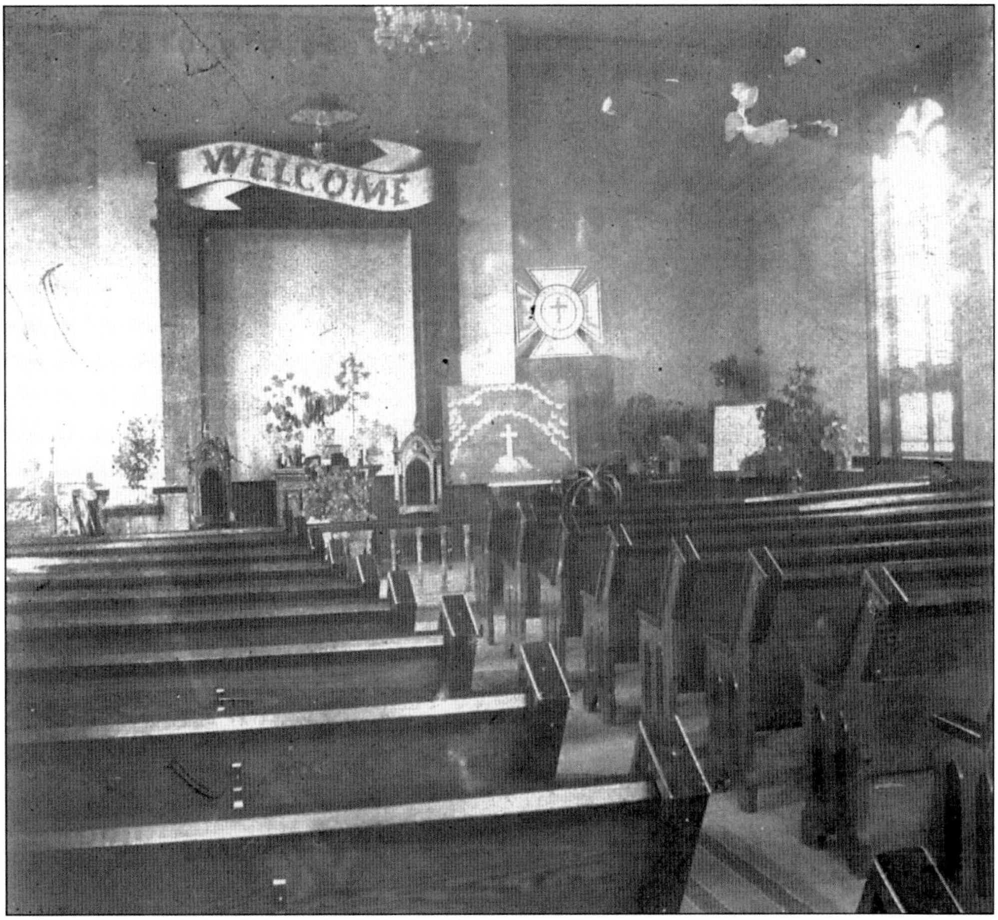

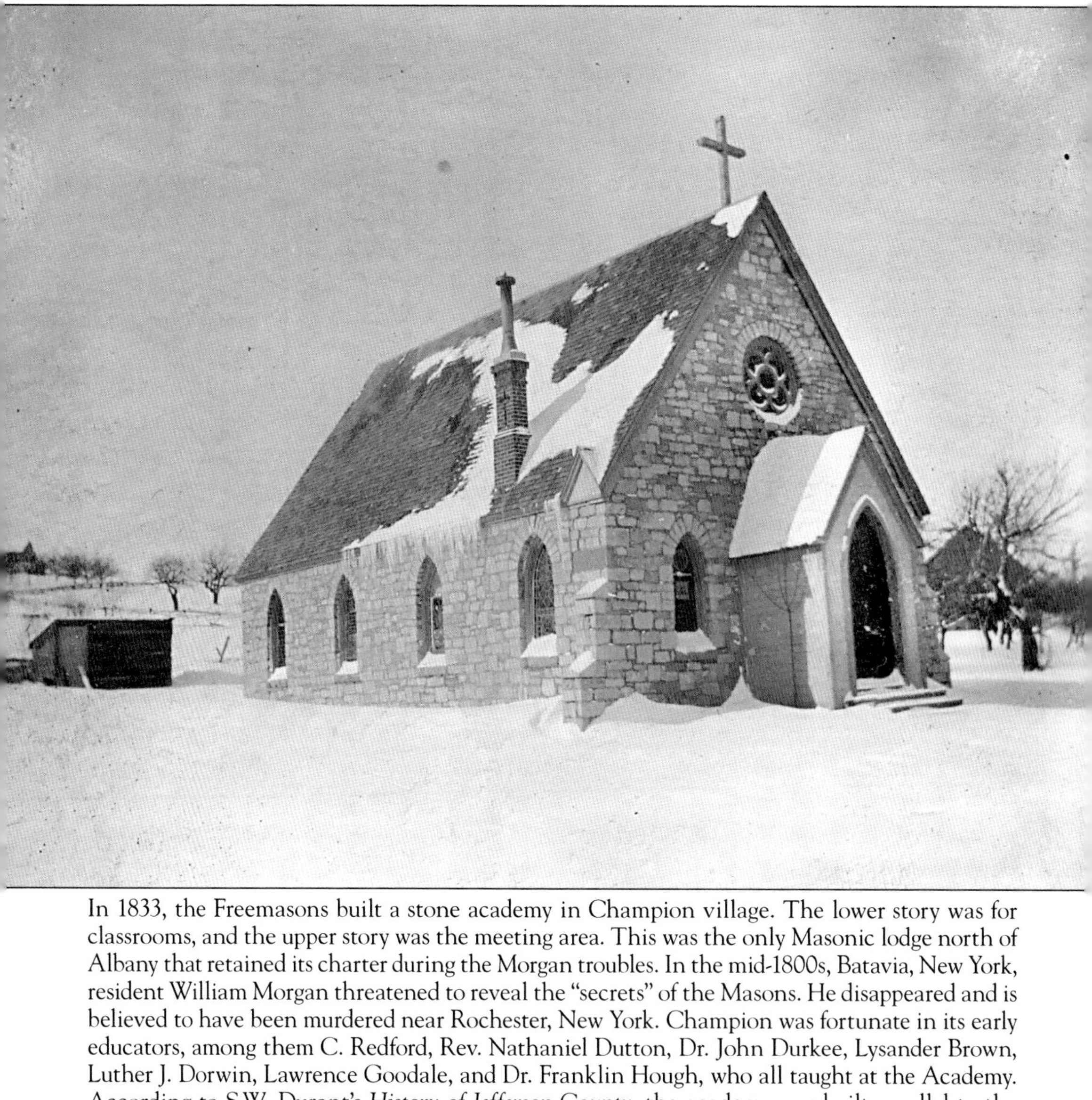

In 1833, the Freemasons built a stone academy in Champion village. The lower story was for classrooms, and the upper story was the meeting area. This was the only Masonic lodge north of Albany that retained its charter during the Morgan troubles. In the mid-1800s, Batavia, New York, resident William Morgan threatened to reveal the "secrets" of the Masons. He disappeared and is believed to have been murdered near Rochester, New York. Champion was fortunate in its early educators, among them C. Redford, Rev. Nathaniel Dutton, Dr. John Durkee, Lysander Brown, Luther J. Dorwin, Lawrence Goodale, and Dr. Franklin Hough, who all taught at the Academy. According to S.W. Durant's *History of Jefferson County*, the academy was built parallel to the road. St. John's Episcopal Church was organized about 1858, but the congregation had to meet in homes of members and in the Methodist Meeting House because it had no building of worship. On April 22, 1867, members met for the purpose of organizing, incorporating, naming wardens and vestrymen, and adopting a name. In 1869, St. John's was willed some money by Roswell Earl, and in 1879, the church accepted the services of Rev. J. Everett Cothell as rector.

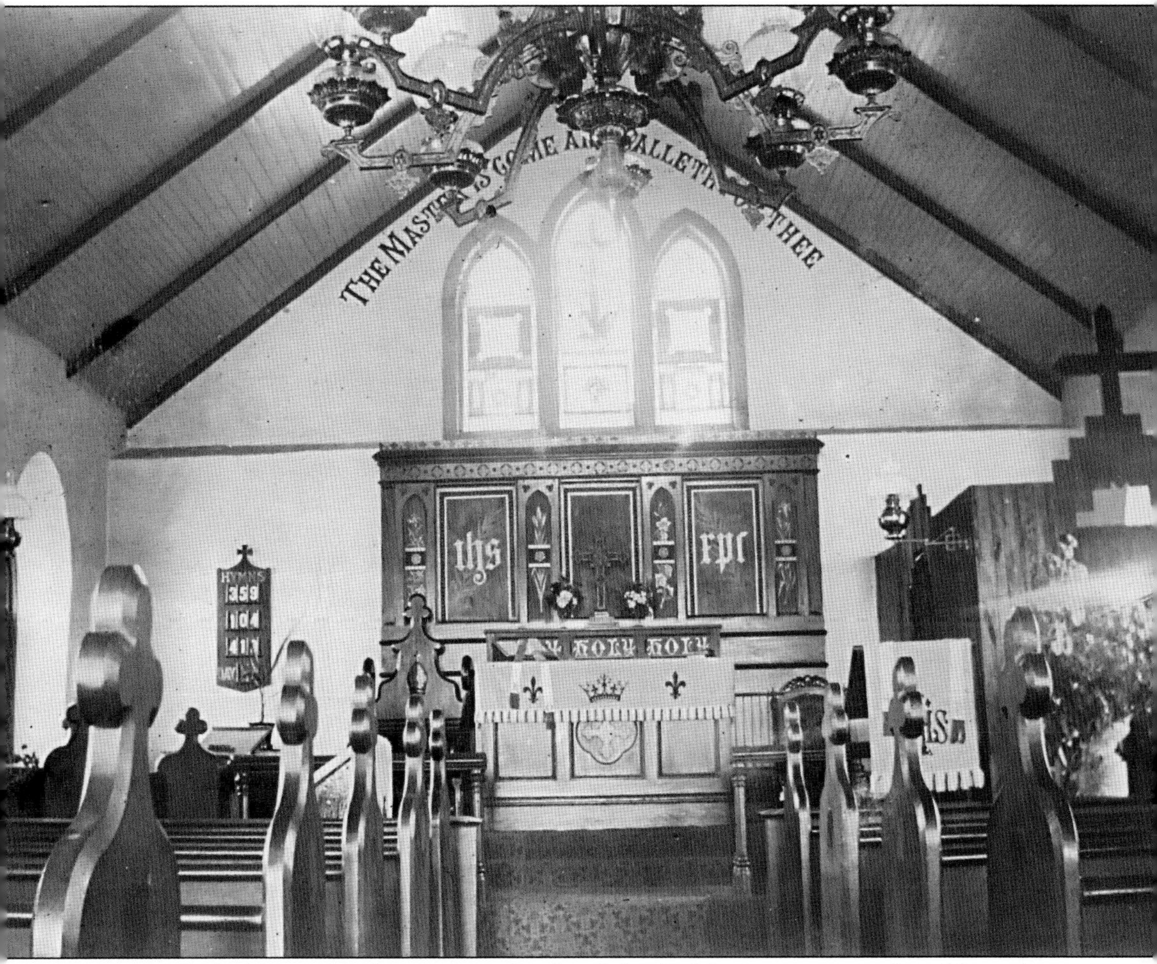

In 1888, the building was either given to the church by the Masons or was purchased from them. On June 28, 1888, the demolition of the old building began, and Rev. R.A. Olin laid a new cornerstone on August 7. The original limestone was utilized for the building. A delay in ordering the windows kept the congregation from worshiping in the new church until December 16, five months after construction began. The Bishop of Central New York officially consecrated the church in May 1889. The church is still active today, under the leadership of Rev. Thomas James of Lamb Road, Champion. Grange No. 18 owns the building itself. This interior photograph was taken around 1900.

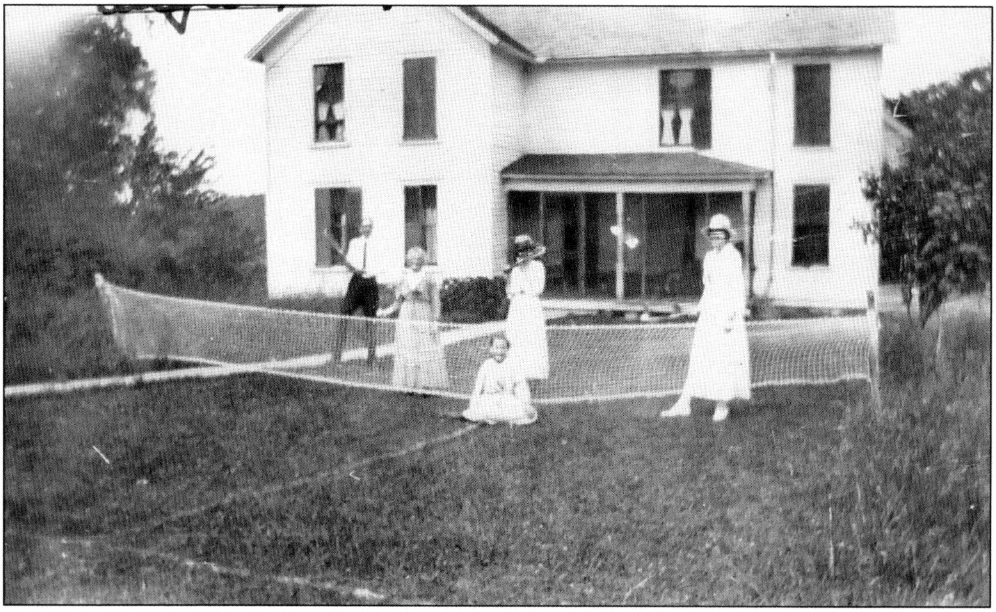

The 1922 photograph above shows a picnic at the Methodist parsonage. Rev. George Smith and his mother, Mary Emma Smith, are on the left. The other women and child are not identified. Below is a photograph taken by Reverend Smith's daughter, Mary Ellen "Nellie" shortly after her marriage to Wolsey Stoddard. It shows her mother with her husband's parents, Wesley and Mary Stoddard, who owned the farm. The wagon is full of hay as opposed to the photograph on the following page, which shows them cutting grain. Mary Ellen grew up in Scotland and lived for a time in London. She came from England to Champion and was married shortly after her arrival. Mary Bach of Bach Road is their daughter. (Both, Mary Bach.)

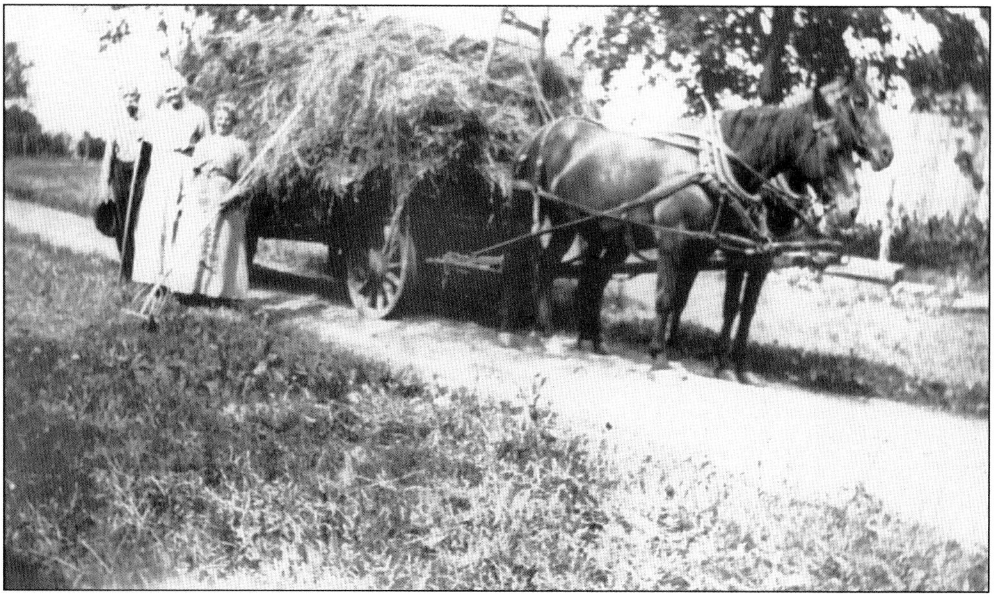

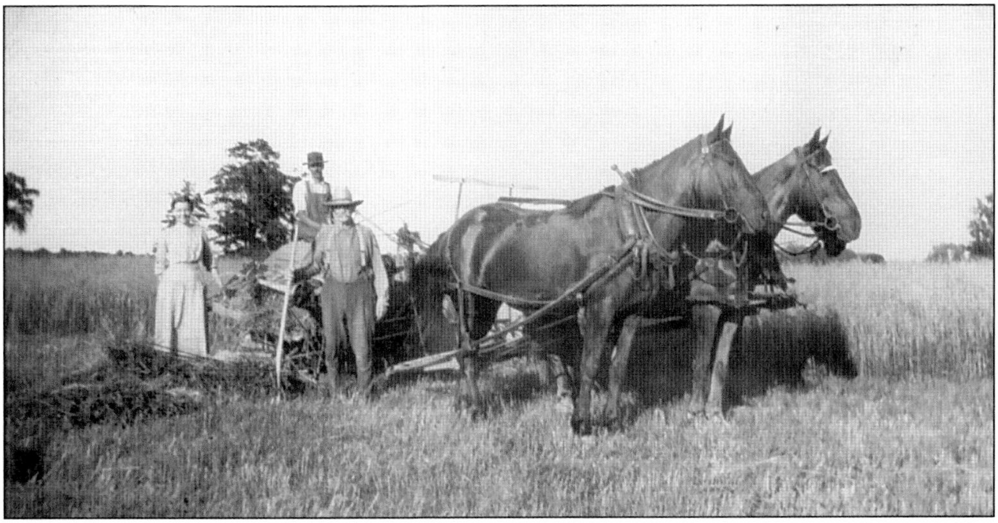

Wolsey Stoddard is shown driving Earl Baker's team while cutting grain on September 24, 1924. On the reverse side of the photograph is the notation "taken by Nellie," who would have been his Stoddard's wife, Mary Ellen. These were days when farmers helped their neighbors, because not everyone had all of the equipment necessary for various tasks. Equipment was sometimes moved from farm to farm as needed. The Bakers owned the next farm on Bach Road. Below, another group poses with a machine that might have been shared; it has a steam engine and could have run several types of accessories. (Above, Mary Back; below, Helen Stott Collection.)

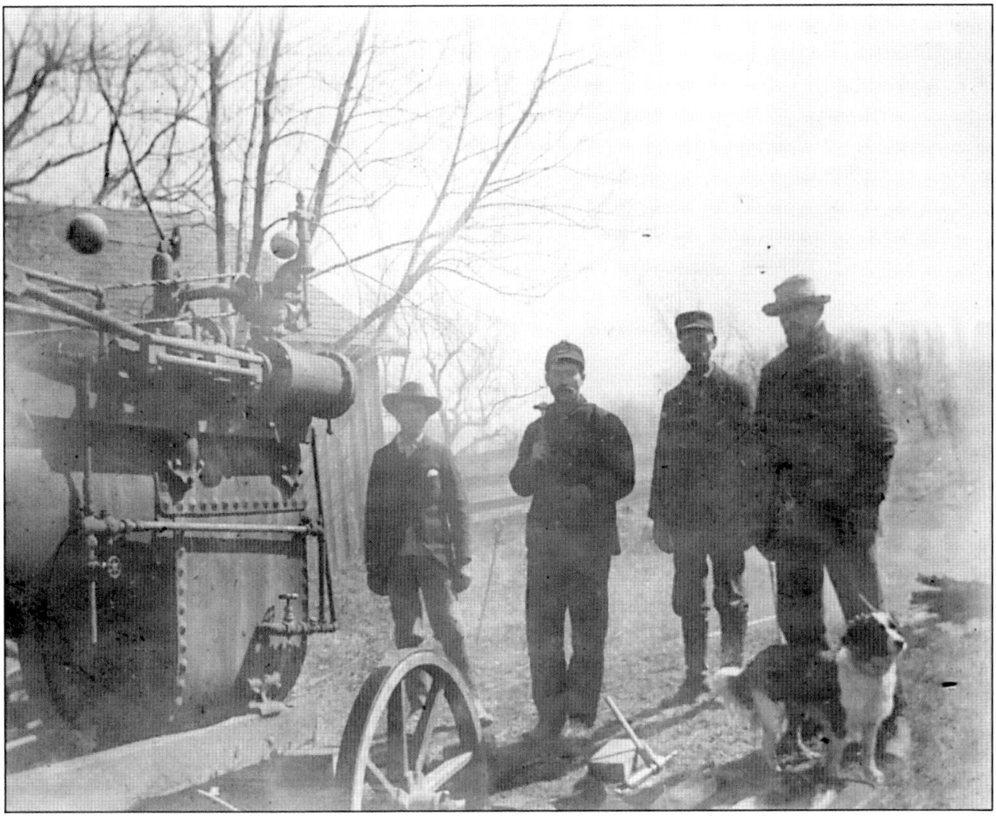

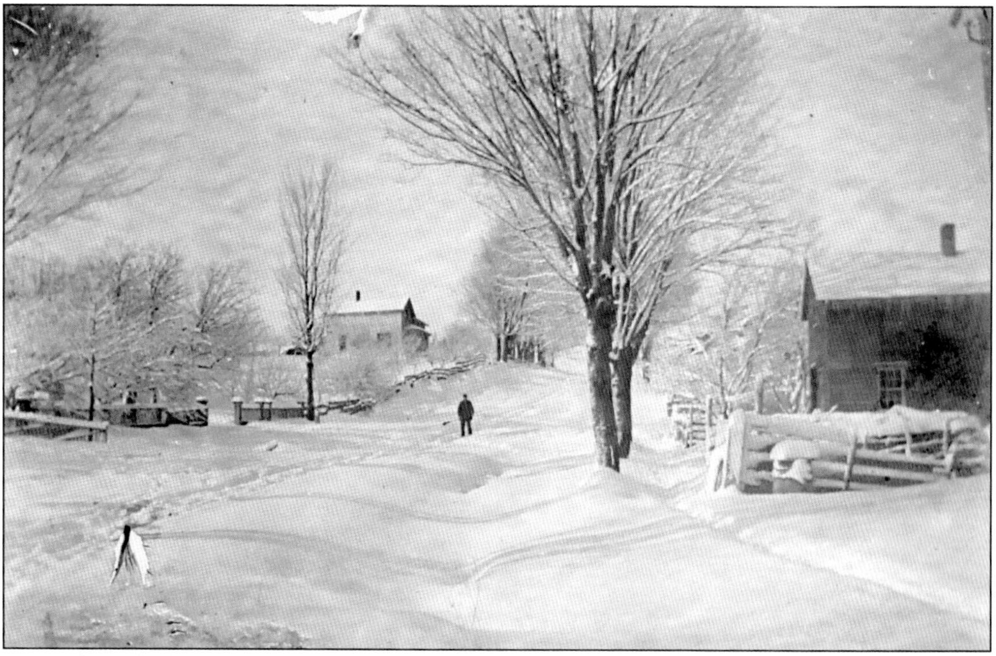

Winter brought hardships and rewards. As the snow piled up, travel was restricted to foot or sleigh. Soapstones were heated and placed at the feet of travelers or in the icy beds of wood-heated homes. The gentleman above is standing in the middle of present Route 126, but barely making a dent in the accumulation. Below, a spirited horse is taking its owner traveling in style. Both of these c. 1900 photographs of Champion village are from the Helen Stott Collection. A stanza from an untitled, anonymous poem sums it up: "When the north wind doth blow, and there's five feet of snow, and the ice devils nibble and gnaw, when snow fills your eyes and the drifts quickly rise, then that is a Black River Thaw!"

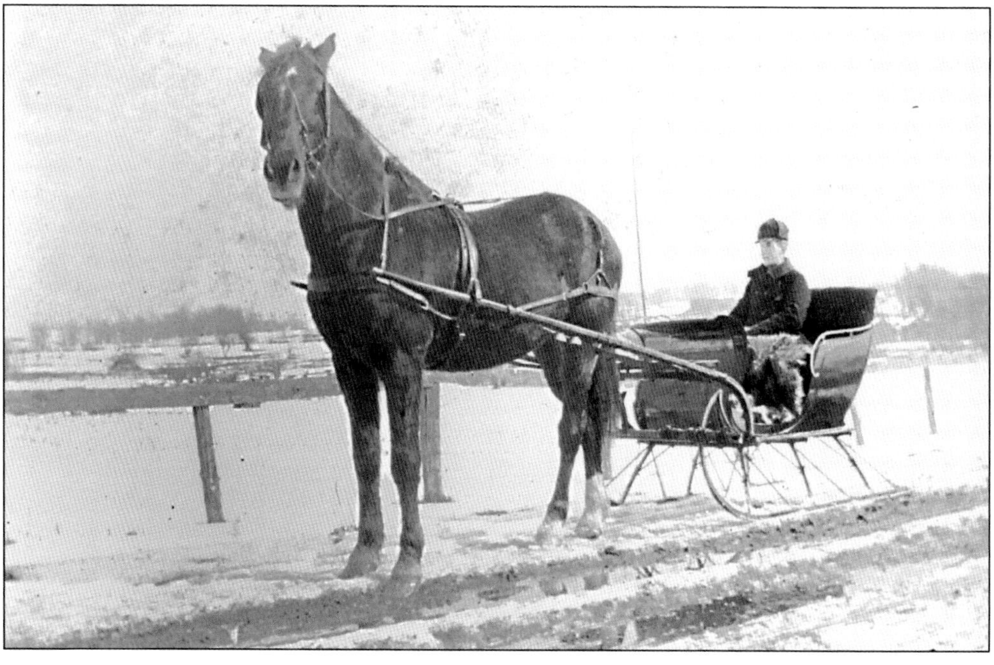

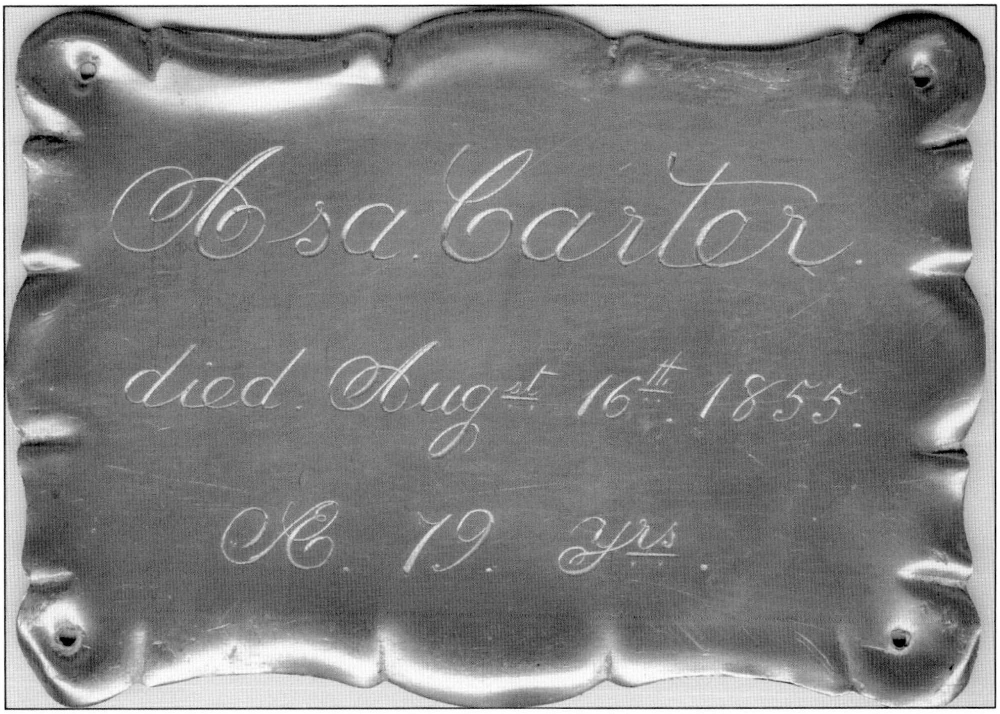

Deacon Asa Carter, son of Jonathan Carter and Abigail Moulthrop, was born on November 13, 1776. At the age of 19, he moved with his parents to Jefferson County, New York, and was a successful farmer. Like his father, Asa was a deacon of the Presbyterian church. He married Roxana Root, who was born on July 25, 1778, in Southwick, Massachusetts, and died December 24, 1863. Asa died August 16, 1855. Of their children, four sons and four daughters grew to maturity. Someone in the family began the quaint habit of collecting the casket plates before they were interred in Hillside Cemetery in Champion. Charles Clark of Adams has several of these in his possession along with daguerreotypes of the people associated with them. (Both, CCC.)

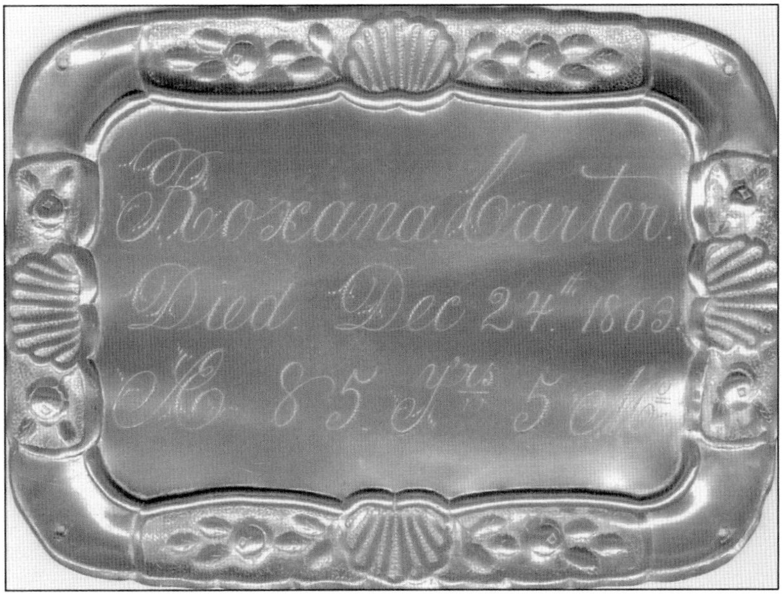

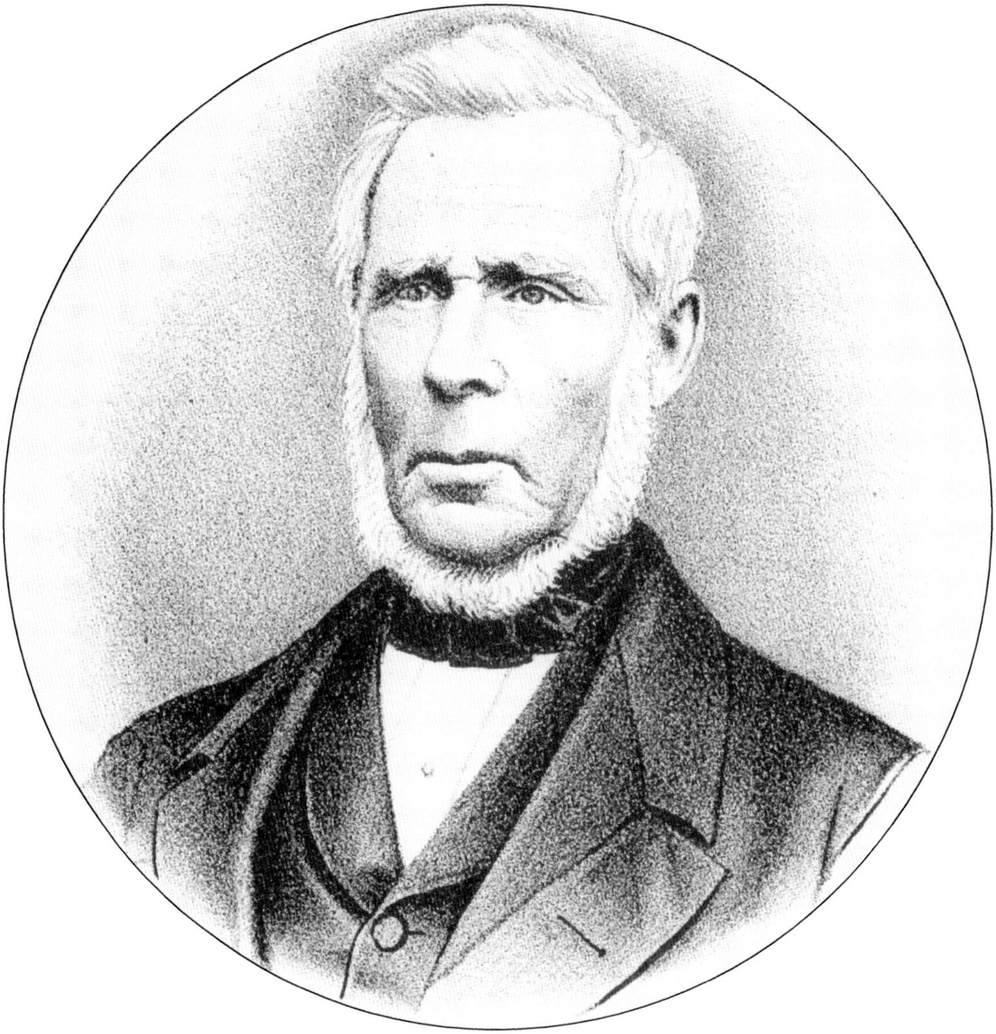

Col. Elias Sage was born February 1799. His family moved to Lowville in 1800, and at the age of 16, Elias was apprenticed to learn the carpentry trade. Any money he saved was invested in real estate. He became the owner of extensive acreage through his work and thrift, and moved his family to Champion in 1815. Sage entered the militia when he was a young corporal in the 14th New York Cavalry. He was soon promoted to sergeant and, step-by-step, he was made colonel of the regiment. Sage's home in Champion is shown below. (Both, Everts.)

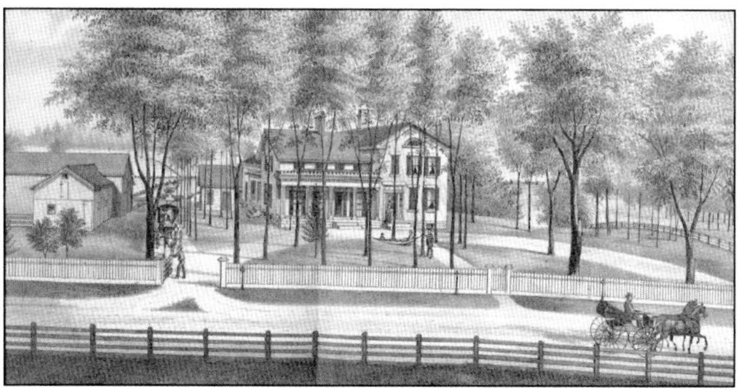

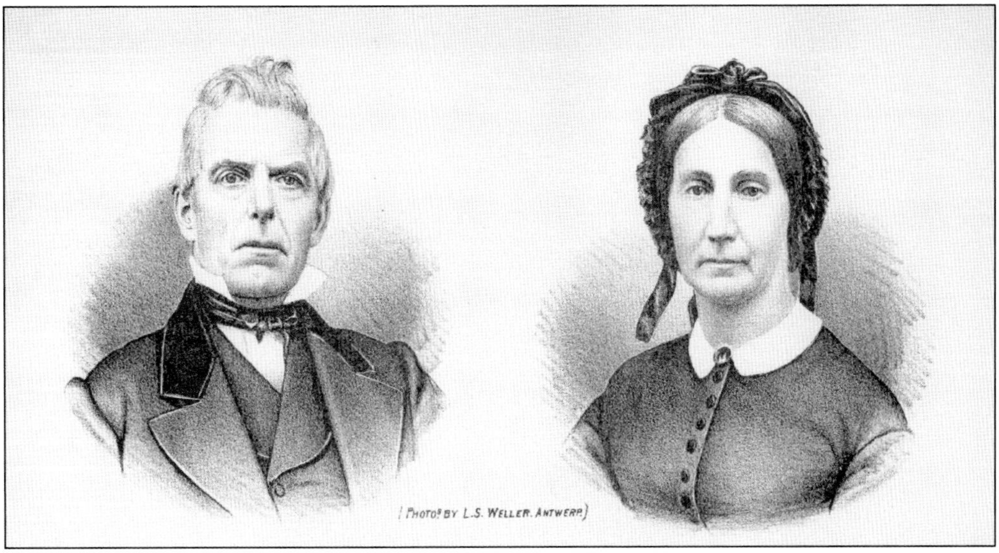

Alphonso Loomis was born in Champion on August 29, 1808, and was the son of John and Achsah Brooks Loomis, who were some of the area's earliest settlers. Alphonso made his home with his father until he was 30 years old, even though he had purchased a farm. In 1838, he married Lucinda Carter and moved to his farm, where he lived until his death in 1875. They had three children—Selinda, Sanford, and Mary. (Both, Everts.)

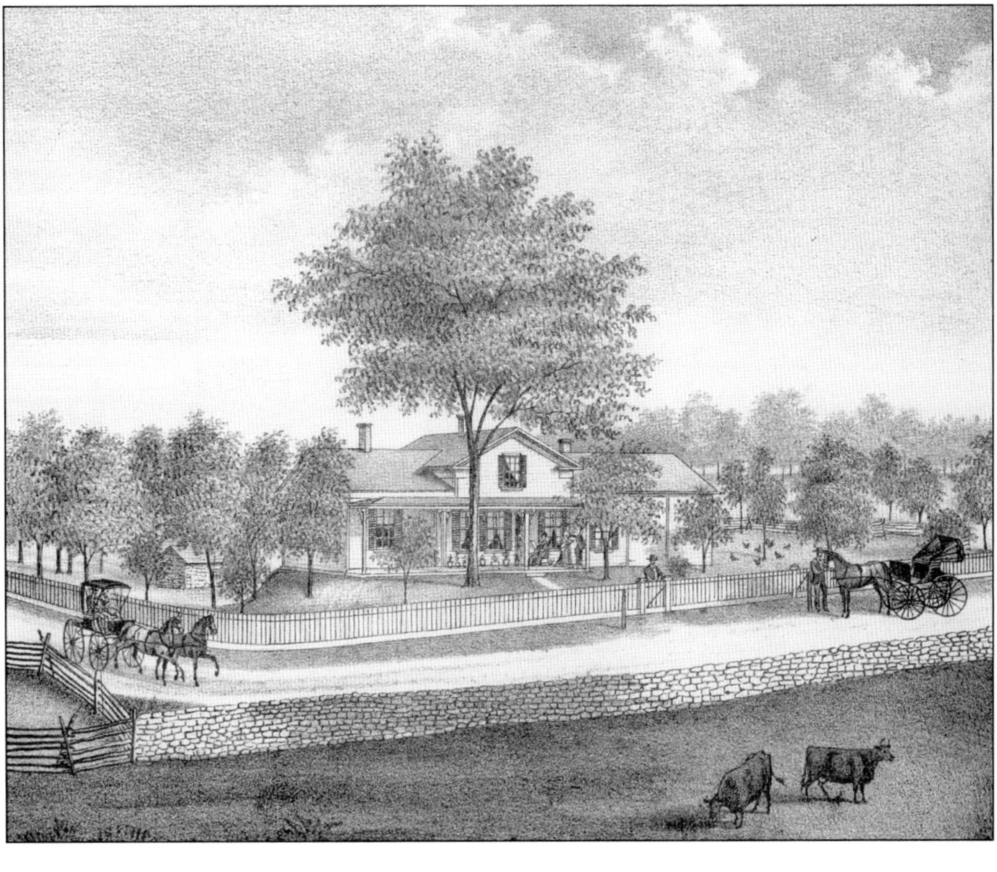

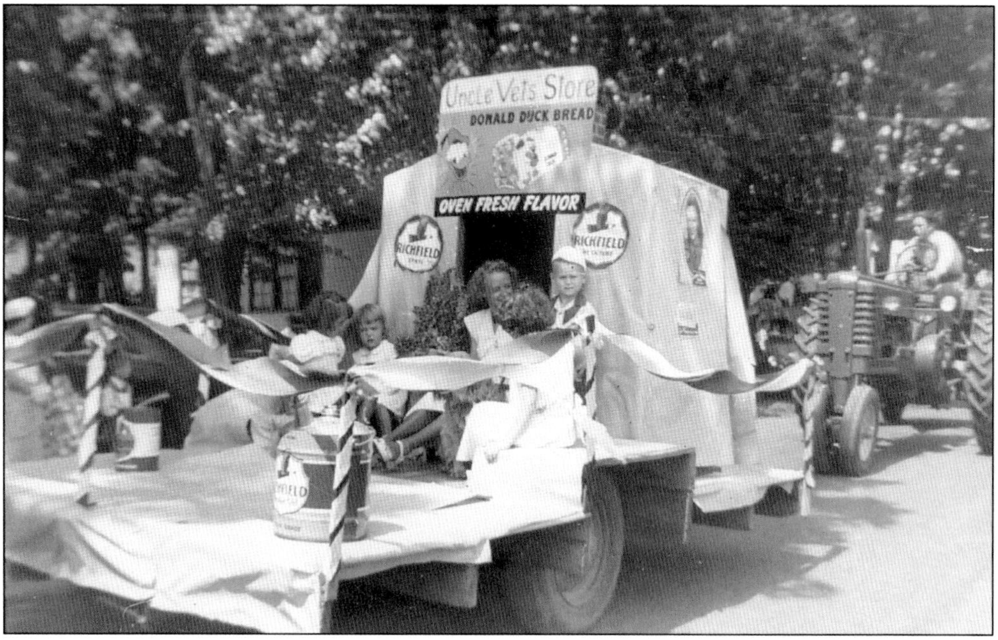

Still an annual event today, a Old Home Day Parade in Champion is pictured here in 1952. The lady in the float's doorway is Rose McCallops Hastings. The little boy may be Larry Archer, Leo Archer's brother. Sylvester Parks, who sponsored the float, owned Uncle Vet's Store. The parade, generally held on July 4, is interesting for several reasons. It forms at the Champion Fire Hall on Route 126, crosses the main road, heads down Church Street past the Grange Hall, St. John's Episcopal Church, past the Second Methodist Church, turns right at the corner of Route 47, goes almost as far as Hillside Cemetery, turns around, and returns to Fire Hall, which makes it one of the few parades residents can catch both coming and going. Below, tractors and farm equipment have always been a big part of the event. (Both, Brian Sech.)

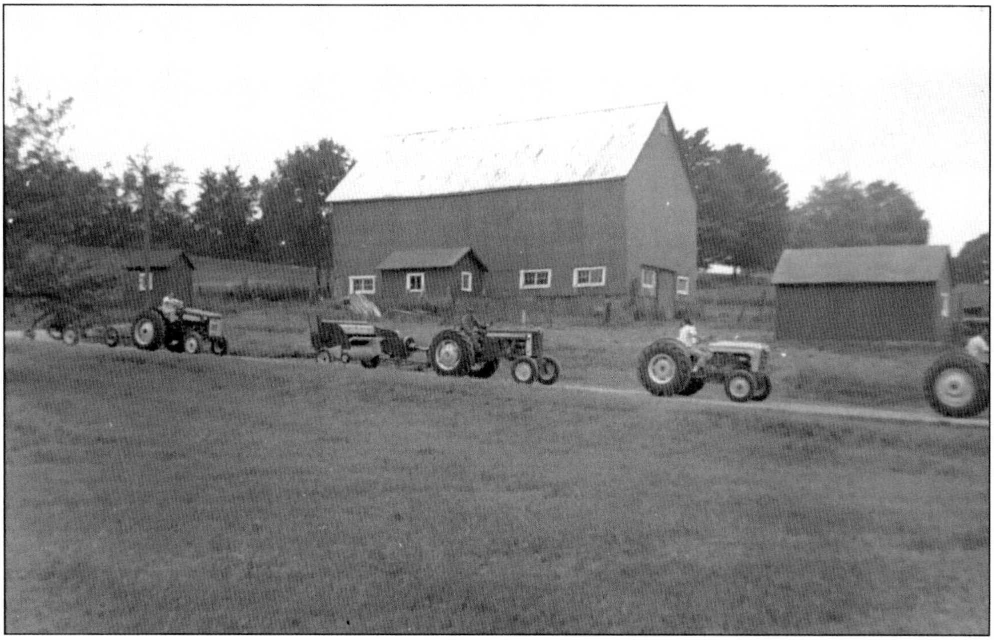

Two

GREAT BEND
THE NEXT VILLAGE

Capt. Joseph Martin founded the village of Great Bend about 1800. By 1805, he and his five brothers—Enos, Samuel, Timothy, Harry and Mason—were all living there. They settled on the road between Great Bend and Carthage that still bears their name.

The founding of Great Bend differed from the founding of Champion in that the bend of the Black River was chosen for its hydropower potential. Egbert Ten Eyck and Olney Pearce were among Great Bend's earliest settlers, and they are given credit for making the first improvements there. They laid the foundation for the hamlet by constructing a dam across the river, and a Mr. Tubbs, also an early resident, did the work in 1806. A sawmill that was built the same year was carried away by high water, but was soon replaced by Henry G. Gardner, who built a second mill. A distillery was erected in 1809, and between 1815 and 1824, Watson and Gates and Charles E. Clark built other improvements and milling enterprises. Great Bend became a place of considerable importance, even in the early years of the town.

The village suffered seriously from a destructive fire on March 5, 1840, but the industries that burned were soon replaced with others that were more substantial and modern. Among several of this hamlet's past enterprises, perhaps the most significant was the pulp and paper mill. During that same period, some other merchants in the town were Chauncey Clark, who ran a feed store; H.H. Clark, who operated a general store; and Bignall and Reynolds, who were also general dealers.

Frank Woolworth, the founder of the famous five-and-dime that for many years was known simply as Woolworth's, grew up on a farm in Great Bend and in later years endowed the Woolworth Memorial Church in the village. It was dedicated on September 15, 1915, and Frank Woolworth, his wife, and daughters were present along with many of his friends from New York City. The church is still an active force in the village.

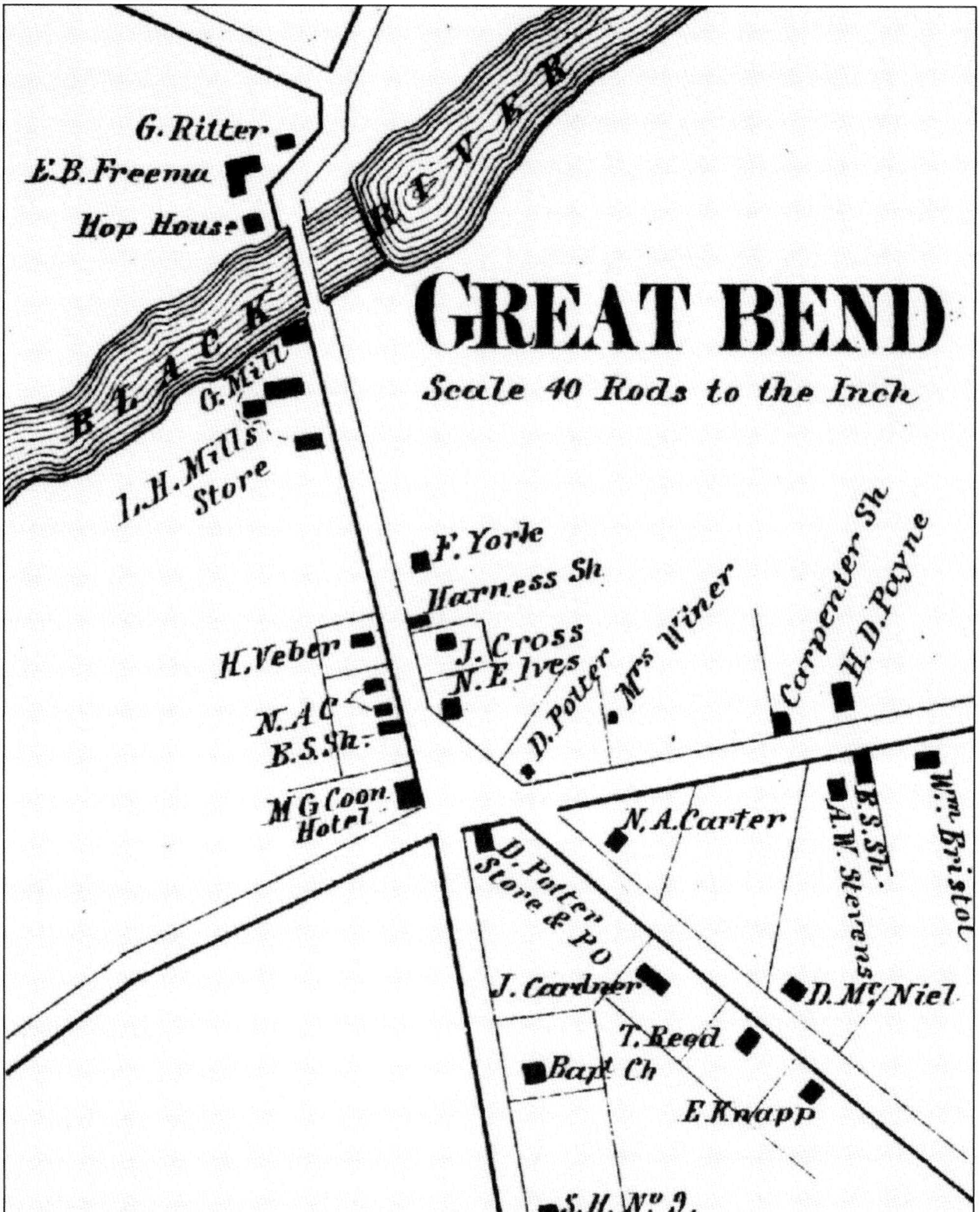

Stone's 1864 atlas shows the village of Great Bend. The map names the principal inhabitants and some of the businesses.

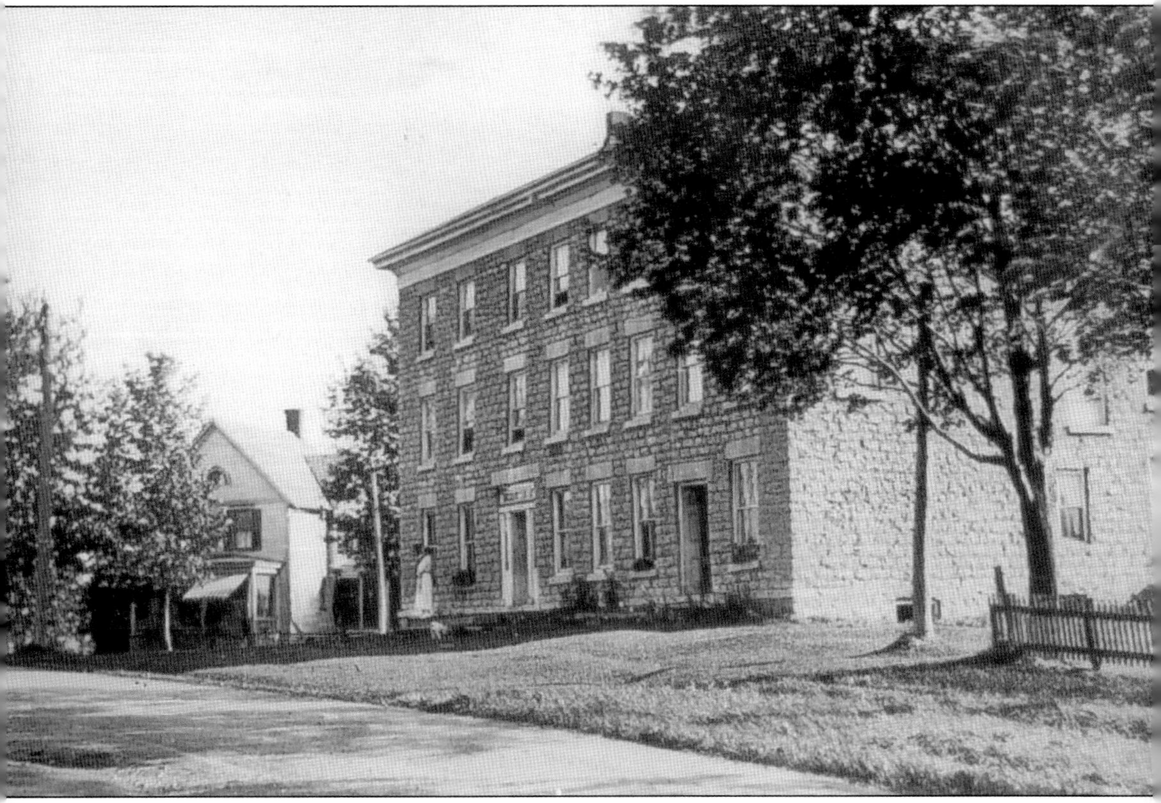

Built around 1829, the old stone tavern at Great Bend was later known as the Jefferson House and famous for its hospitality in the stagecoach era. It is still standing at the crossroads in Great Bend. Probably the burning down of Hubbard's Inn in Champion and the increased use of the four-horse stagecoach in 1828 brought more passengers to Great Bend, which prompted the tavern's construction. The third floor of this building, which is one of the most picturesque and historic stagecoach taverns in northern New York, was given over to a ballroom. The home to the left belonged to Dr. Albert A. Joslyn. A veteran of the Civil War, Joslyn enlisted in Company H, 186th New York Volunteer Infantry, at the early age of 15 and was the youngest soldier in the regiment who carried a musket. Joslyn read medicine first in Connecticut and later continued his studies with Dr. N.D. Ferguson in Great Bend. Eventually, he moved to Lewis County, where he continued to practice medicine. (SEC.)

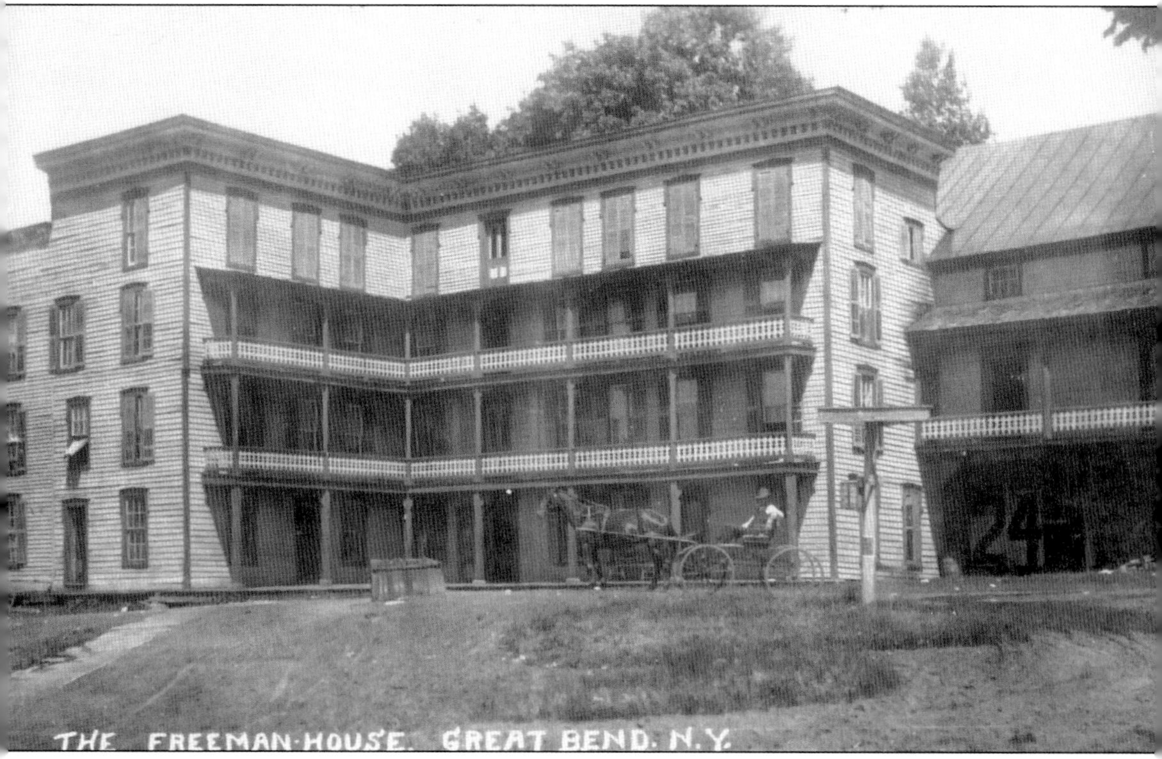

The Freeman House of Great Bend, dismantled in 1920, was one of the well-known hotels in the town of Champion, although technically, it was located in the town of Wilna, which was on the opposite shore of the Black River across from the gristmill and paper mill. It had its beginnings in a small hostelry purchased by Erastus Freeman in 1851. After buying the hotel, he gradually added on to it until his death in 1873, which was when the ownership and management passed to his sons John and George. After the opening of Pine Camp as a military maneuver field in 1910, it was frequented by many soldiers. It was on the night of August 29, 1910, that a private of the 10th cavalry shot and killed a private and a corporal of the 24th infantry at the hotel. At the time that the hotel was torn down, it was owned by the old Taggart's Paper Company, which later became the Sherman Paper Company.

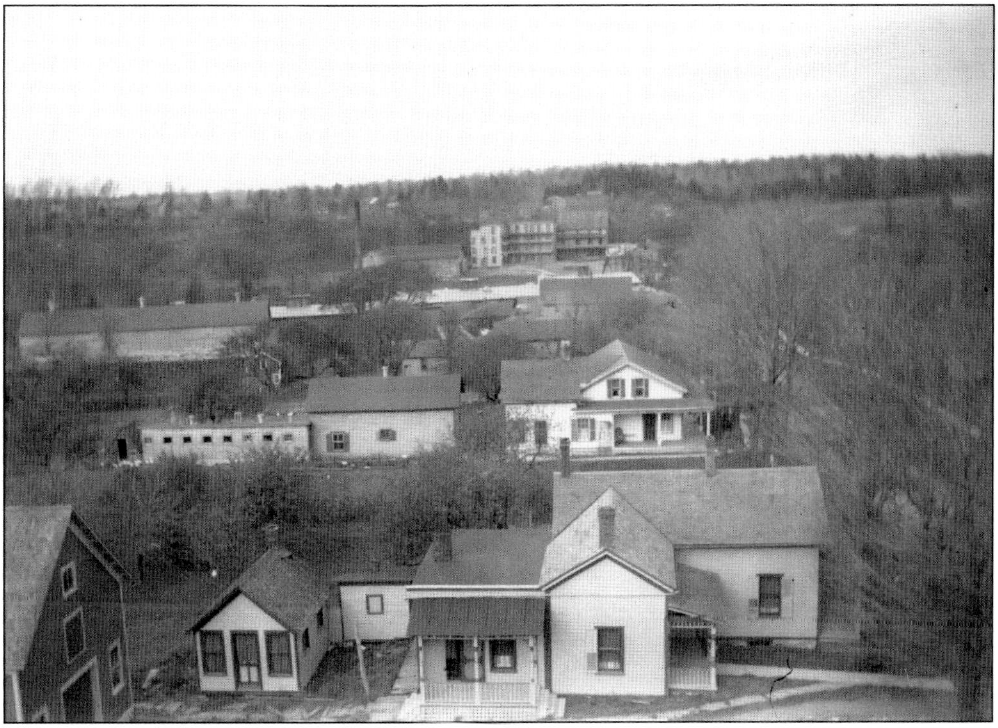

The photograph above shows the mills on the bend of the river, and one can clearly see the Freeman Hotel in the background, on the other side of the Black. Seen below are the bridge, the dam, and the incredible power that was harnessed to run the mills on the bank. (Both, JCHS.)

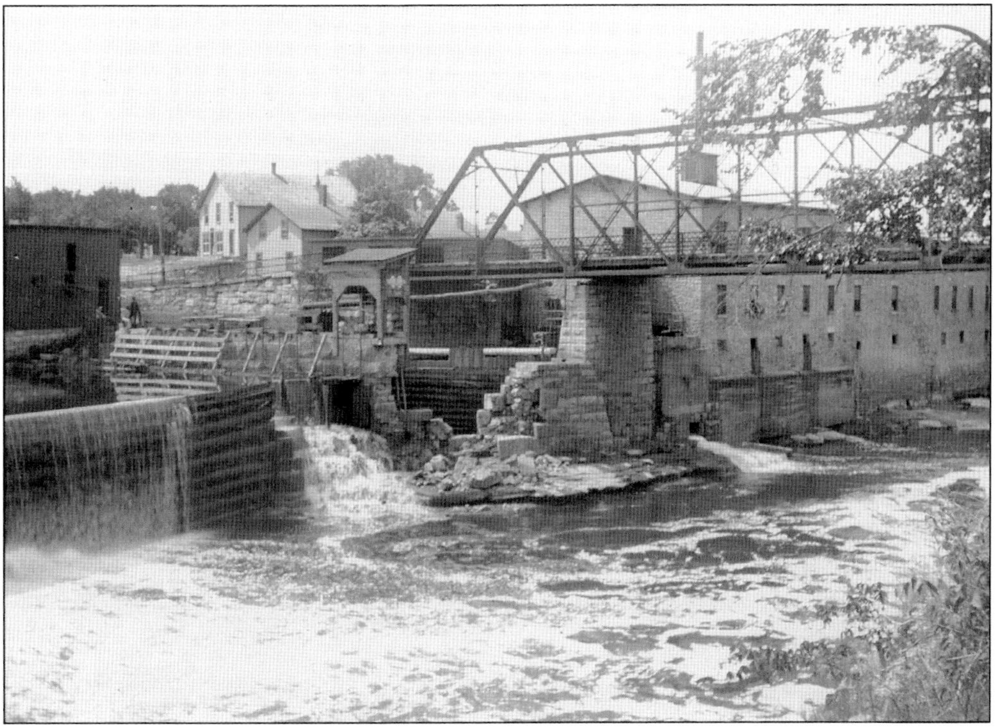

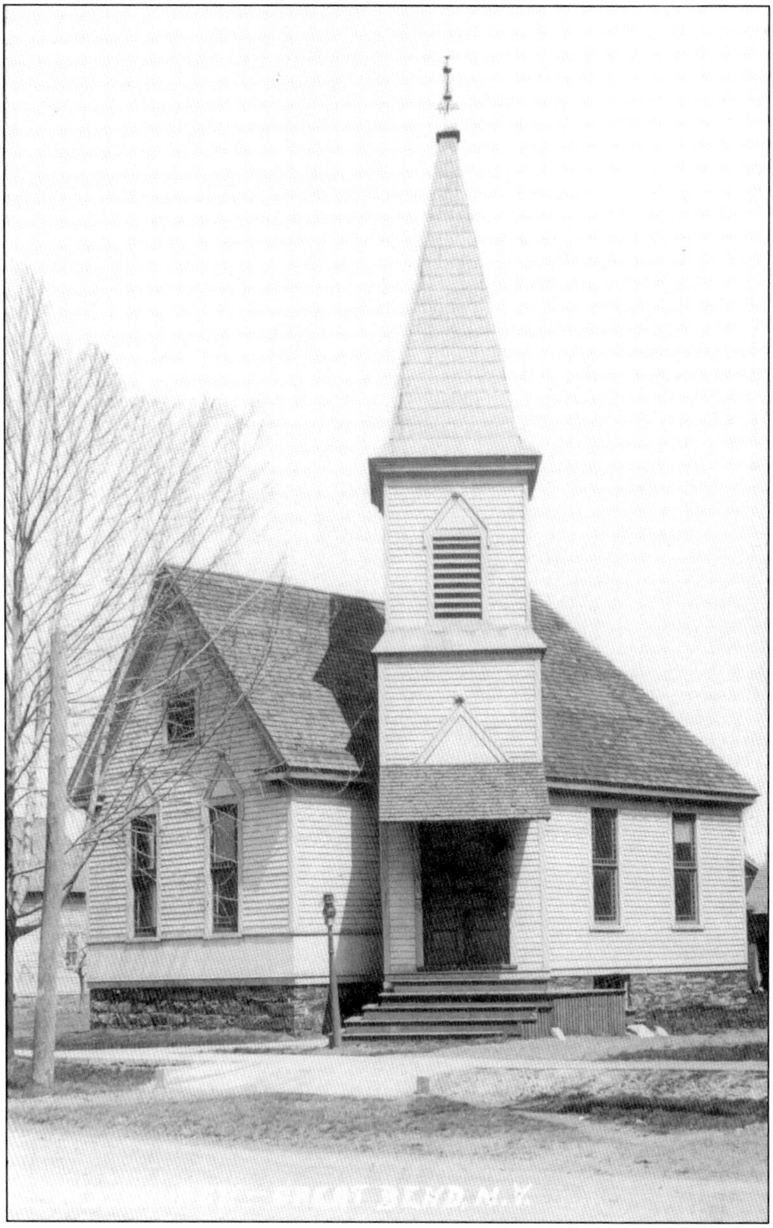

Nathaniel Salisbury and Gardner Baker organized the First Methodist Church in Champion, located in Great Bend, in 1826. The house of worship was built in 1887 at a cost of $2,300, approximately its present value. It seated around 200 people and was dedicated about four months after the old church was abandoned. Local preacher Wilson Pennock, Jason Francis, Josiah Townsend, and Elijah Francis were the first trustees of the church. This church building, which was modern in style, had a 50-foot tower, was nicely furnished and carpeted, and was heated by a furnace. It was dedicated free from debt with a membership of 54 in 1900. Henry Ernest was the pastor. The Sunday school had about 80 members, with Edwin Sweet as superintendent. In 1915, the property was sold to Floyd Miller, who remodeled the building and converted it into a home. It was later the Jawarski residence. That same year, the present Woolworth Memorial Church that faced Champion Street was built. (SEC.)

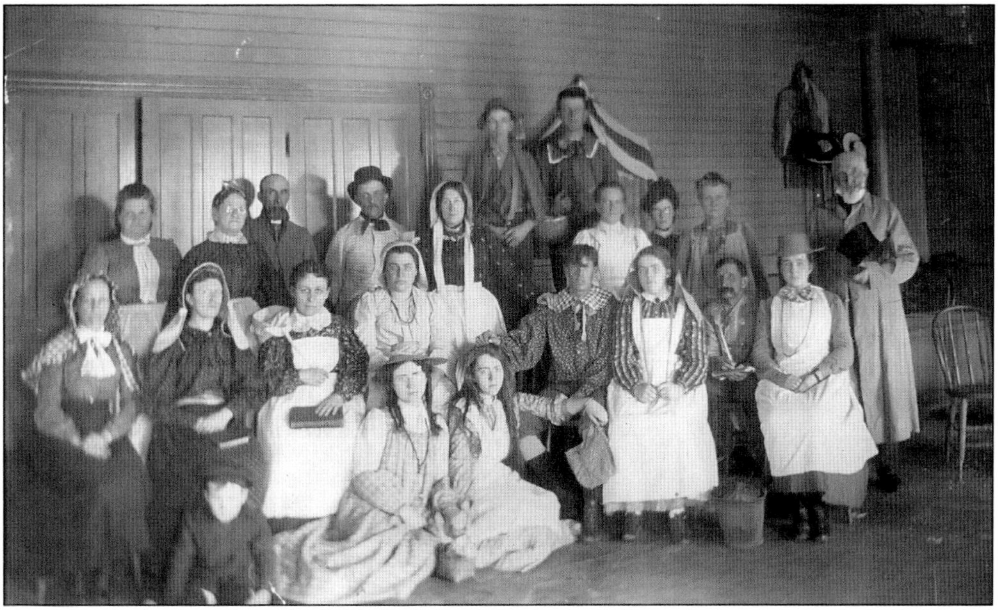

A Great Bend Methodist Church program on March 6, 1903 is shown above. Pictured, from left to right, are (first row) Paul Merrit, Clare Morgan, and Nellie Stewart; (second row) Mrs. Will Pennock, ? Merrit, Mrs. J. W. Higby, ? Robinson, Ray Peebles, Mae Stewart, Sam McCallops, and Vera Pennock; (third row) ? Stewart, ? Pennock, ? Peck, Will Pennock, E. Mae Ricket, Clark Shew, Will Morgan, ? Woodard, Florence Peck, ? Morgan, and ? Pennock. The interior of the church is pictured below. (Both, SEC.)

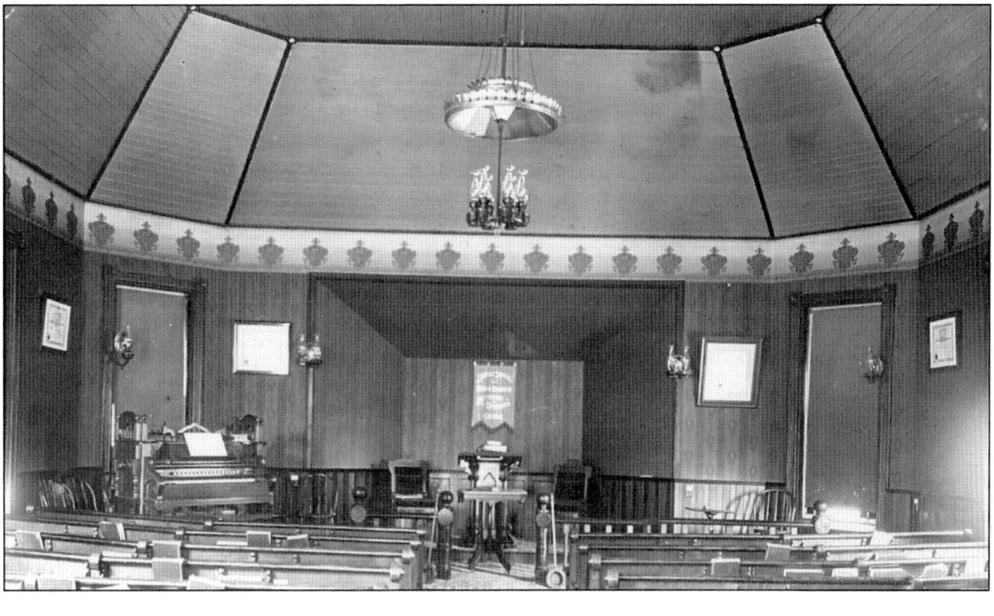

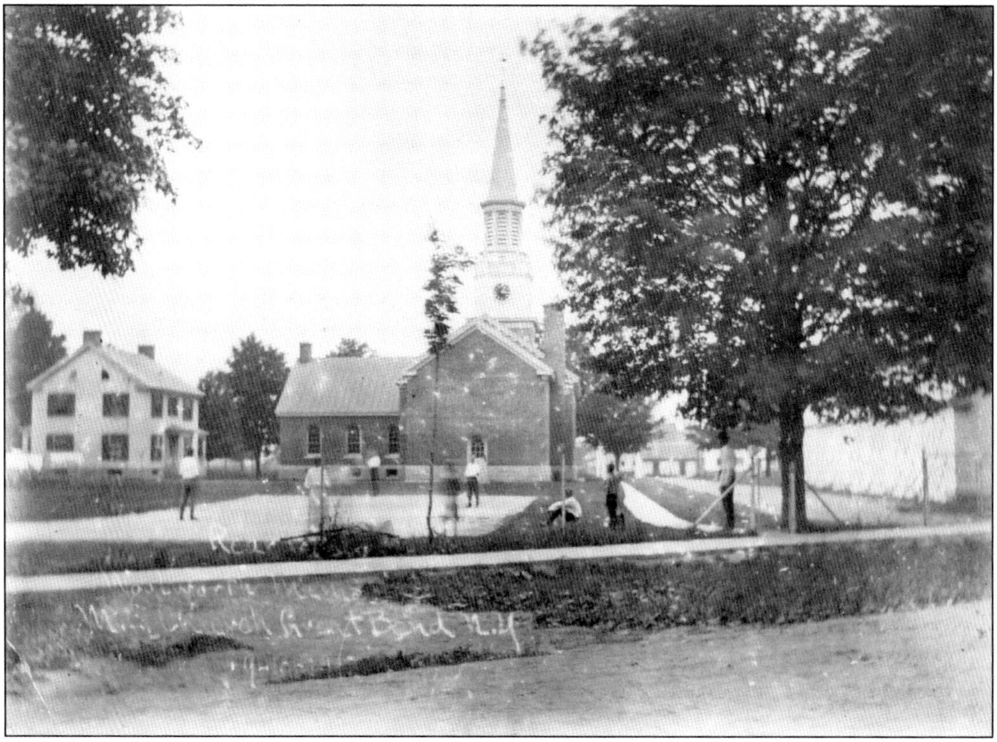

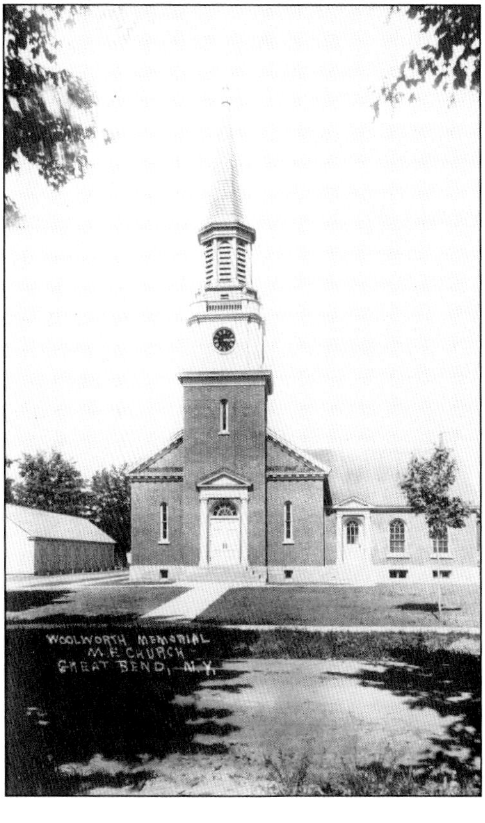

Shown here are early photographs of Woolworth Memorial Church in Great Bend. The above photograph shows village tennis courts with the church in the background. Also visible is one of the stone houses for which the area is noted. At left, another early photograph includes the horse stables to the left of the church. (Both, SEC.)

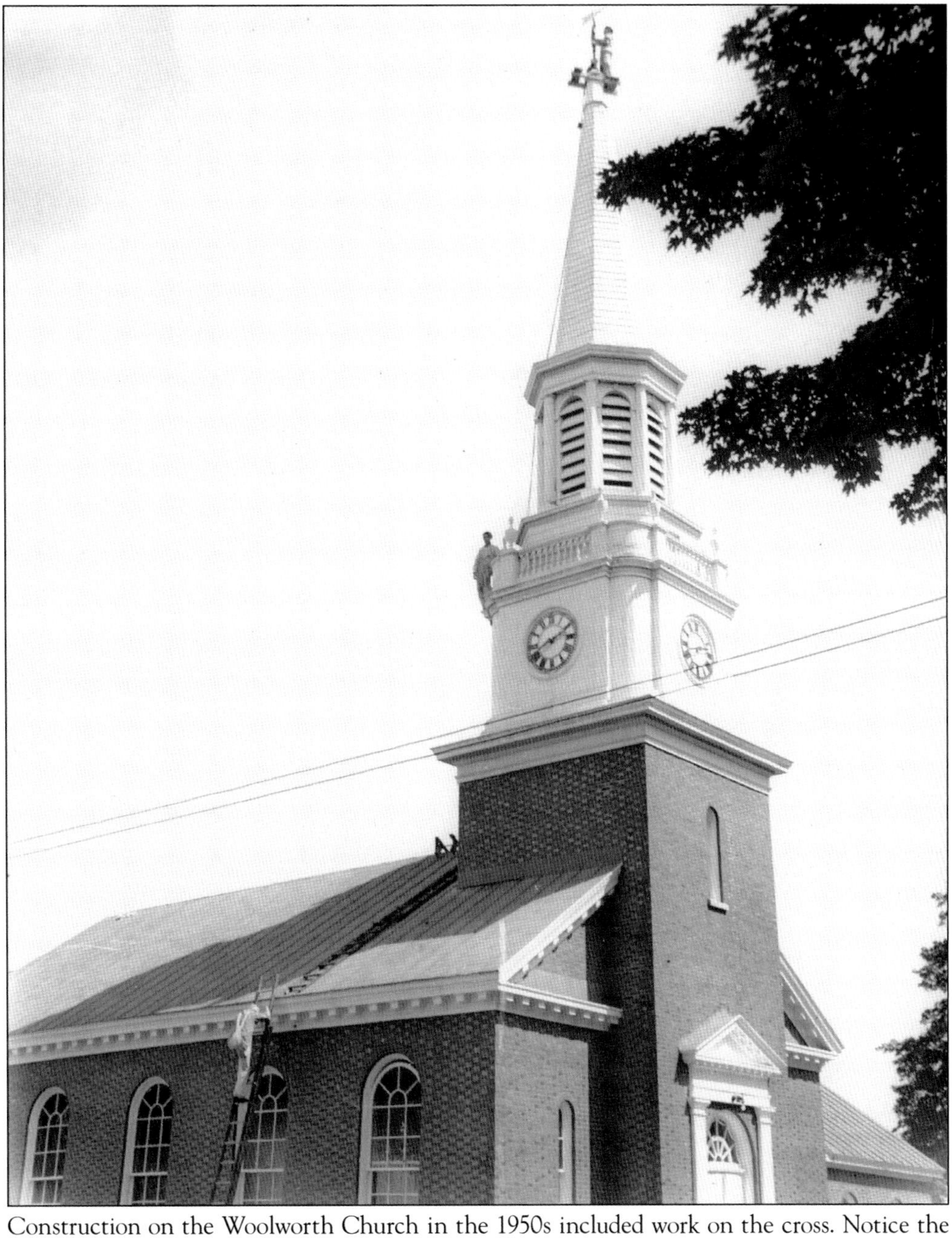

Construction on the Woolworth Church in the 1950s included work on the cross. Notice the men on the ladder, roof, and steeple, and by the cross. (Bisha Collection.)

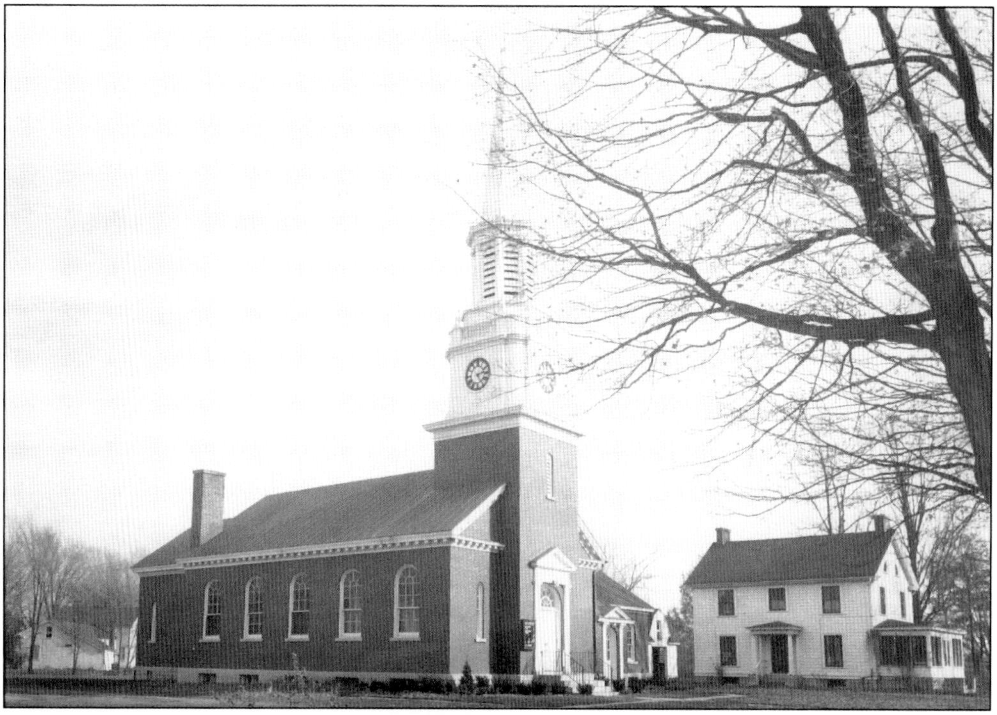

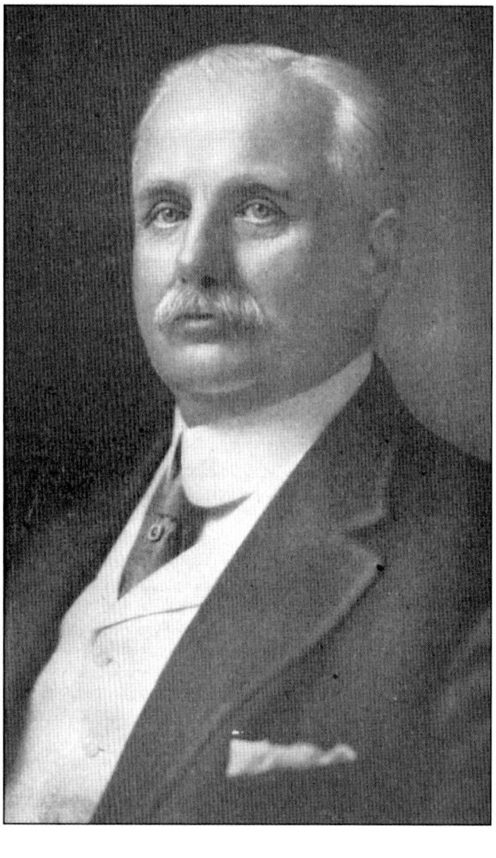

Built by Frank W. Woolworth as a memorial to his father and mother, this church was presented by him personally to the trustees and congregation on September 15, 1915. It was dedicated by Bishop John W. Hamilton, the architect was Case Gilbert of New York City, and the contractor was Fred Wright of Adams, New York. Frank W. Woolworth is pictured on the left.

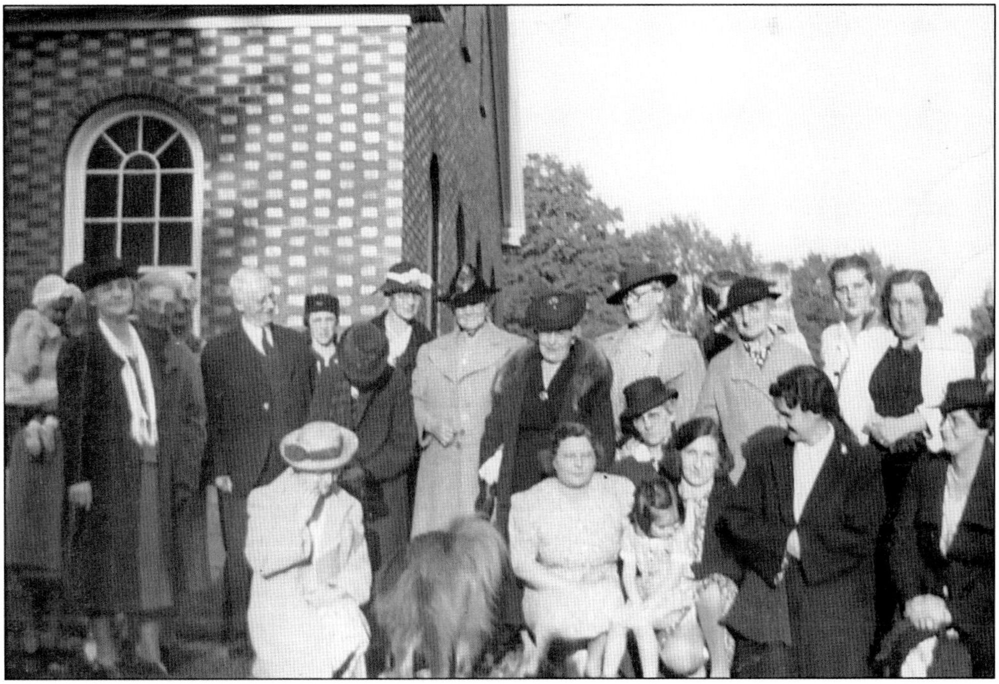

Congregants are pictured outside Woolworth Memorial Church. They are, in no particular order, Mildred Hammill, Lillian Call, William Mayhew, Cora Laughlin, Agnes Hartman, ? Miller, ? Neggris, ? Jeffers, ? Brownell, ? Pratt, ? Morrow, Rev. ? Barrett, ? Barrett, ? Taylor, Carrie Sisson, Eva Jonas and baby, ? Reynolds, Alice McCallops, Vera Keller, and? Dodge. Seen below is a harvest festival at the church. (Both, JCHS.)

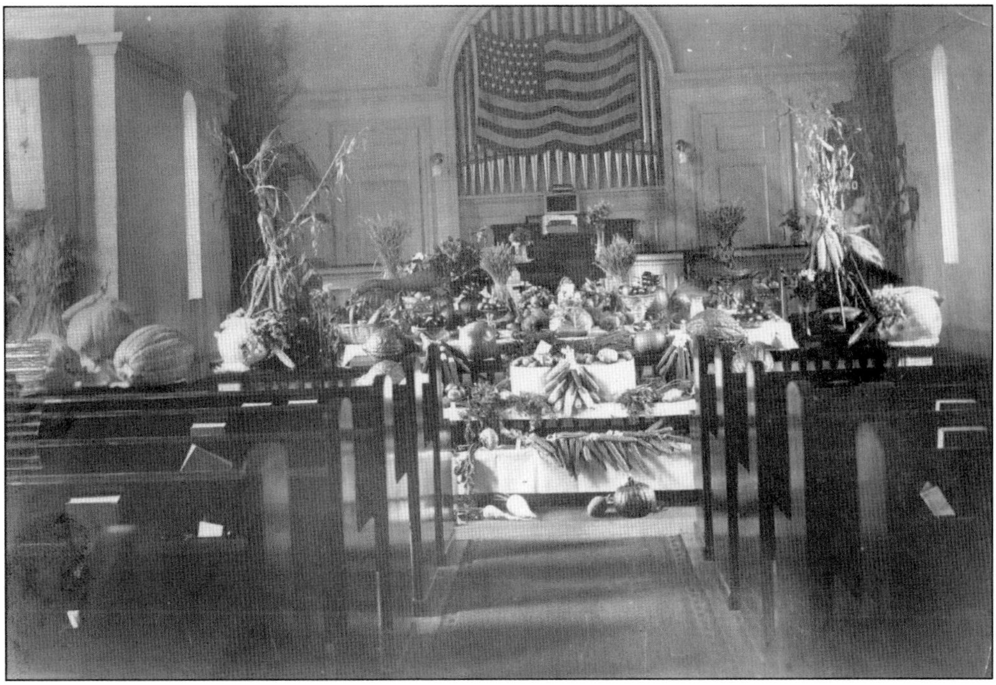

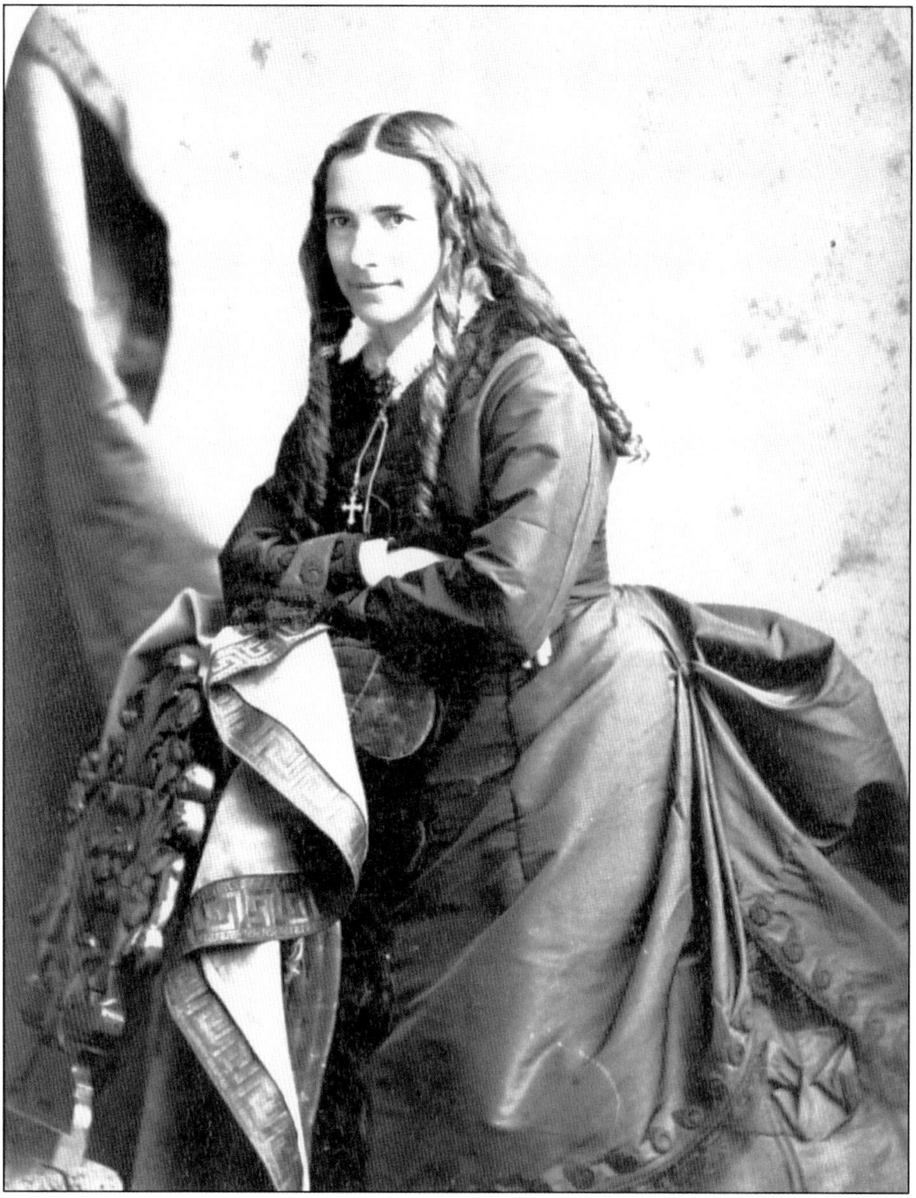

Mary Bradford Sterling Clark was the wife of George Clark of Great Bend and the daughter of James Sterling, the "Iron King" of Northern New York. Born in 1830, Mary married George in May 1851. It was through her work and guidance that Trinity Chapel was built. Truly an angel of mercy, Mary was always dressed in black, with her long grey curls topped by a black bonnet while she went about her work caring for the sick and poor of the area. She never failed to go where she was needed and could do some good. Mary started the first Sunday school class in November 1872, meeting first at the Jonas Shoe Shop, then later in the finishing room of the paper mill. Children and community members made what donations they could toward building their own church—giving pennies, nickels, and dimes. In 1874, her husband donated land, and ground was broken for a church. On September 25, 1875, Bishop Huntington consecrated the chapel, and on August 1, 1875, the Sunday school met and marched to the new chapel singing "Onward, Christian Soldiers." (CCC.)

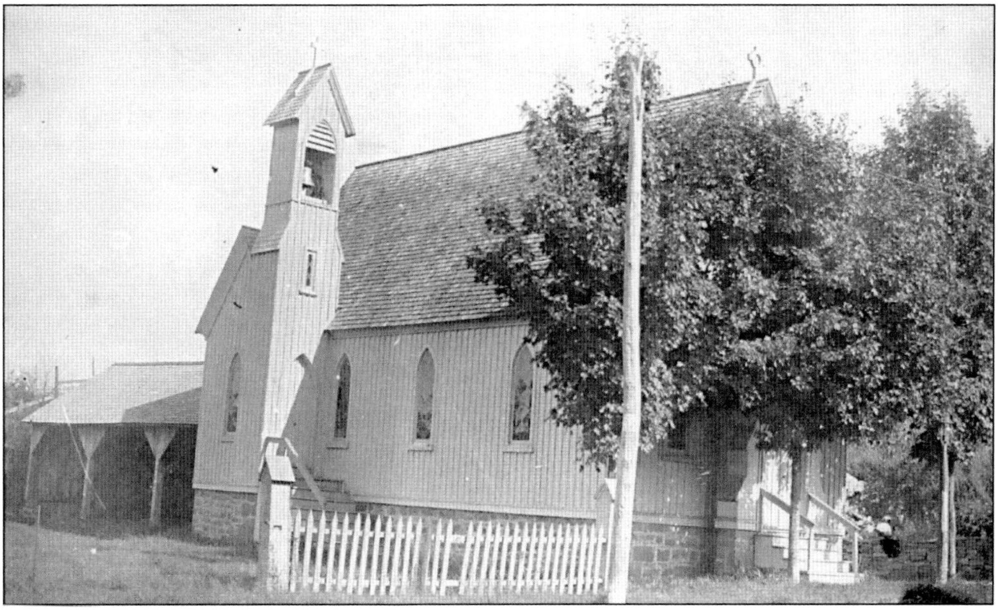

Trinity Chapel was built on property across the street from George Clark's mill. In 1873, Clark's wife, Mary, became the first Central New York deaconess in the Episcopal diocese. She was the chief instigator for building the chapel, which used a Richard Upjohn design and was dedicated on September 25, 1875. While most Upjohn churches were brick, the board-and-batten construction of the chapel gave it a distinction of its own. In 1977, the 4 River Valleys Historical Society was formed for the express purpose of preventing the removal of the chapel from Great Bend to the Partridge Berry Complex at Black River. Below is a church group after a performance.

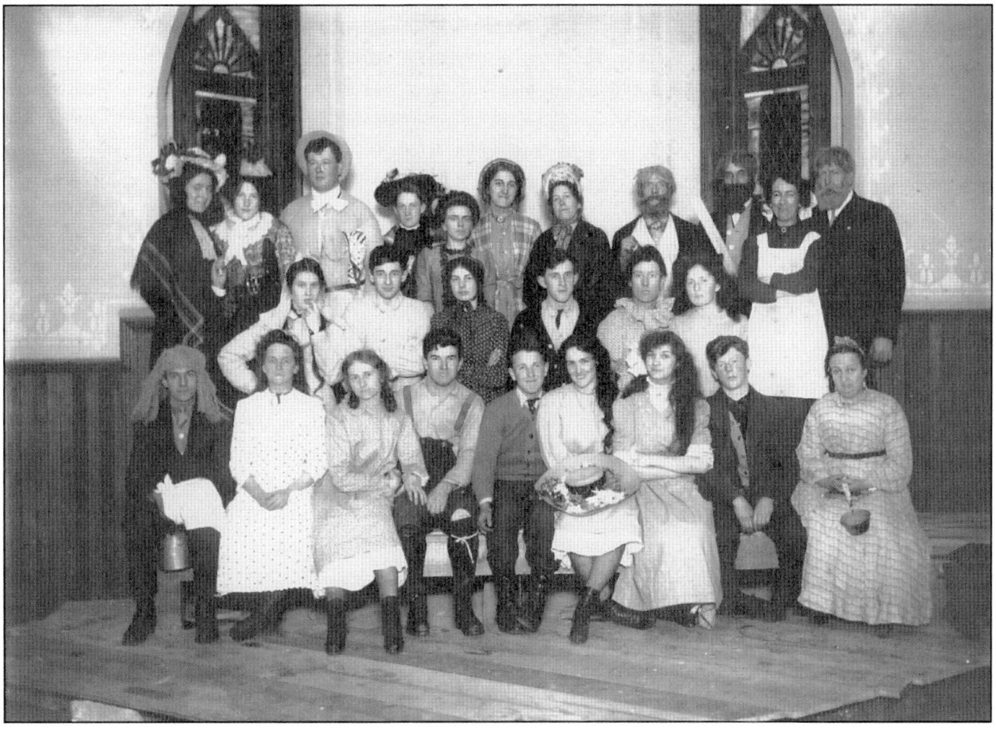

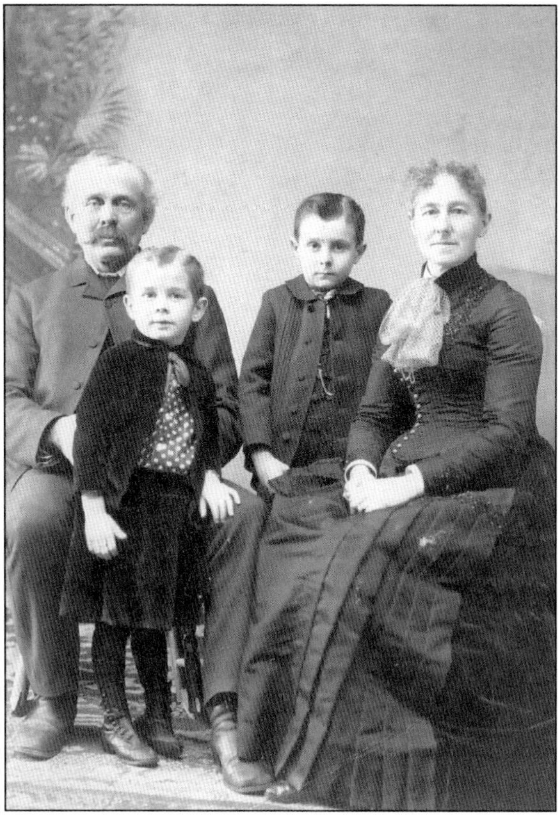

The Chauncey Clark family poses in this photograph. Chauncey, born 1843, and Gertrude (née Buck), born 1844, are shown with children Jay (left) and Fred. Chauncey was the owner of a gristmill, sawmill, woodworking mill, and shingle-manufacturing facility, the latter built by the Sisson brothers of the village. During the construction of the paper mill at Deferiet, Chauncey catered to the demand for meats in the vicinity for two years. He always dealt in cattle of all kinds, and operated a dairy with 20 to 25 cows. He bought and sold lands extensively, and eventually was the possessor of nearly 1,500 acres. Below, Chauncey and Gertrude are pictured later in life. (Both, CCC.)

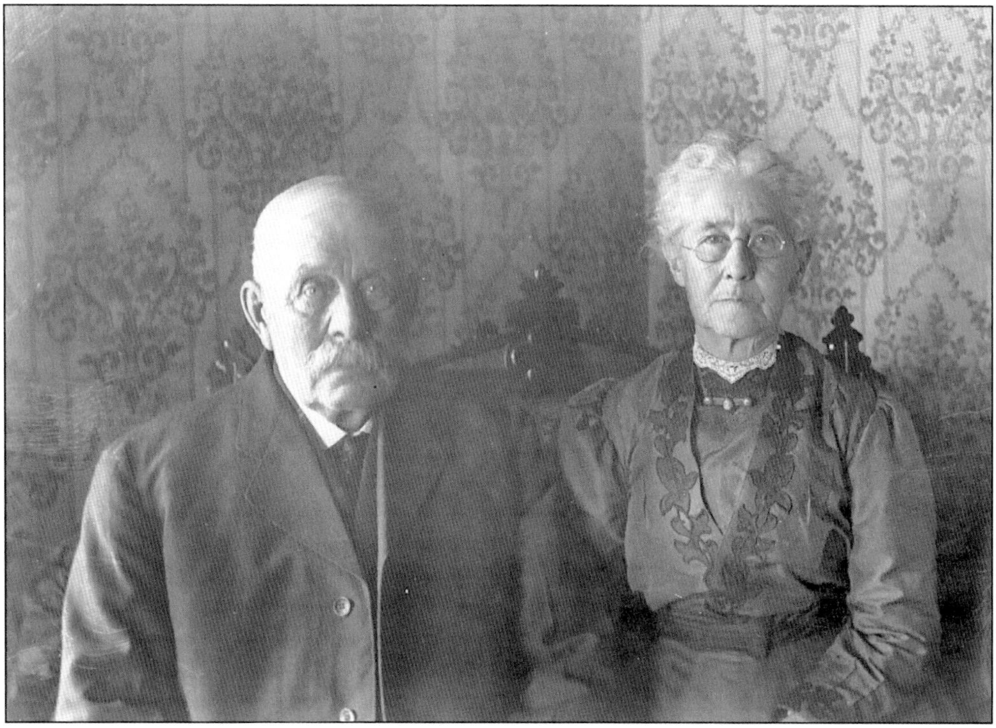

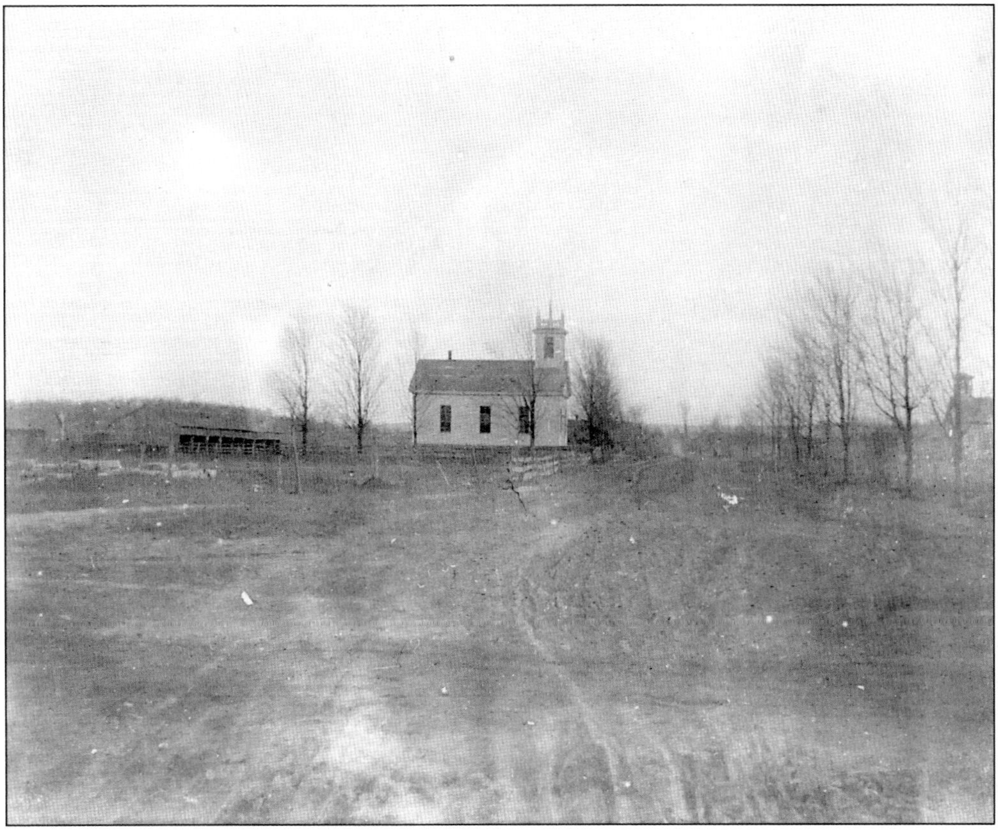

The old Baptist church and school are seen in both of these photographs taken at the Great Bend intersection. The image above, made in 1897, shows Champion Street before other buildings were built on the corner or in between. The photograph below is of the Knapp and Pressaw General Store and the corner of what are now Routes 47 and 3. The elementary school can be seen in the middle-right. (Both, SEC.)

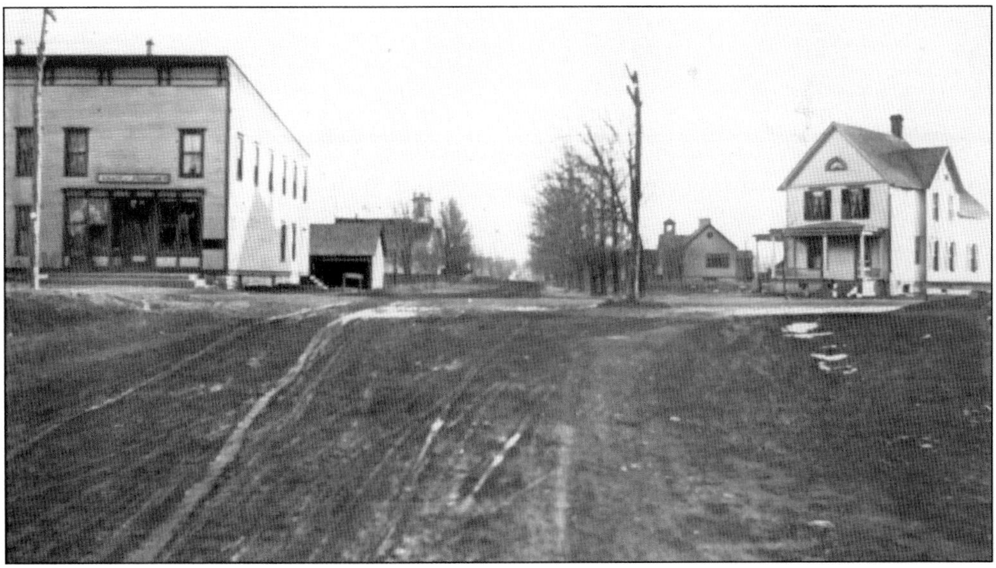

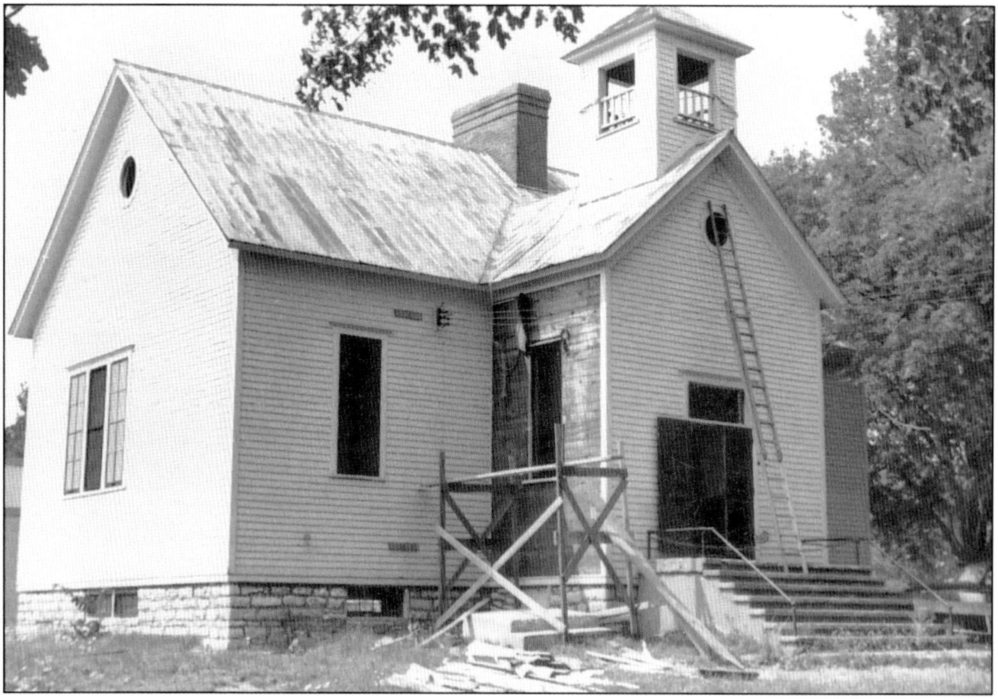

At a special meeting held on June 3, 1873, the school board voted to build a new educational facility on a lot across from the old school, half an acre of land that was purchased for $200 from Edwin and Samantha Carter. Wesley Briggs erected the main building at a cost of $1,150. He also purchased the old stone school for $150. In 1907, a new school was built on the same site by the Sisson brothers, who took the 1870s school in the deal and sold it to M.J. Pfister. He moved the former school across the road and onto a site between the old stone school and the railroad tracks, and it was renovated into an apartment house. The new school cost $4,000. Below is an undated class photograph at the school. (Both, SEC.)

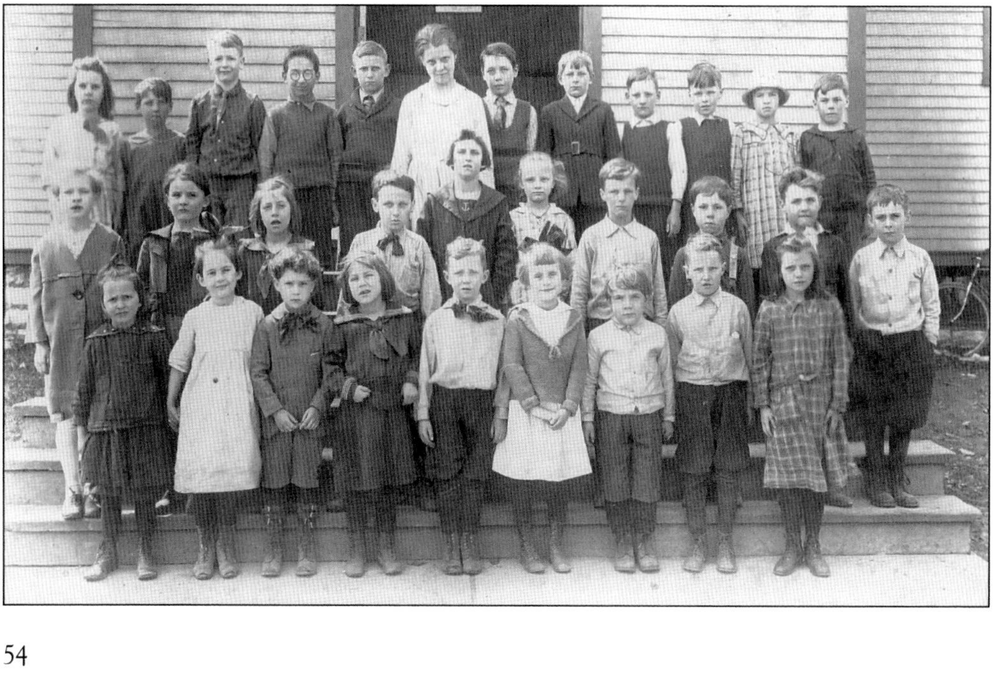

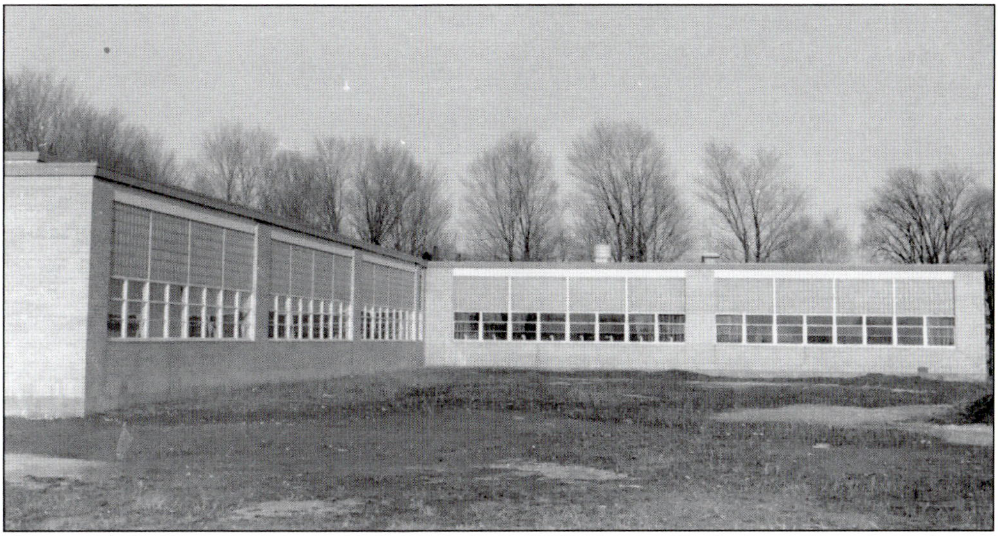

The new Great Bend School originally opened in 1951 with two classrooms, a gymnasium/auditorium, kitchen, office, and locker and shower rooms. In 1953, with funding provided jointly by the federal and state governments and taxpayers of the school district, an addition was constructed in order to accommodate a large number of children from Camp Drum. Until that time, the school was so crowded that first and second grades were held in the dining and recreation rooms of the Woolworth Memorial Church. With the addition, the school was capable of educating 350 pupils. Madeline Jerome Sisson and Irma Edward Jawroski, pictured below, headed the cafeteria staff. (Both, SEC.)

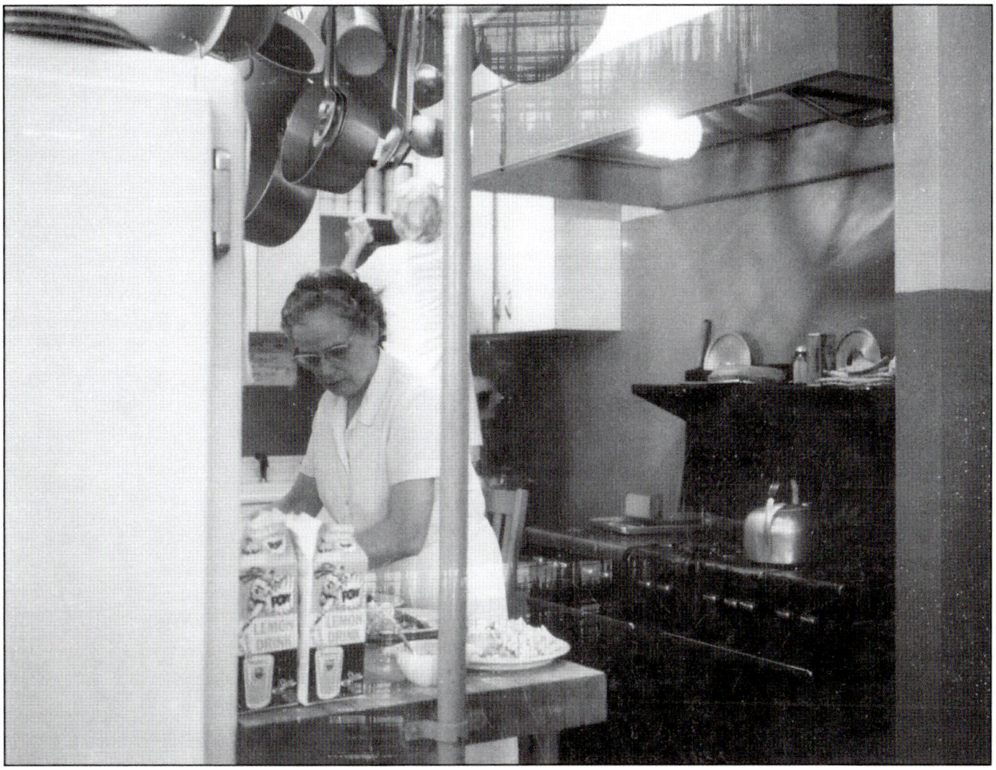

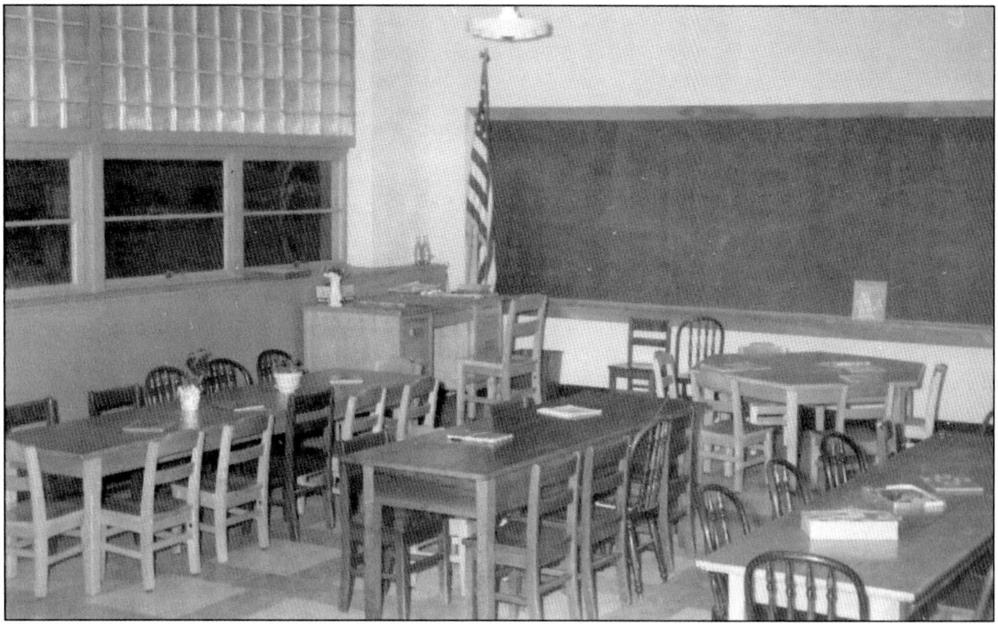

This classroom, awaiting its pupils, shows the glass block windows that were state-of-the-art at the time. The photograph below shows fifth-graders who, according to the *Carthage Republican Tribune*, "[are] demonstrating how very comfortable their special posture chair and desk sets are, and how well the light floods the room from the wide windows on the right while the glass brick above lets in a soft light." (Both, SEC.)

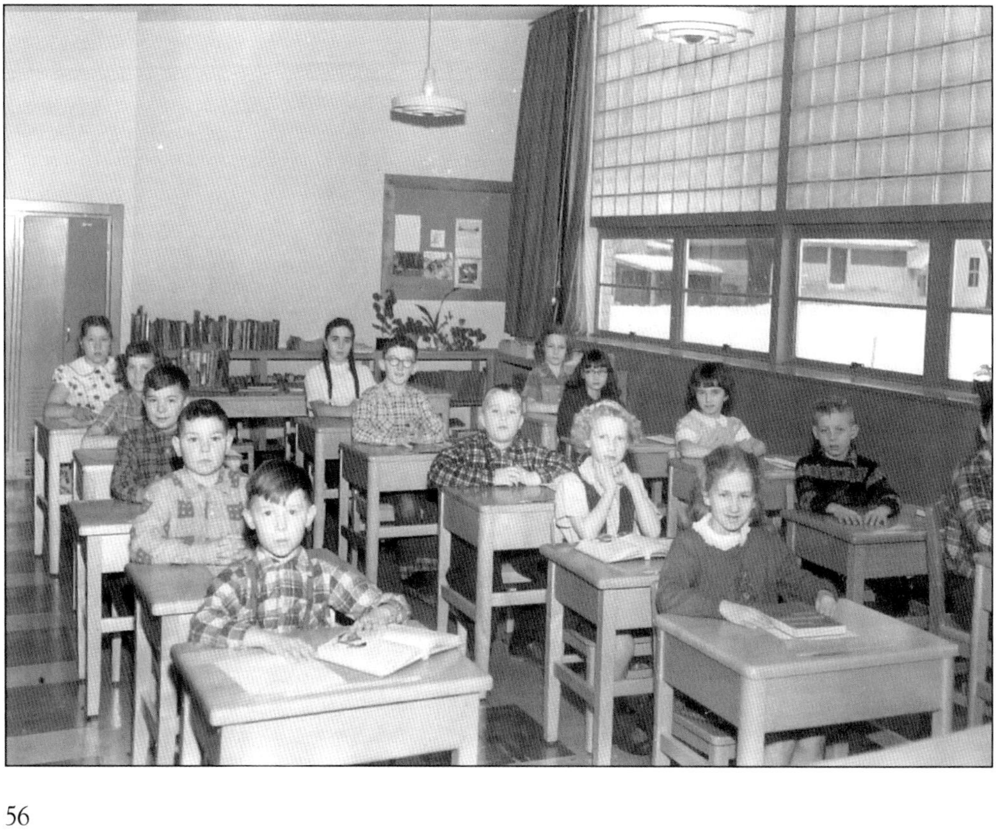

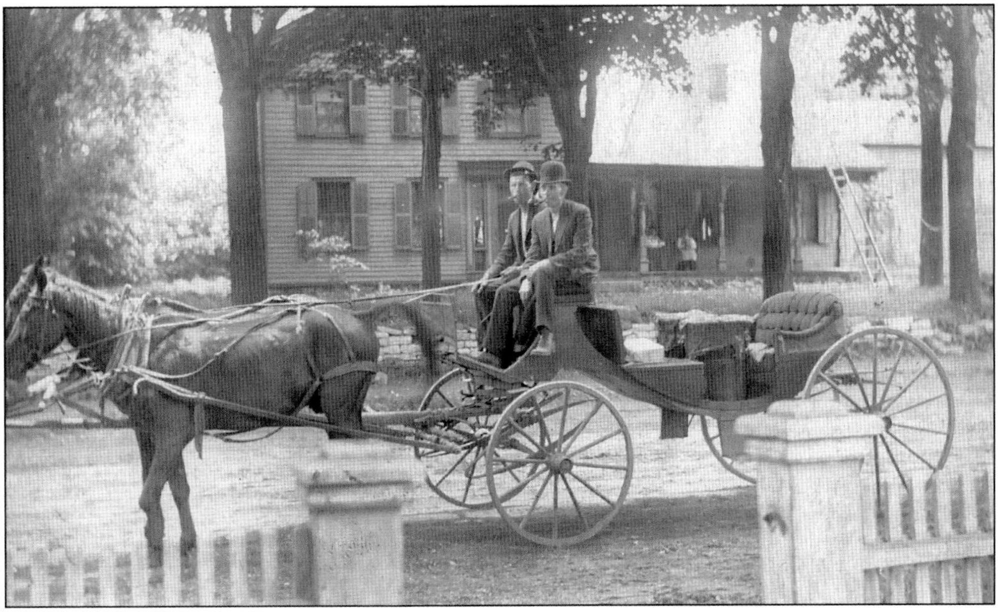

Daniel Potter probably built the Flint Sisson House around 1840. He owned all the property on the south side of Route 3 from Great Bend's Martin Street Road to the bridge over the Black River at Deferiet. Among the owners of this house were Cicero Potter, Alexander LaClare, Jude Cross, Egbert and Selinda Flint, Almeron and Esther Ricket, and Jerome and Madeline Sisson. Today, it belongs to their daughter JoAnna Sisson Emerson and her husband, Terry, who operate it as the Grand View Bed and Breakfast. In the above photograph, two draymen, or carters, drive a wagon toward the mill area. Women on the porch are peeling potatoes. Below is the same home with an enclosed porch. (Both, CCC.)

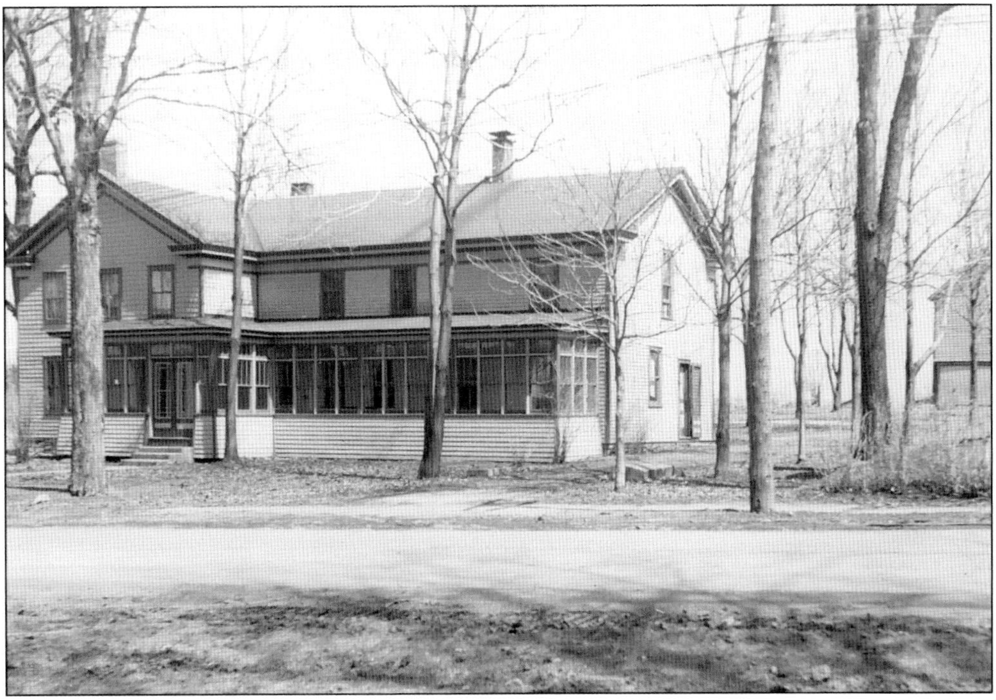

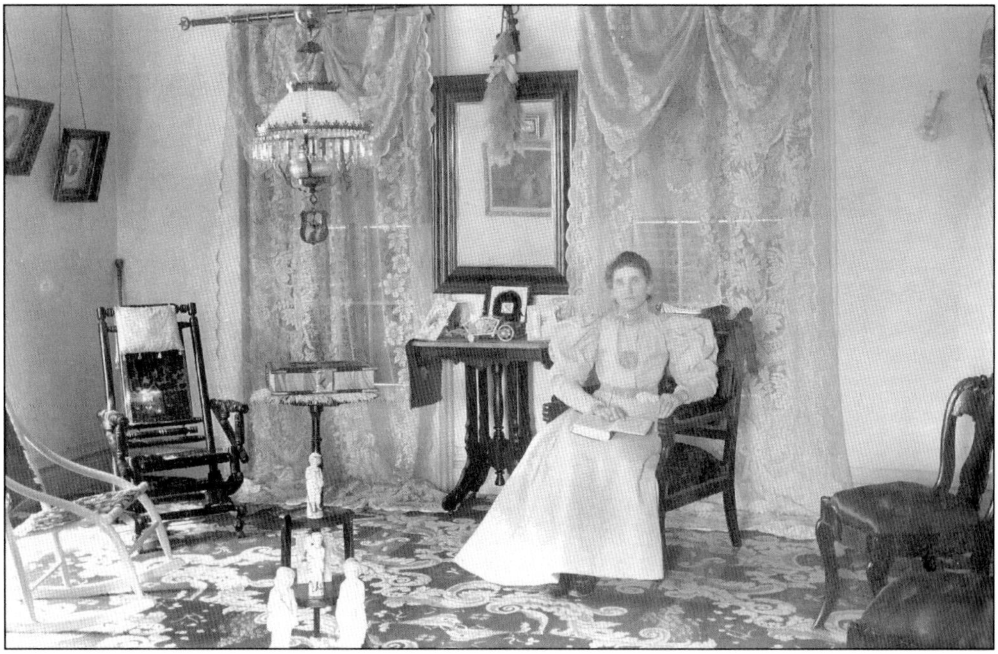

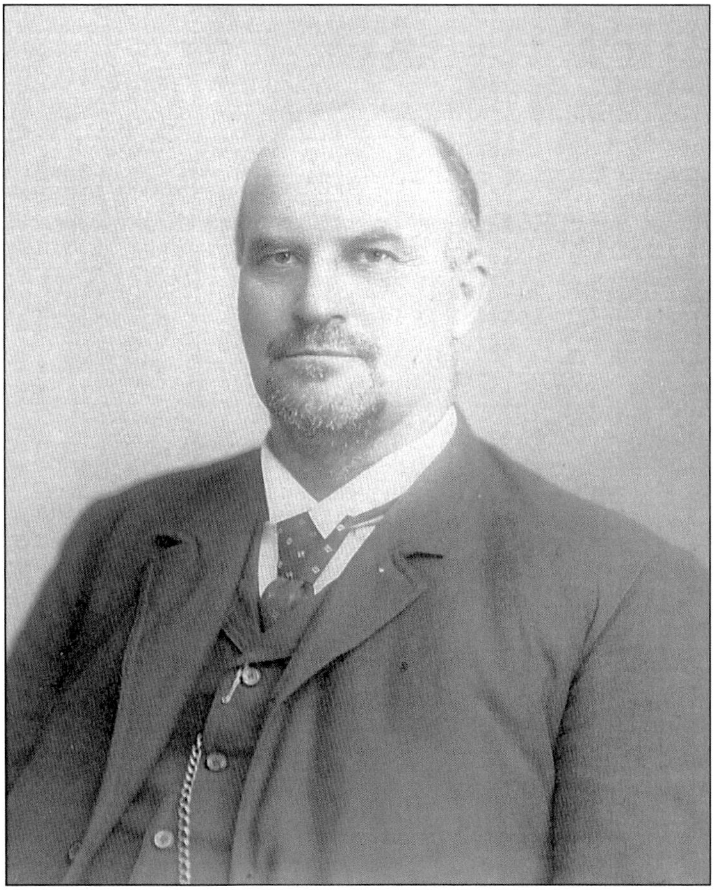

An unidentified woman is pictured sitting inside the Flint Sisson House. Egbert Flint was responsible for some of the more decorative aspects of the home, including the stained glass in its exterior doors. Flint (left) met an untimely end when a train startled his horses, throwing him from his carriage and killing him. (Both, CCC.)

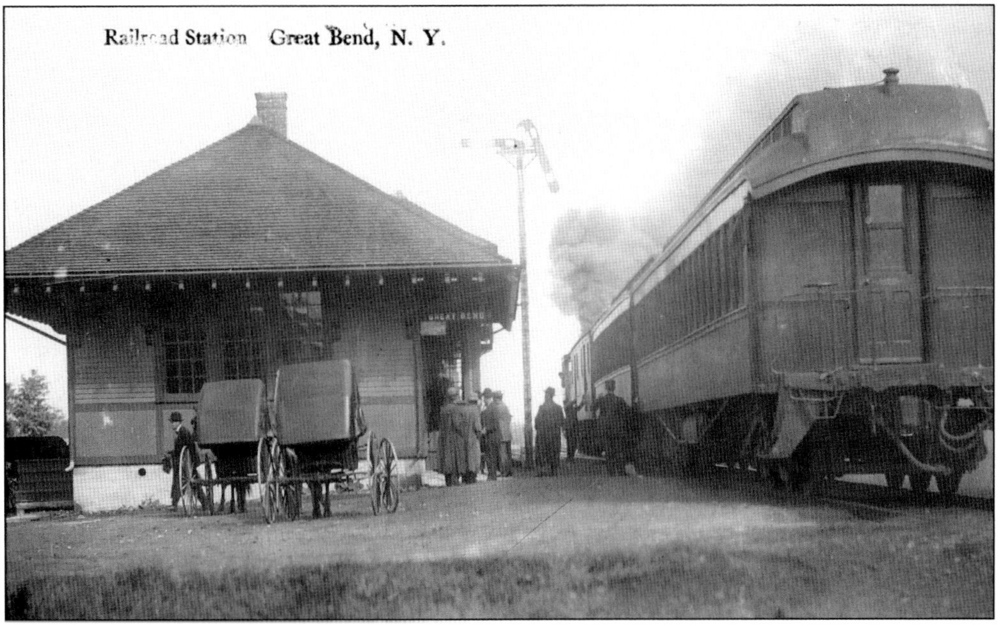

A train at this station startled Egbert Flint's horses, in the incident that led to his death. The primary reason for the railroad in this community was transporting paper made at the mills in Great Bend. Below is a sled bringing rolls of paper from the mill to the railroad depot. (Above, SEC; below, JCHS.)

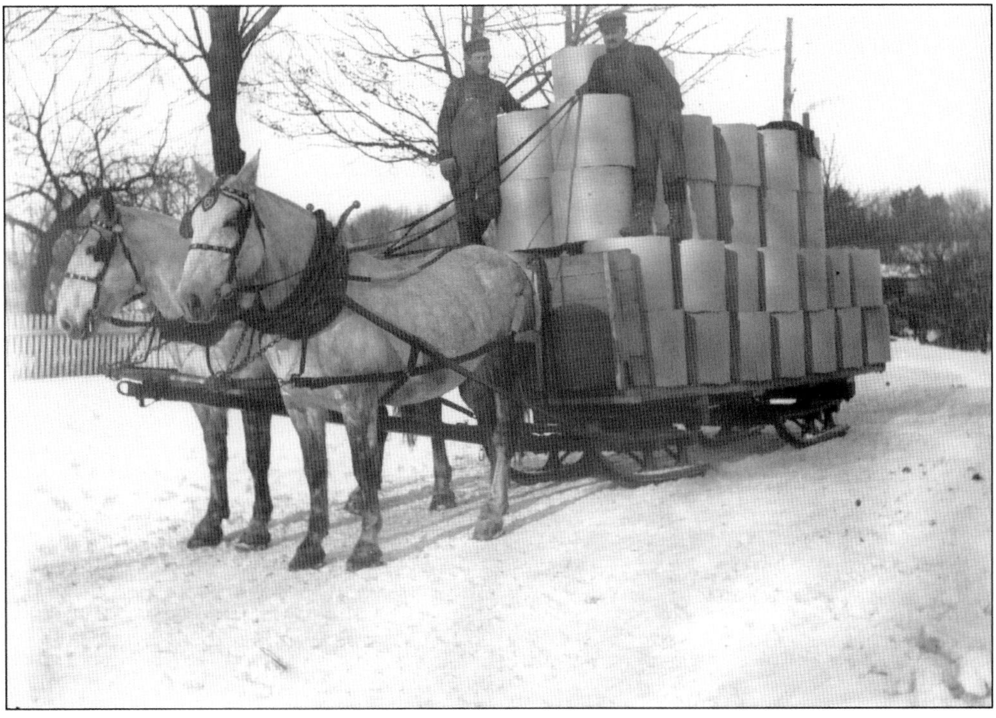

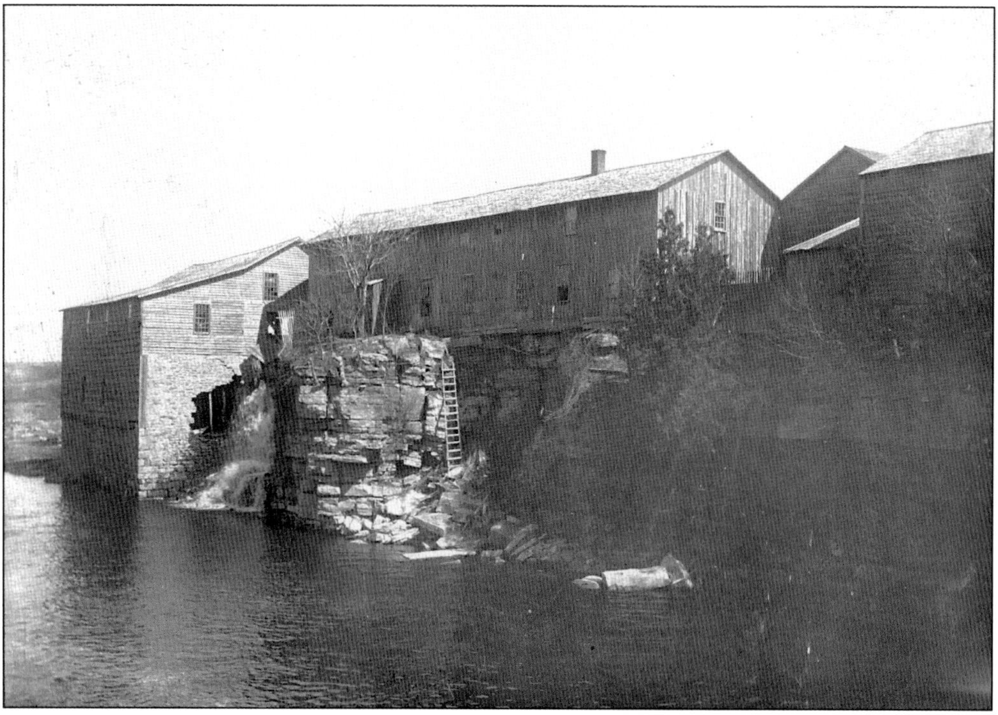

In 1809, a distillery was put into operation. In 1816, the premises were purchased by Watson and Gates who, in 1824, sold them to Charles E. Clark. The large fire that occurred in Great Bend on March 5, 1840, destroyed the entire business portion of the village, including the gristmill and bridge. The loss was estimated at $20,000. The mill was immediately rebuilt on an extensive scale. (Both, SEC.)

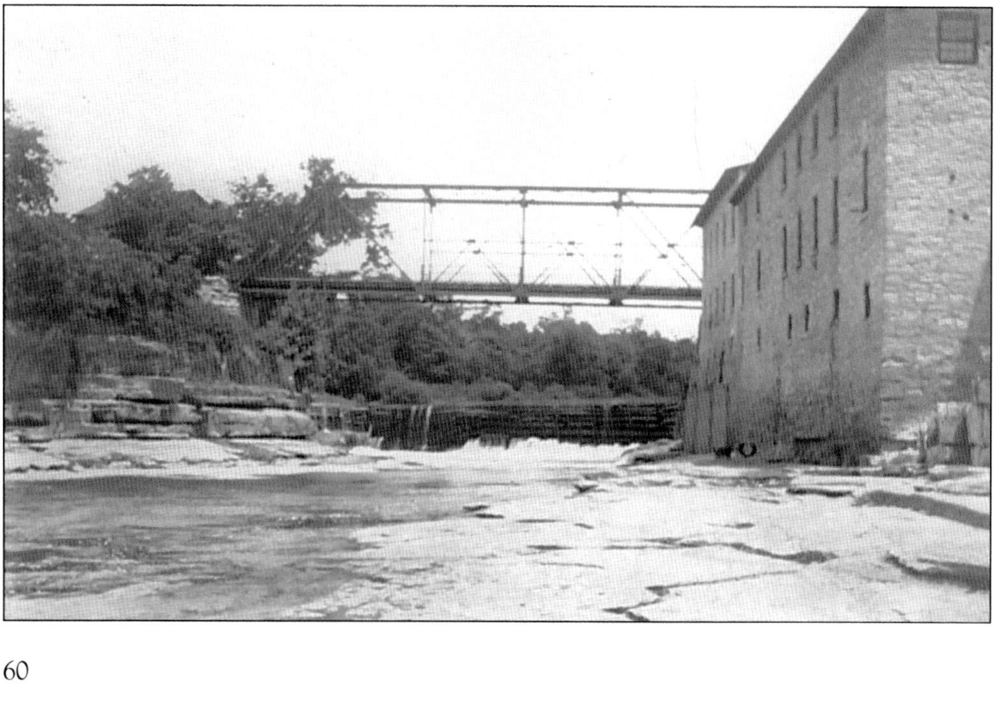

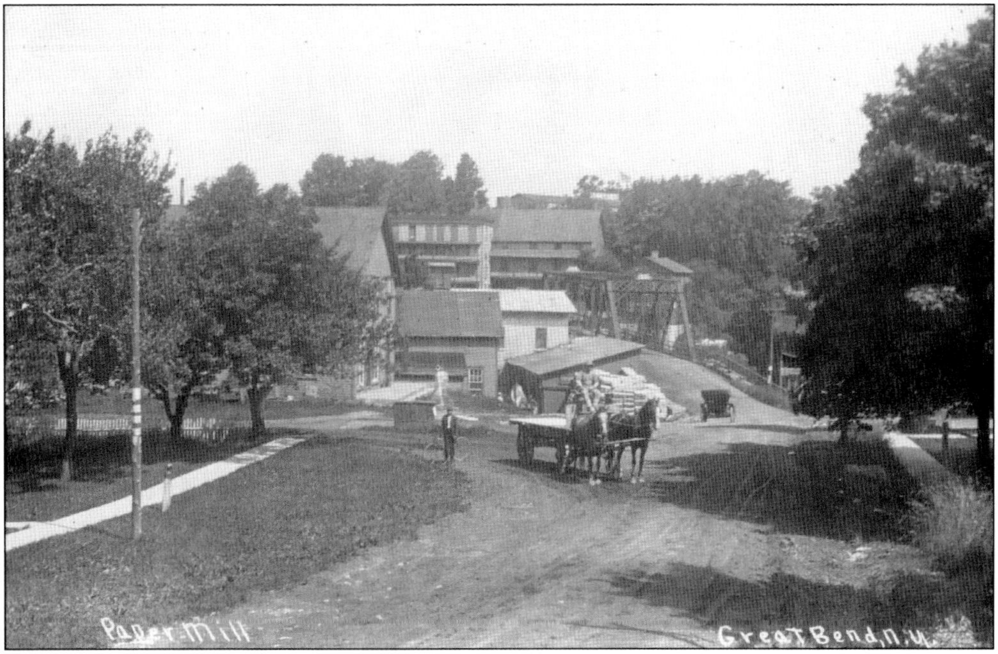

Looking toward the bridge and industrial section of Great Bend about 1900, one can see a series of paper mills harnessing the Black River's natural power to produce strawboard, known as "brown hanging paper." There were a number of people associated with the industry in the village, including, but not limited to, George Clark, Lewis Milles, James Sterling, John Harrigan, Frank Fletcher, F.X. Zaph, E.F. and Ida Thompson, E.H. Thompson, W.K. Peck, John H. McLean, O.F. Dodge, and George C. Sherman. Below is the old log dam that controlled the water for many years. It is shown shortly before its collapse in 1914. (Both, SEC.)

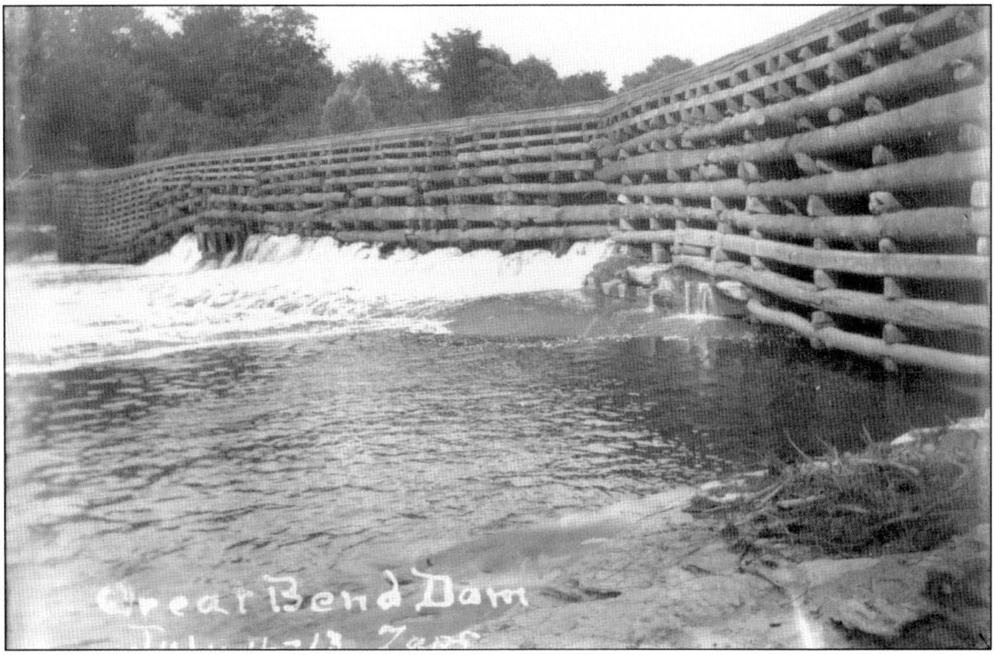

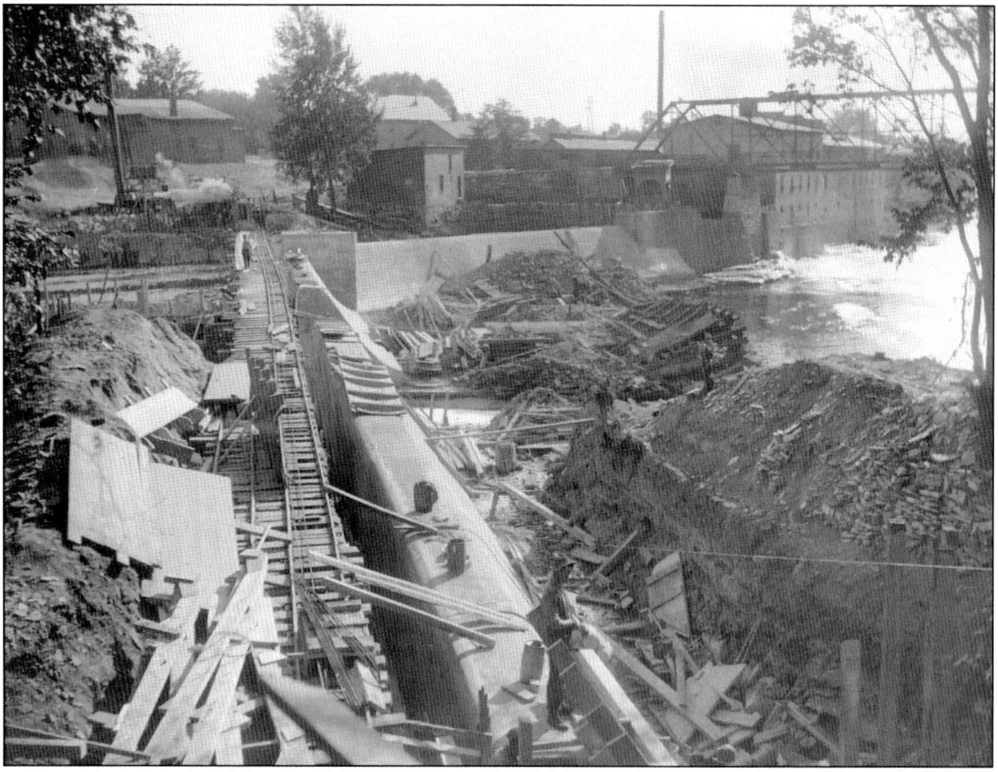

This photograph shows the construction of the new concrete dam. After the collapse of the log dam, D.M. Anderson sold his interest to George C. Sherman, who changed the mill's name to Sherman Paper Company. The mill was one of the few run by waterpower until February 28, 1927, when the obsolete water turbine was replaced with a steam-turbine drive. Below, Sgt. ? Green and his mule team bring wood to a mill site. The bearded man at right is O.L. Sisson. (Both, SEC.)

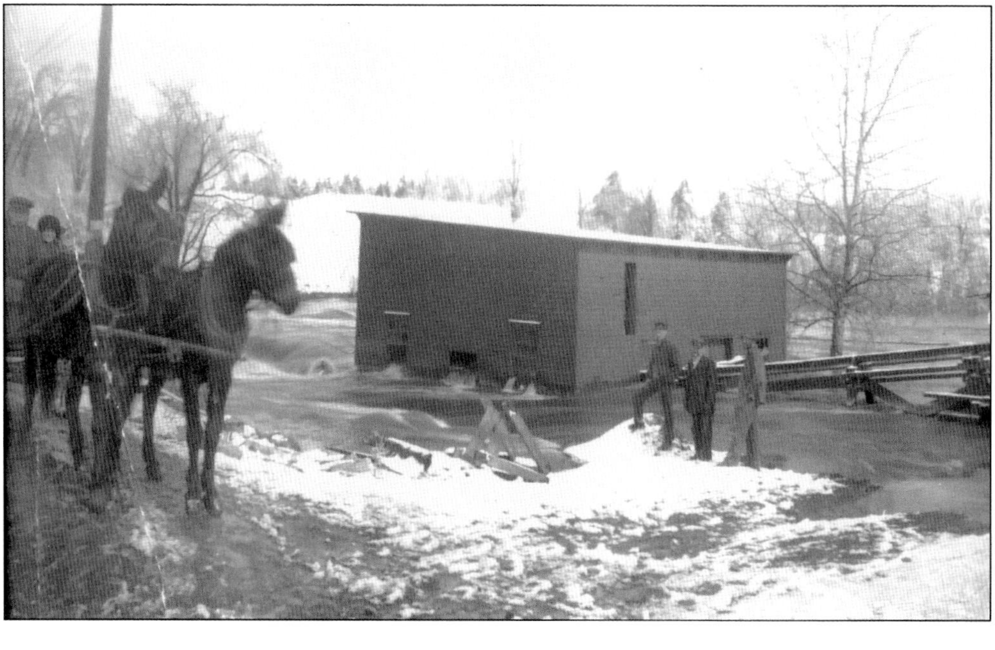

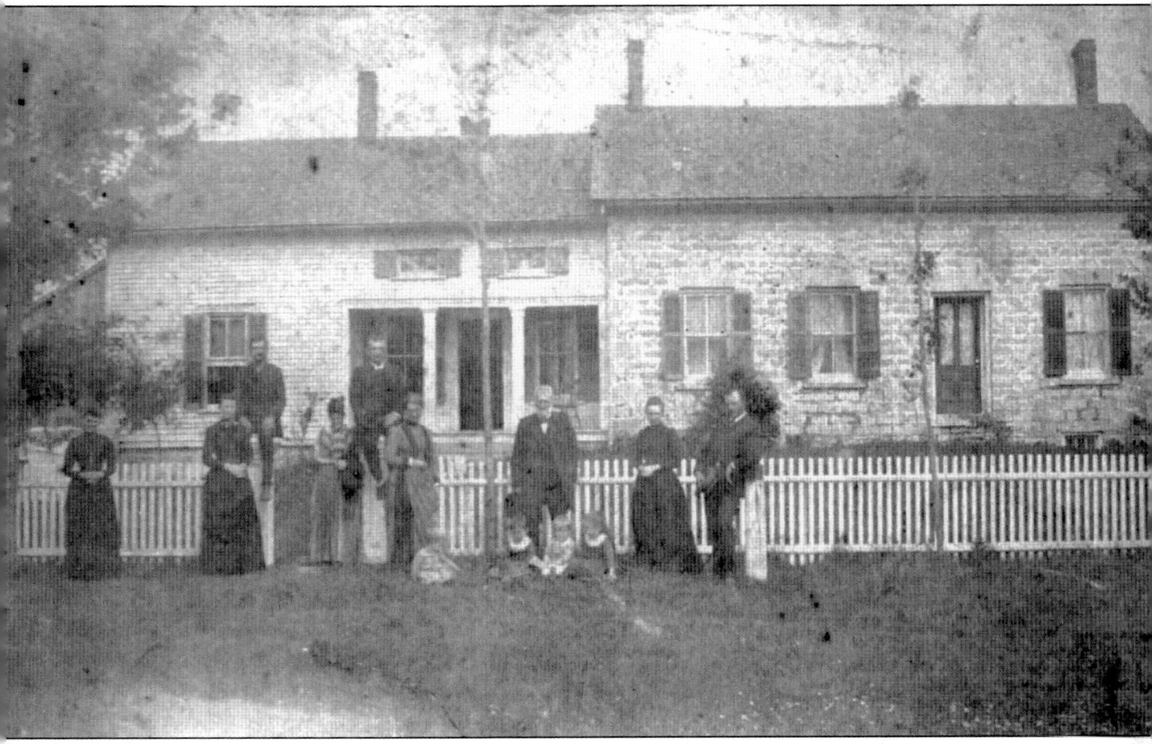

This 1900 photograph of the John Peck Farm includes many members of the Peck and Pennock families. Joseph Peck Jr., a Revolutionary War veteran, constructed the house in 1827. The farm, which he cleared and developed, sits in a portion of the town known as the Pennock Road and has remained in the family since the time of its construction. John C. and Wilma Fargo Peck bought their farm from his grandmother, Mary Flint Peck, in 1946. John E. Peck, son of John C., worked the farm for many years before moving to the next farm, the Pennock-Peck farm in the 1970s. (Peck family collection.)

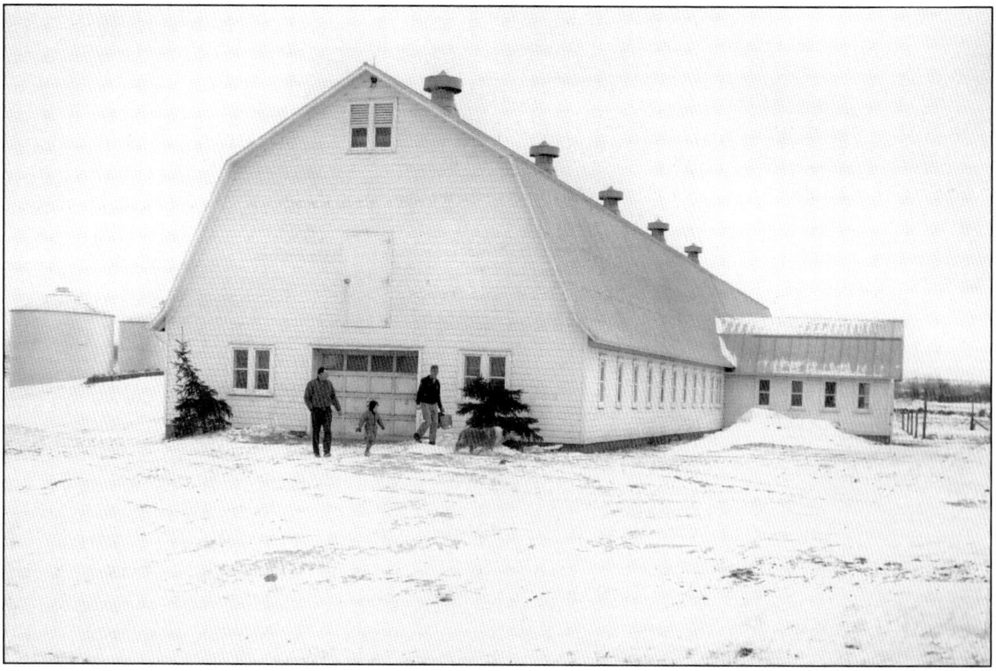

This aerial view of the Peck Farm (below) was taken in 1958. The 1968 photograph above shows the Peck men in front of their barn. The land has been in the Peck family for over 200 years and was originally awarded by George Washington to Joseph Peck for his service in the Revolutionary War. The 56.5 acres that Joseph settled in 1803 have expanded to 347 acres. Over its lifetime, the land has produced everything from potatoes and apples to maple syrup, but for the last 100 years, it has been milk production that has kept the Peck families going. (Both, Peck family collection.)

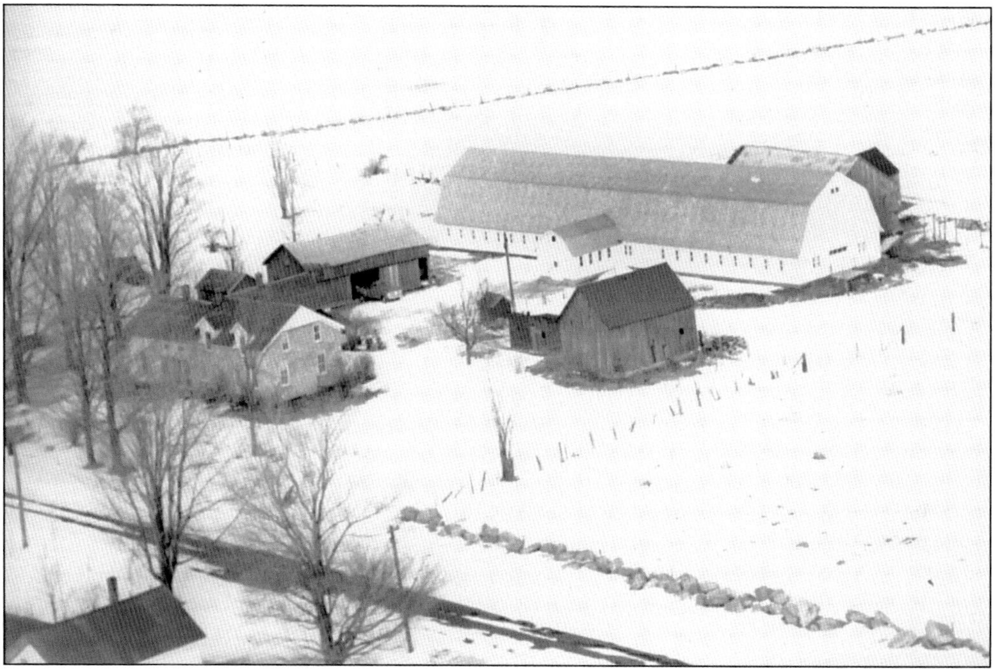

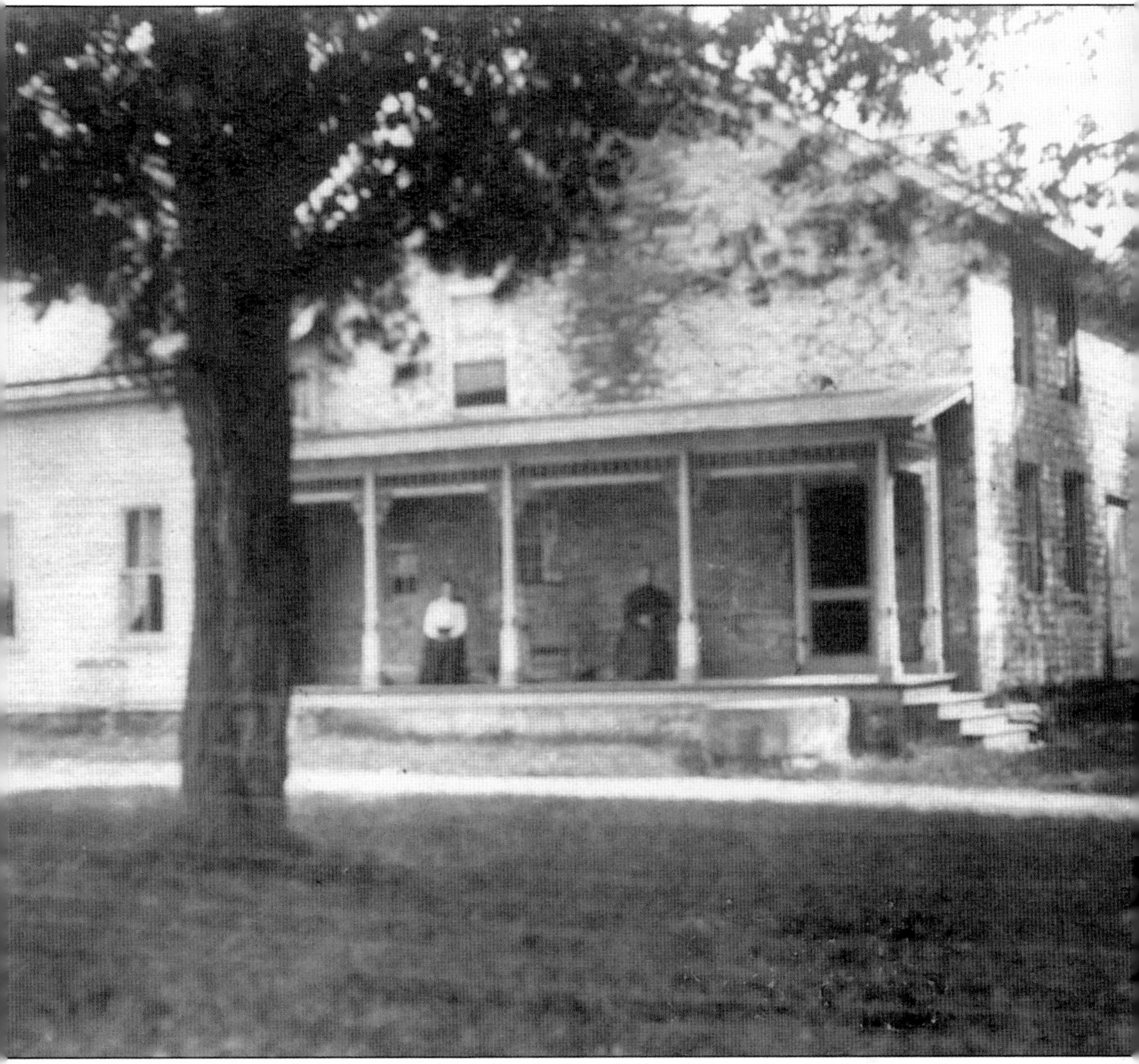

On one of two century farms in the Peck family, Rev. Wilson Pennock built this fine old limestone mansion with his own hands. It is located about a mile from Great Bend on the east road that runs to Champion. Constructed around 1825, the property is next to the old Henry Peck farm, which also has a fine old native limestone house. Rev. Wilson's son, Emory J. Pennock, was born there on February 28, 1832. In 1852, Emory Pennock married Cordelia M. Lewis, daughter of Abel P. Lewis. On February 16, 1865, Rev. Pennock deeded his farm to his son Emory, making reservations that he and his wife should have use of such portions of the house and farm as needed, be furnished with fuel, wood, light, wholesome food, medicines, medical care, conveyance to go visiting, and care of rooms. (Both, Peck family collection.)

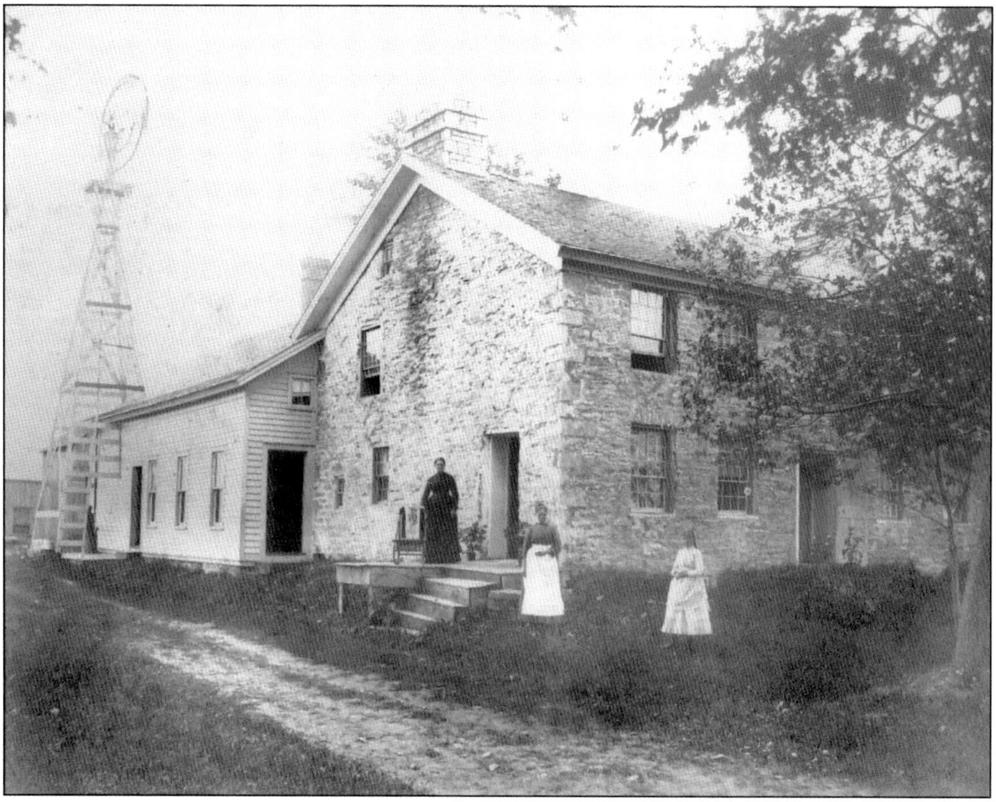

Among Emory's seven children was William E. Pennock, who married Emily A. Peck, daughter of John F. Peck. Rev. Arthur F. Pennock, DD, died in 1931. In 1944, Wilma Fargo Peck came to the farm, where she married, raised a family of five, and worked alongside her husband in the barn or picking up rocks in the fields. She recalls taking a day or two off when she gave birth. She also remembers that they had a tractor quite early, as her husband did not really care for horses. Below, the Peck family is pictured around 1970: (first row) Barry Peck, Cory Peck, John D. Peck, and Brian S. Peck; (second row) John C. Peck, Wilma Peck, John E. Peck, and Harry Peck. (Both, Peck family collection.)

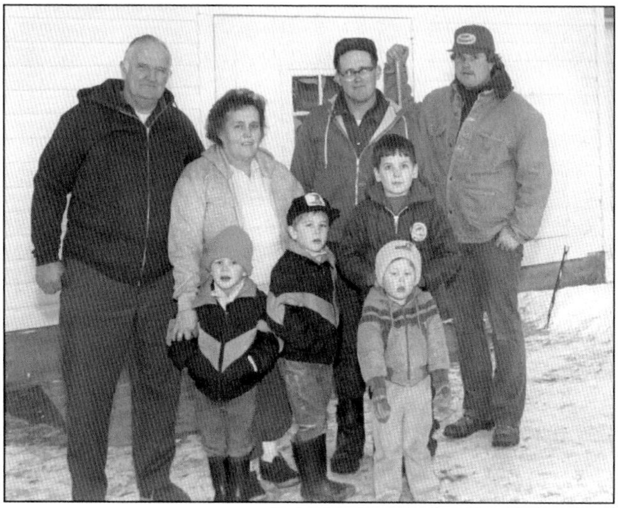

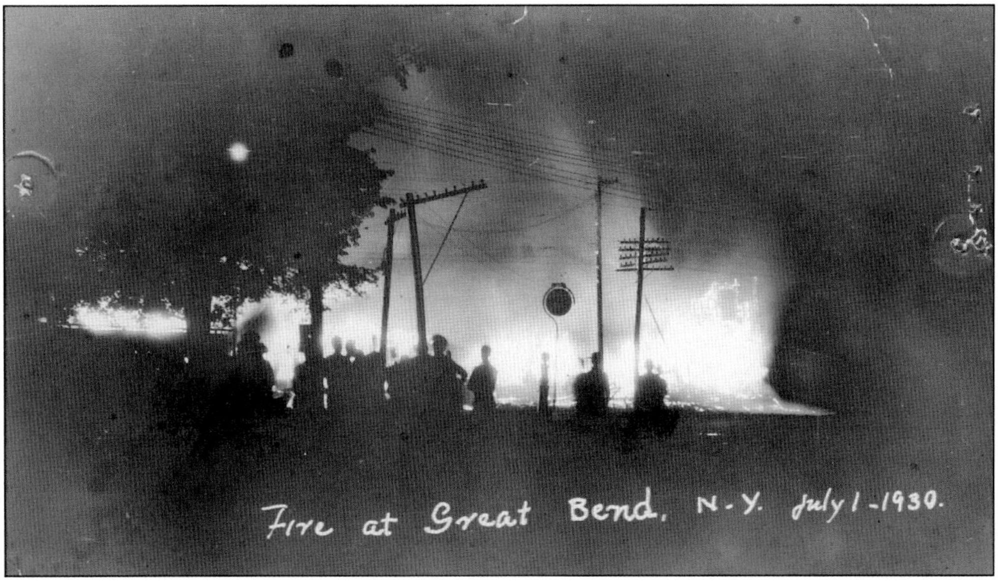

Frank Krakowka owned the Great Bend Bakery on Champion Street, pictured here on fire. The building was a total loss. Afterward, the Great Bend Fire Department sent Krakowka a petition to express sympathy for his loss in the fire and also to express hope that he would continue doing business in Great Bend. Fire departments from Watertown, West Carthage, Carthage, and Black River also responded. Each was sent $25, because departments were paid for every fire they responded to. Below is the first Great Bend Fire Department on January 1938. From left to right are Paul Snyder, Leonard "Mose" Wilton, Floyd Rendle (chief), Harold Comstock, Joel Bacon, Jerome Sisson, James Call, Fred Sterling, James Green, and C.B. Dodge.

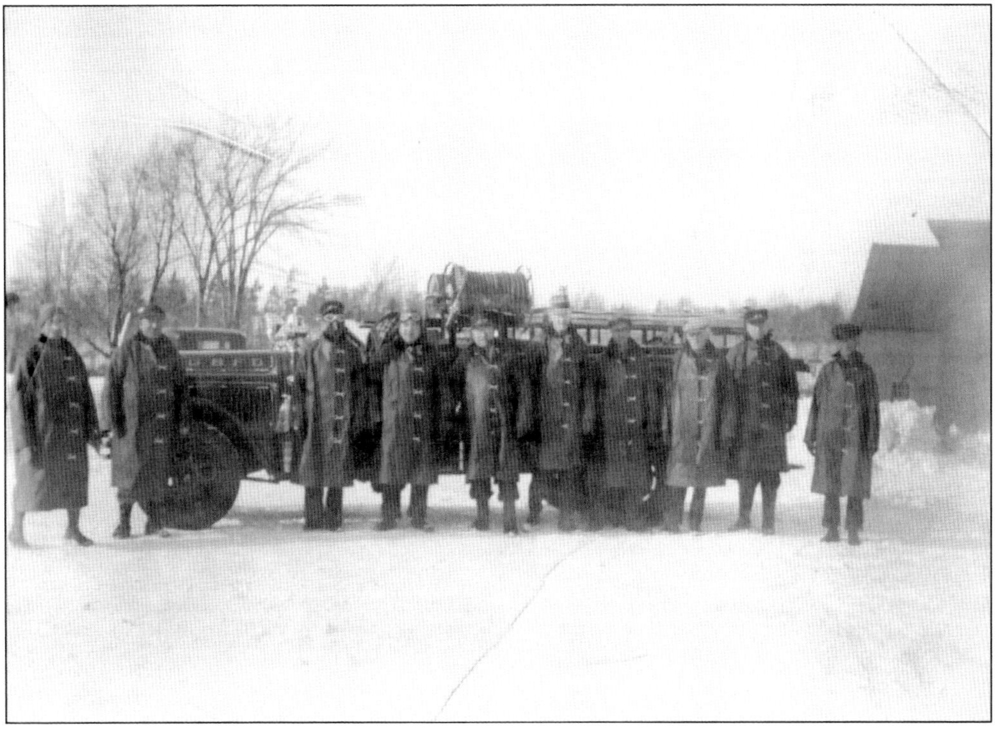

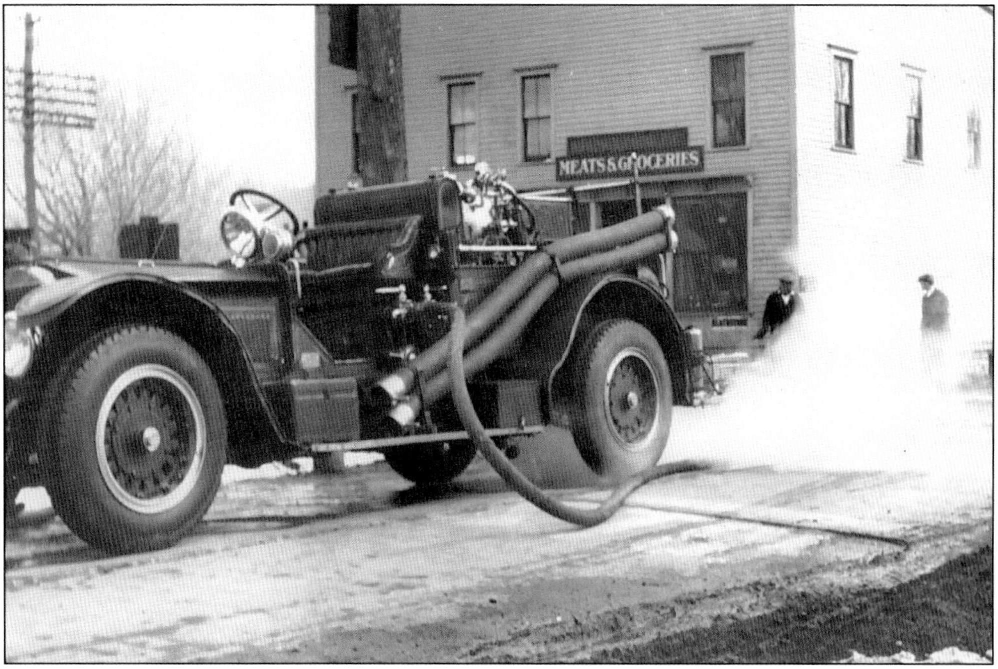

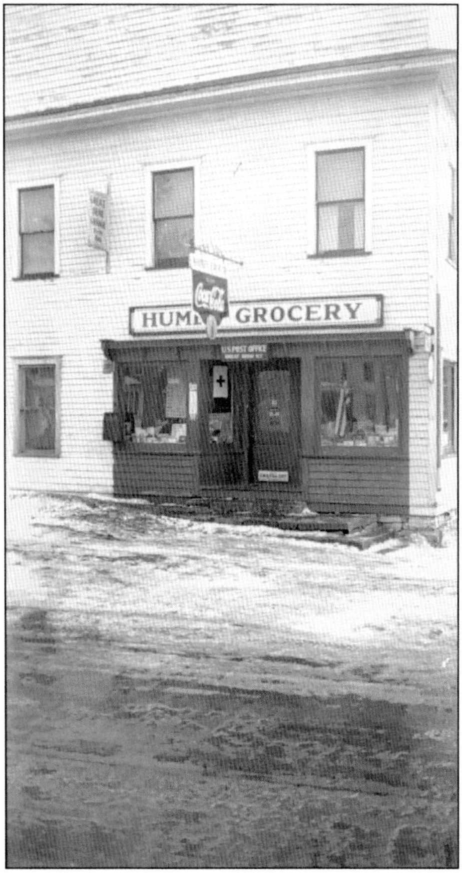

On October 22, 1942, a fire that caused $9,000 worth of damage left four families homeless when it completely destroyed an apartment house along with all its contents in the center of Great Bend. The fire also threatened the whole eastern section of the village before five fire departments brought it under control. An oil stove in the barbershop on the ground floor of an old building caused the disastrous blaze. The structure where the blaze started had until two years earlier been a general merchandise store operated by George E. Sheldon.

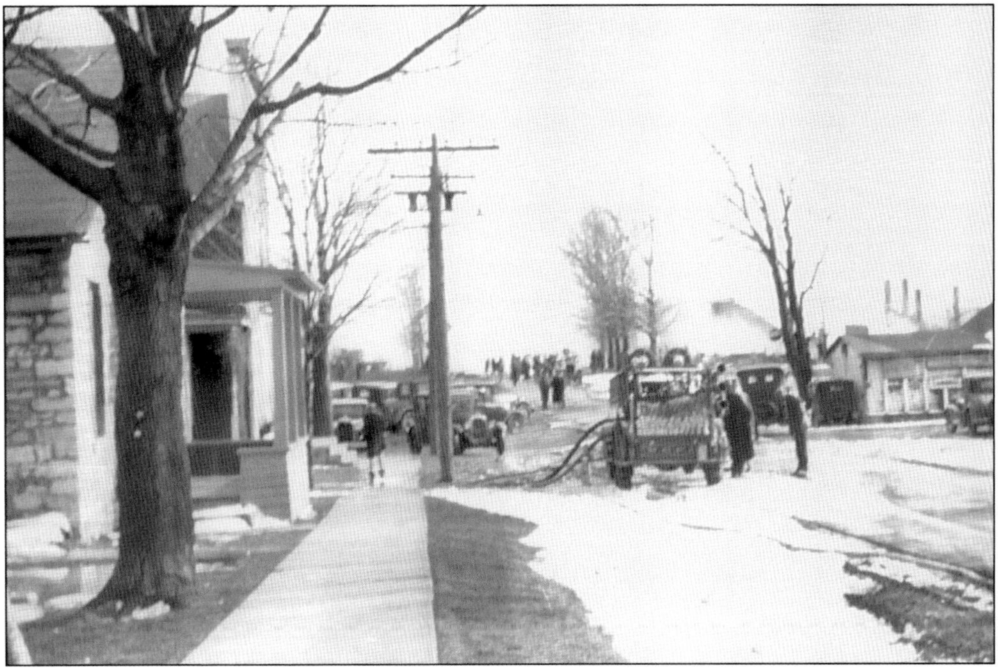

Peter Bell, the barber who discovered the blaze, sounded the alarm that brought the Great Bend Fire Department to the scene. The departments of Pine Camp, Black River, Deferiet, and Carthage also responded. The photograph above shows the first Great Bend pumper in action. Below is a photograph of the store in 1917. Over the years, parts were added, demolished, and the structure was altered. The young man marked with an X grew up to be Dr. E.C. Soults. His father, Albert, was one of the supervisors of the Taggert Mill, later Sherman Paper. (Both, SEC.)

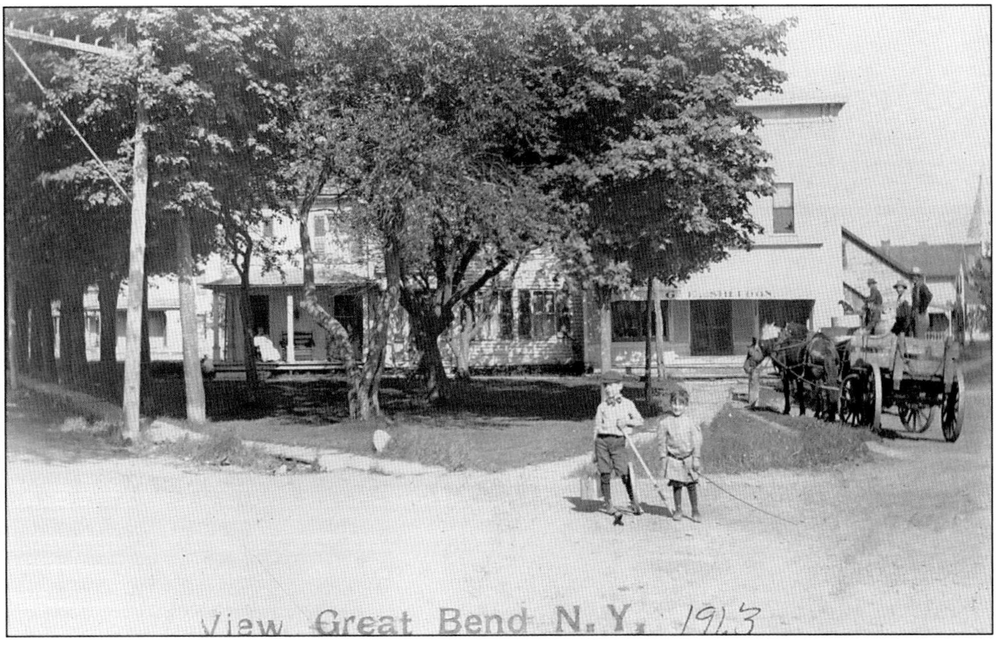

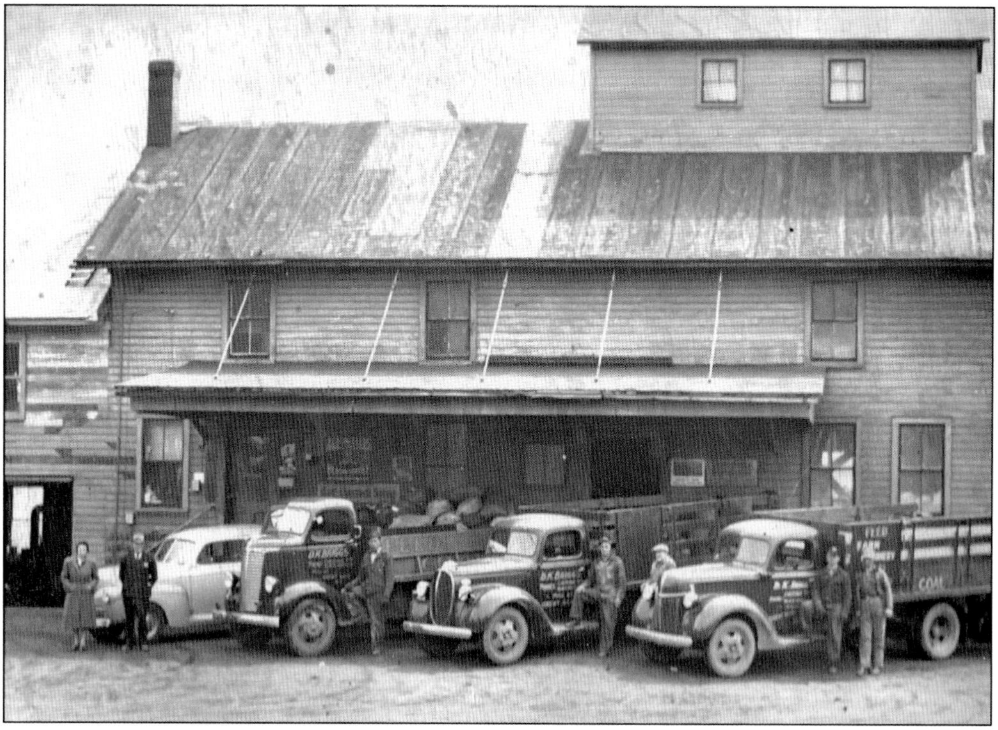

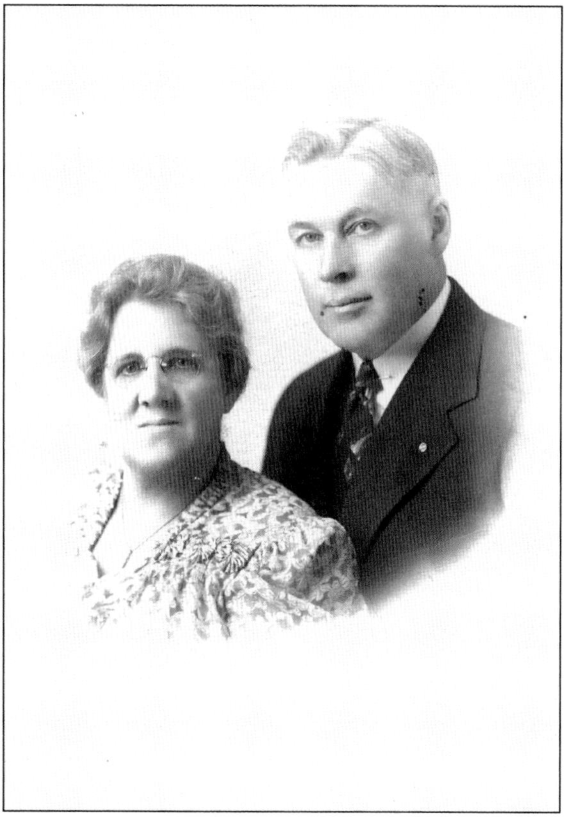

Pictured above, from left to right, are Ethel Bullis, Dax Briggs, Theodor Mosley, Harry Fargo, Frank Briggs, Merle Cross, and Bing Fargo. Darius K. Briggs started in the feed and coal business in Great Bend in 1922. He sold his enterprise in 1925, but reacquired it in 1927. Briggs manufactured dairy and poultry feeds in both mash and pellet forms under the labels Briggs and Beacon Feeds. He later added bulk fuel oil, lumber, and hardware to the business. The photograph on the left is of D.K and his wife, Ollie, who were married in 1923. She was a member of the Woolworth Memorial Church and directed the choir. The store is currently owned and operated by Bill Nier. (Both, Bill Nier.)

Three

DEFERIET
THE MILL TOWN

When Baroness Jenika de Feriet was born in 1776 to Francois Louis de Feriet, Seigneur of Verny, she never expected to leave a legacy. To escape the horror of the French Revolution, she fled to England, where she was persuaded by James LeRay de Chaumont and his daughter to immigrate to America. Many believed that the French émigrés, who came to northern New York, would build a "new France" and restore power to Napoleon. Jenika lived lavishly, as if she were still in France, but became disillusioned and eventually returned to her homeland.

The St. Regis Paper Company was established on February 4, 1899, when George Sherman and David Anderson filed a certificate for incorporation with the State of New York. George Eggleston Dodge, Ferris Meigs, and Titus Meigs financed the new venture, with Dodge as the first president. St. Regis was chosen as the name since the St. Regis River flowed through the first timberlands the company had purchased. A spectacular engineering feat was undertaken in constructing a canal to channel the water from the Black River to power the mill. Teams of horses and over 1,000 men, the majority of them Italian, were employed to build it. Excavation of the canal and construction of the mill were simultaneous, even through the harsh winters. A major reorganization occurred in 1900 when George Knowlton Jr. became the second president. By the time the first paper rolled off a machine on July 31, 1901, an entire village had been created and constructed for the laborers. Deferiet was a company-owned town.

The uniqueness of Deferiet was unmistakable. The residents were a melting pot of Americans, Poles, Italians, and many other nationalities. In order to keep the mill in operation, they had to work collectively. They blended together even though some knew only their native languages, but many nonetheless Americanized their names.

Even though they never forgot their native customs, these immigrants adapted to their new country through worship, learning the language, expressing the importance of education, and getting involved in community activities and sports. Their love of God and country was obvious.

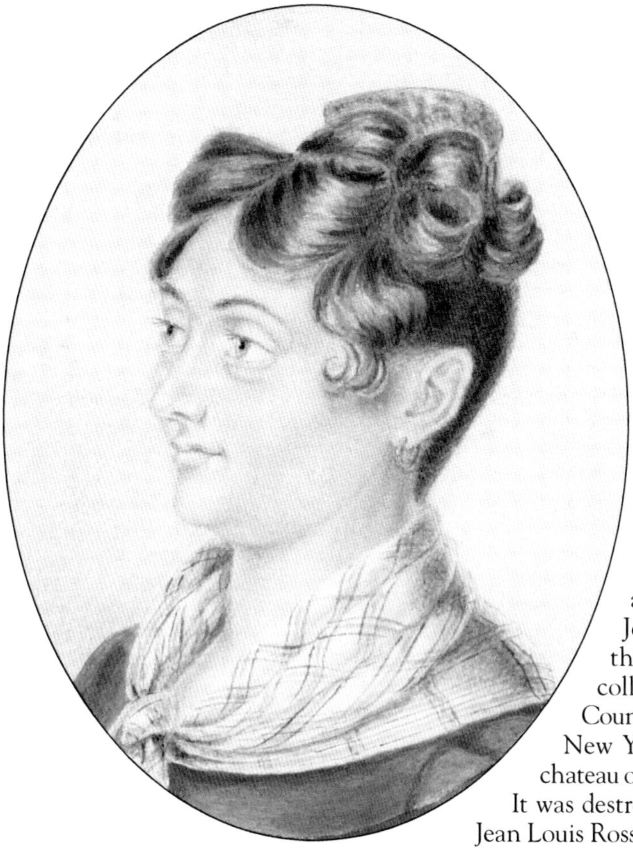

There is a certain mystery to Jenika de Feriet. She was born in 1776 near Paris, France, and was named after a Polish ancestor. She is believed to have held a court position during the reign of King Louis XVI. She was educated, a linguist, grew exotic plants in her greenhouse, knew shorthand, and owned the first grand piano in Jefferson County. Jenika sketched this self-portrait, which is part of a collection of her items at the Jefferson County Historical Society in Watertown, New York. The sketch below is of the chateau of the Feriet family in Verny, France. It was destroyed in 1944. (Left, JCHS; below, Jean Louis Rossignol collection.)

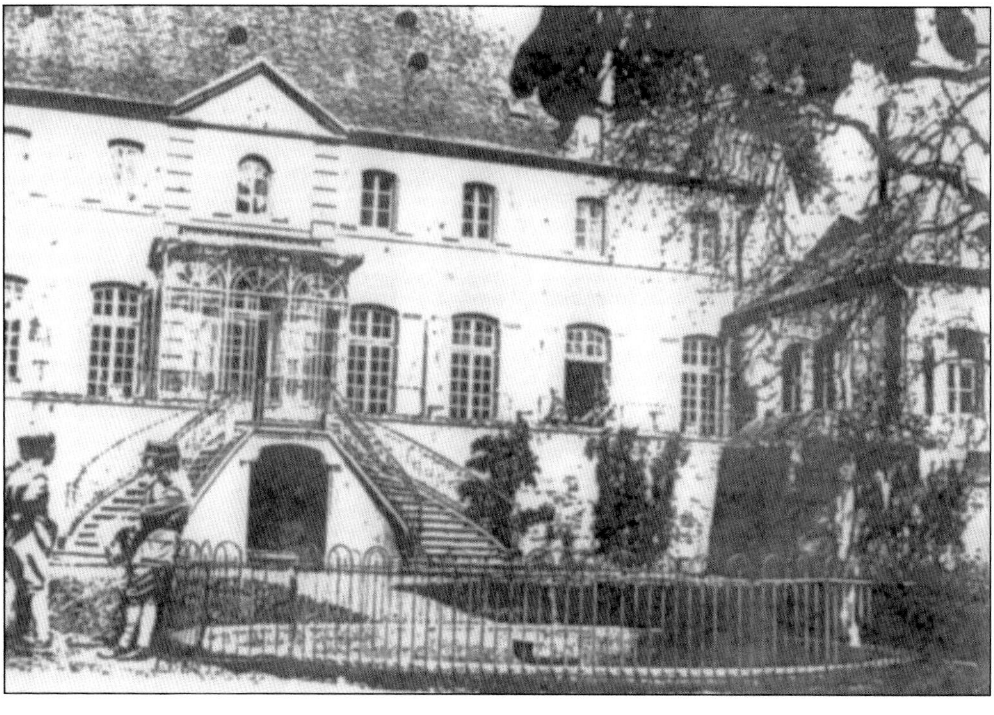

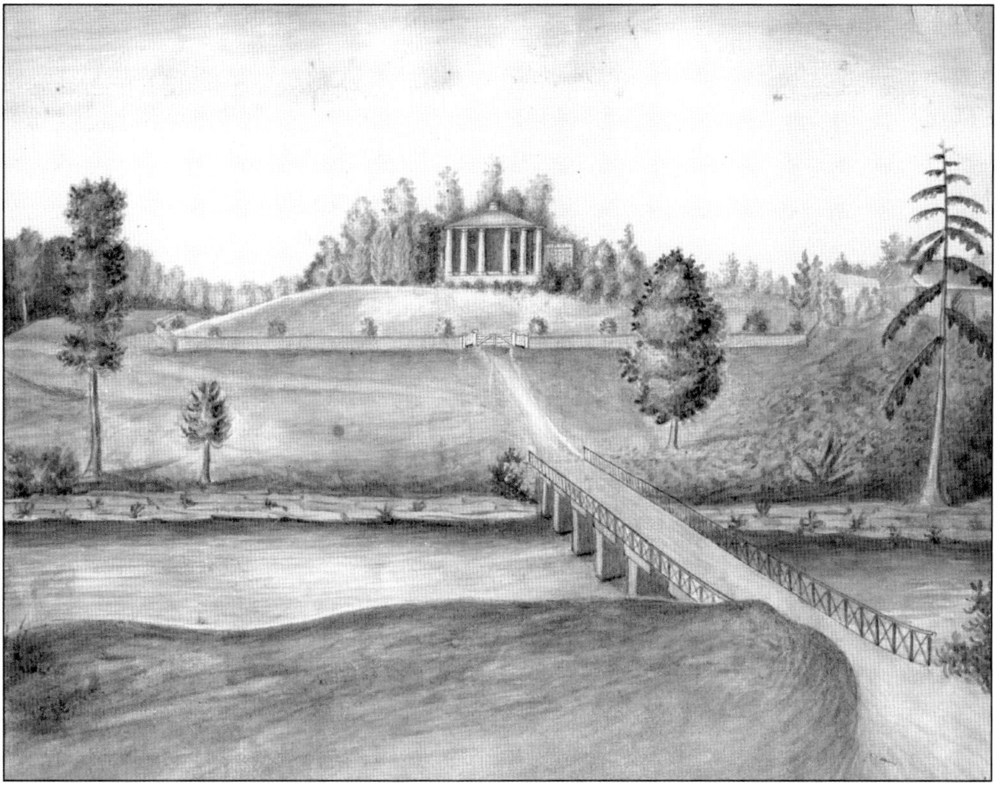

The Hermitage was built on the great bend of the Black River. Jenika, an accomplished artist, painted this watercolor (above) in mainly shades of green. In 1838, she visited her brother Louis in New Orleans, Louisiana. While there, she had a lithograph made of her painting. Notice the Southern flair to the lithograph. Her brother died in New Orleans on May 8, 1845. (Both, JCHS.)

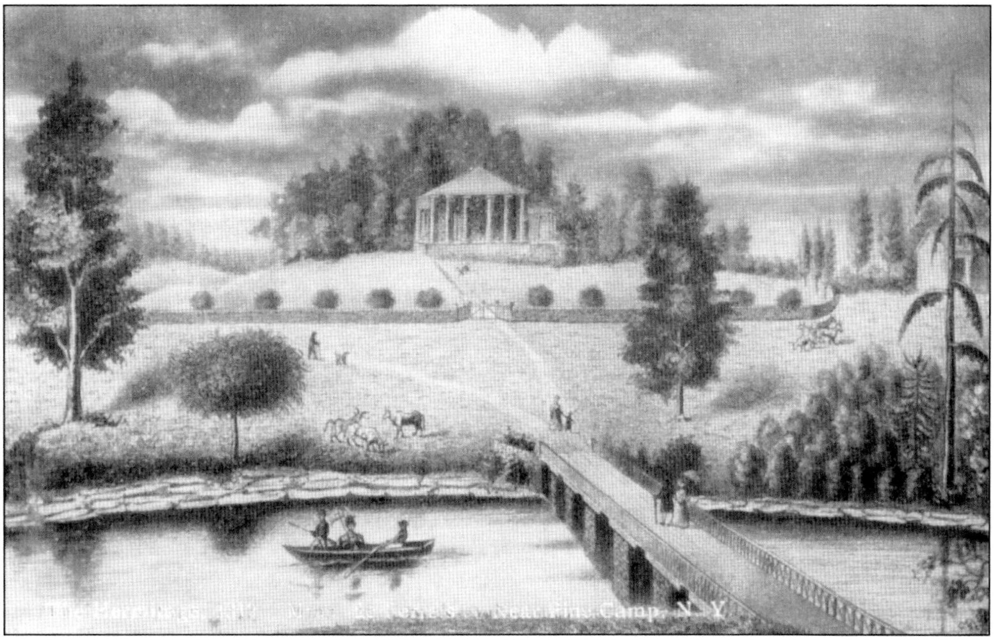

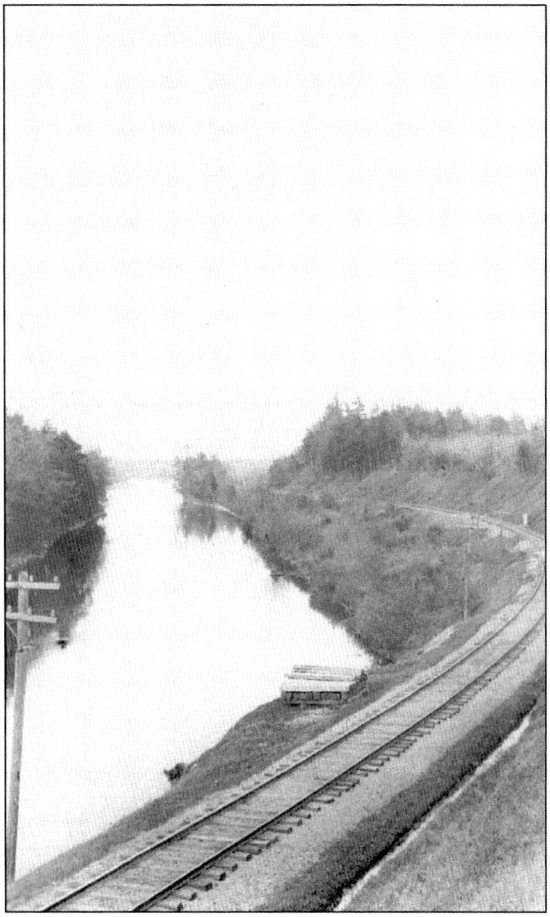

Excavating the land to construct a hydraulic canal was an immense project. To dig, blast, and construct this 4,400-foot-long and 20-foot-deep channel took over 1,000 men and many horses and cost thousands of dollars. The horses were kept on a farm across the river from the mill. Not only did the water furnish power to the mill, it made Deferiet an island. (Deferiet Archives.)

This photograph of Deferiet was taken from Wilna Avenue toward the Black River. Over a period of two years, this unique village was founded and built by the St. Regis Paper Company for its workers. By October 30, 1901, crews had constructed 52 houses with electricity and sanitation provisions, a general store, and hotel, and a school district was created on May 16 that year. The village was first called Eggleston, but the name was changed to Deferiet in 1901.

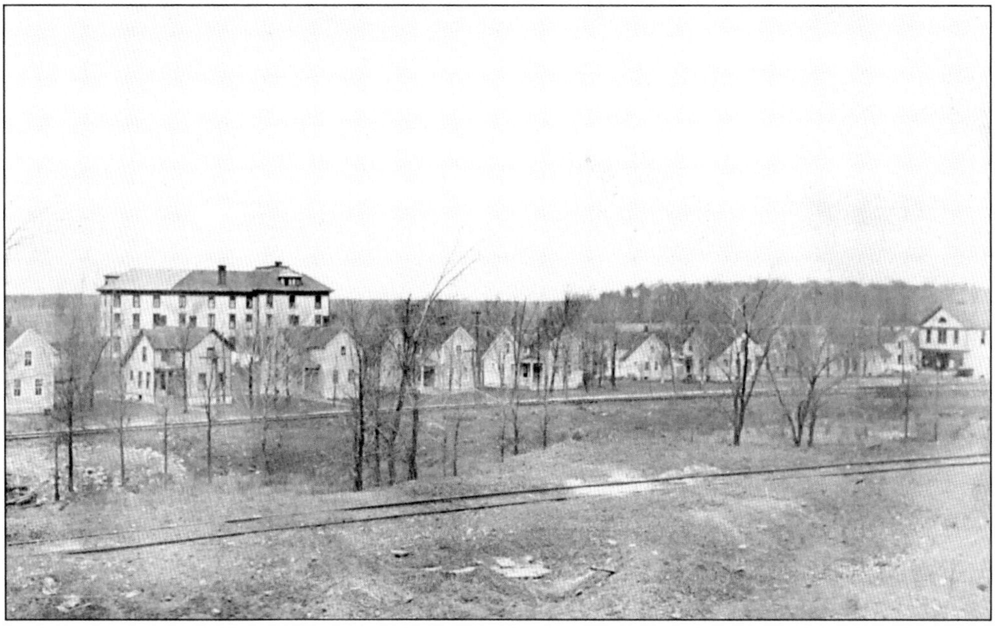

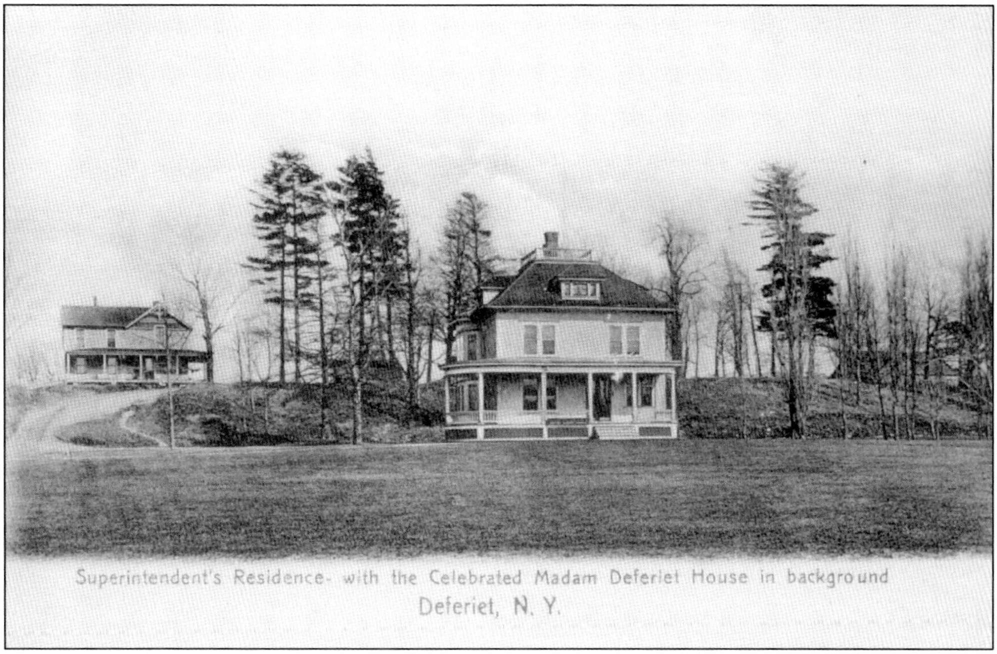

William Decker was the first superintendent of the paper company, and Patrick Moran was the last superintendent to live in this residence. The Reynolds family bought the de Feriet mansion (background) in 1856. After a fire in 1871, they rebuilt, leaving what they could of the original structure. Frank Reynolds, who was born in the mansion, sold 250 acres of his land to the newly formed St. Regis Paper Company.

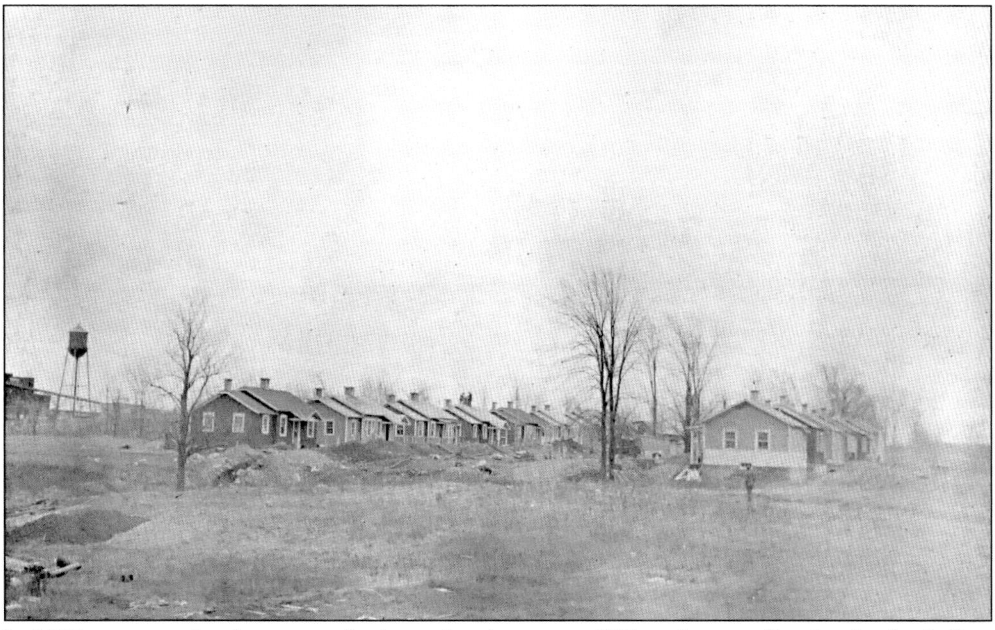

In 1915, construction began on the bungalow houses on Wilna Avenue. Previously, the Italian Block had been built on the far end of the street. The two-story homes on the western end had not been started.

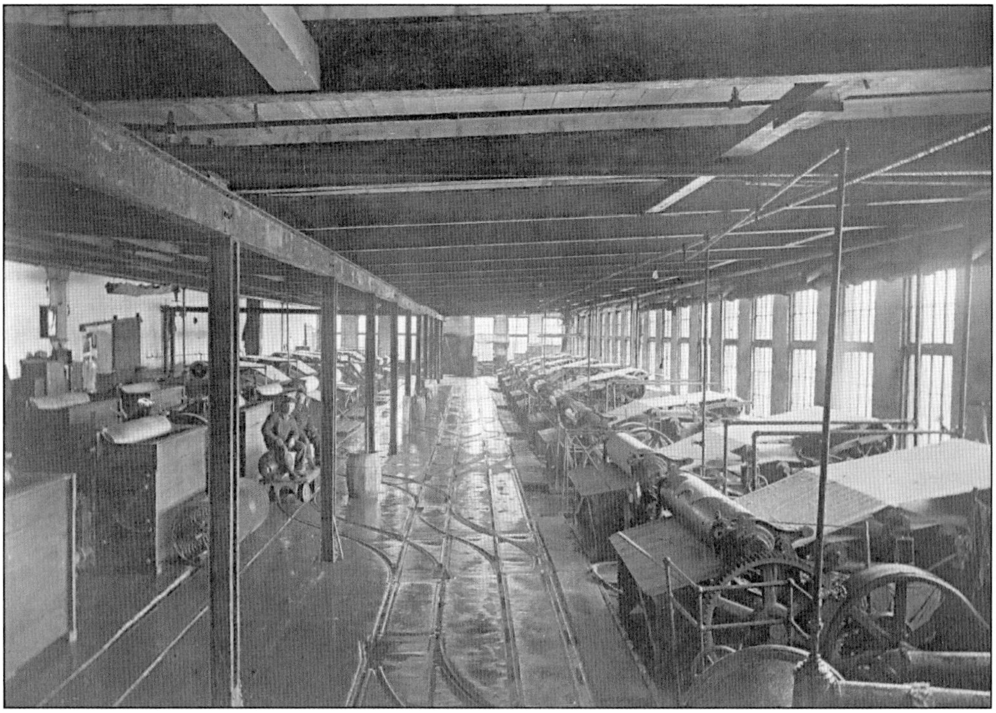

The above photograph shows the primitive machines used in making paper at the St. Regis mill at the turn of the 20th century. Roy Genter is one of the workers posing in the photograph below. On July 1, 1915, Roy and two others were arrested for an assault that occurred during intense violence at the beginning of a strike. Notice that some workers are not wearing shoes. Identified in the photograph below are Roy Genter, Eugene Godfrey, Ray Seeder, and William "Bill" Bacon.

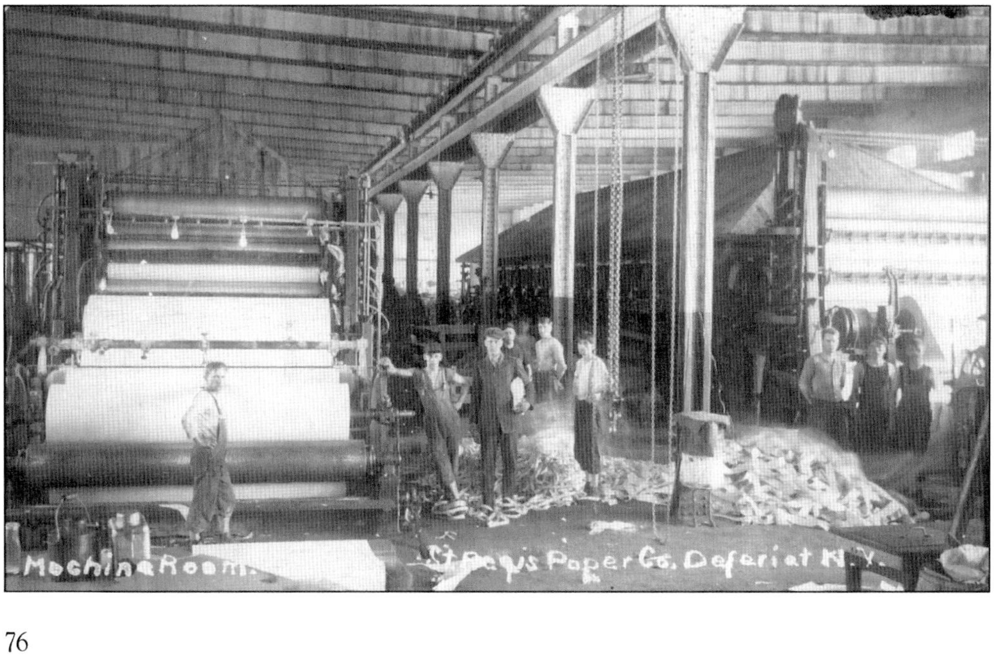

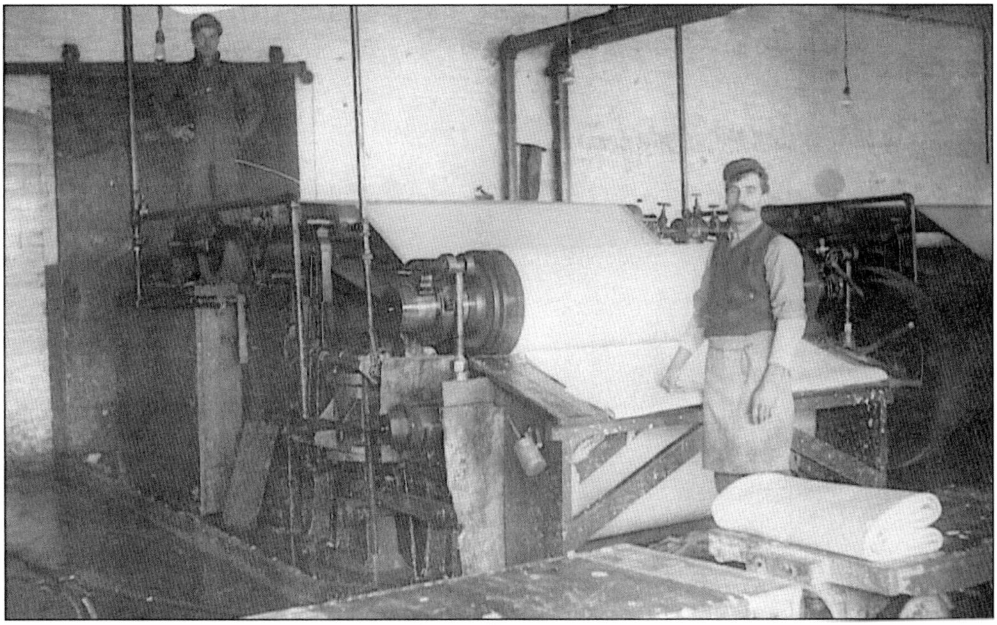

In front of the paper machine is Michael Powell (originally Pawelczyk), who was born in Poland and immigrated to America in 1906. He married Josephine Wojcik. They lived in the new Polish Block, and just one month after the strike started in May 1915, their son, Lawrence, drowned in the Black River. One month later, they were evicted from their home. Michael died in 1921. (Stephen Powell collection.)

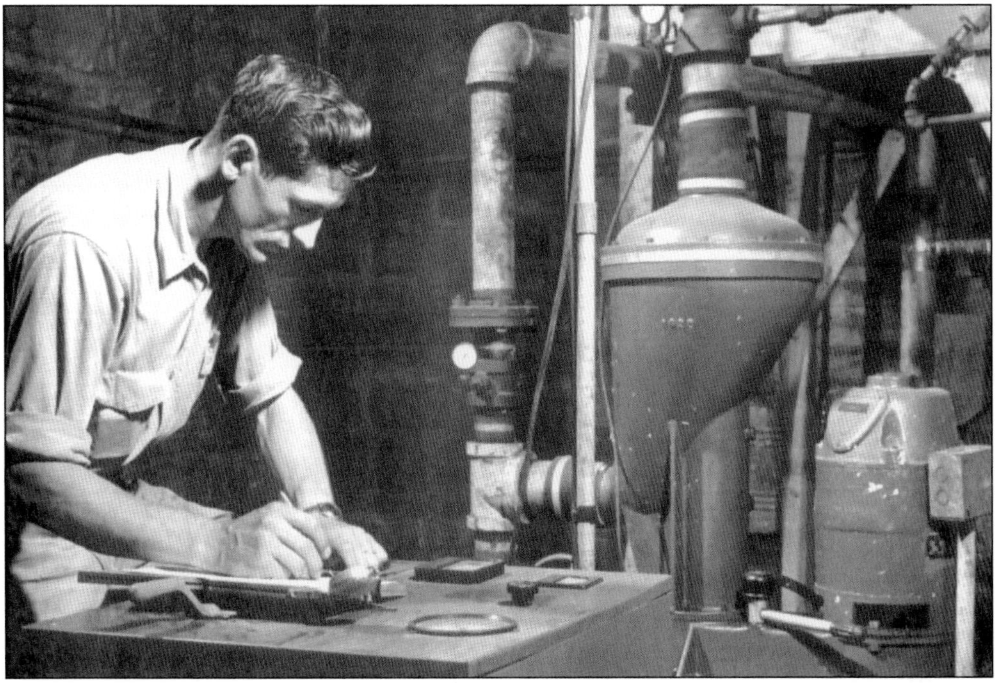

The machinery at the mill was improved and updated over the years. Here, Frank Miterko, head chemist in the paper lab, is calculating formulas for the process of making paper. In the background, chemical storage tanks can be seen. (Monica Miterko Vincent collection.)

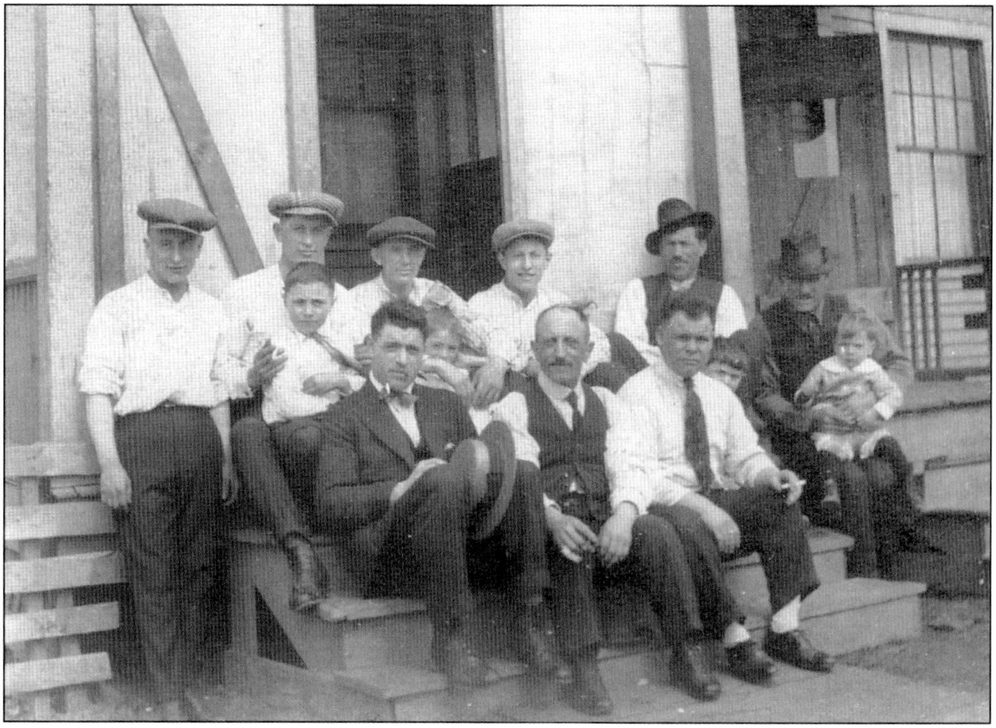

In this c. 1920 photograph, some workers are enjoying time off from the mill with their children. The photograph below was taken in front of the yard office. In the first row, Ernie Griffith is third from left, Nicholas Kochubinski, with mustache and standing in front of the door, is 11th from left; and Frank Cosmic (originally Kusmis) is third from the right. At far left in the third row is Alex Brzezinski, and the rest are unknown. (Below, Francis Burke collection.)

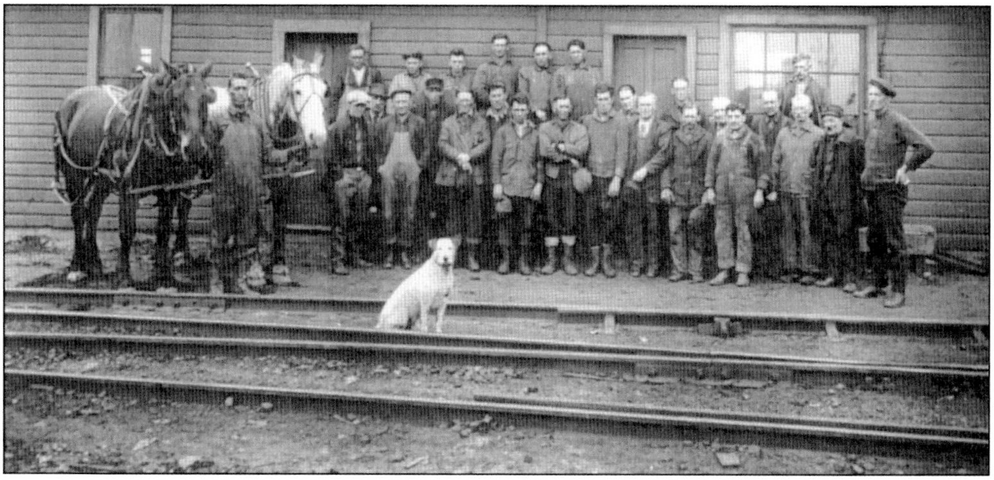

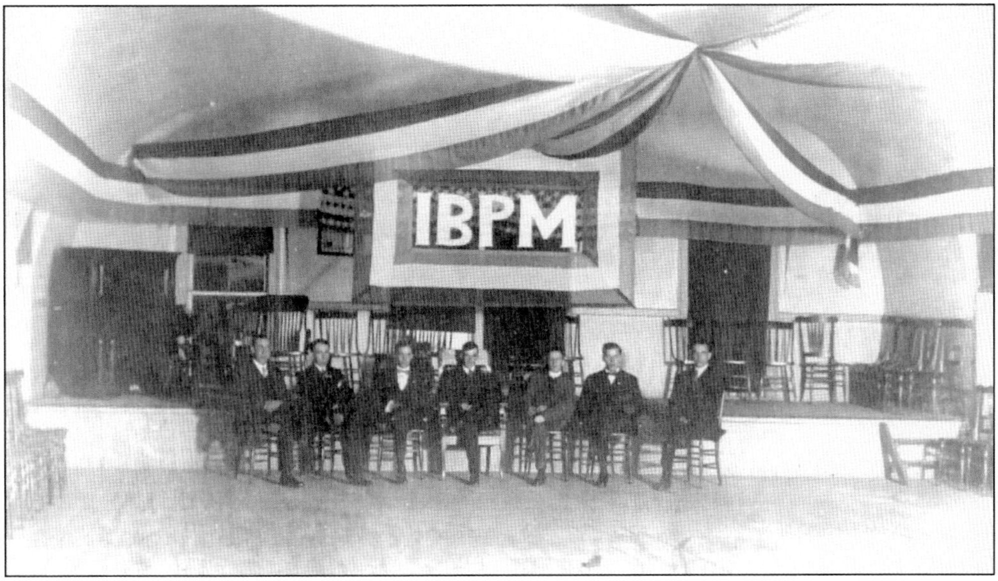

Local 45 of the International Brotherhood of Paper Makers received its charter on June 20, 1902. On June 29, 1912, Local 56 of the International Brotherhood of Pulp, Sulphite, and Paper Mill Workers received its charter. Here, a group of papermakers meets in the assembly hall over the store. In the photograph below, union men meet at the Old Fargo Inn. Pictured are, in position from left, (first row) Local 56 president Eugene Moody, first; Frank Callahan, second; Gilbert DeLosh, sixth; Norman Lovejoy, seventh; and Thomas Dowling, last; (second row) Alexander Zando, second; and Joe Russell, sixth; (standing on porch) Marco Zando, second.

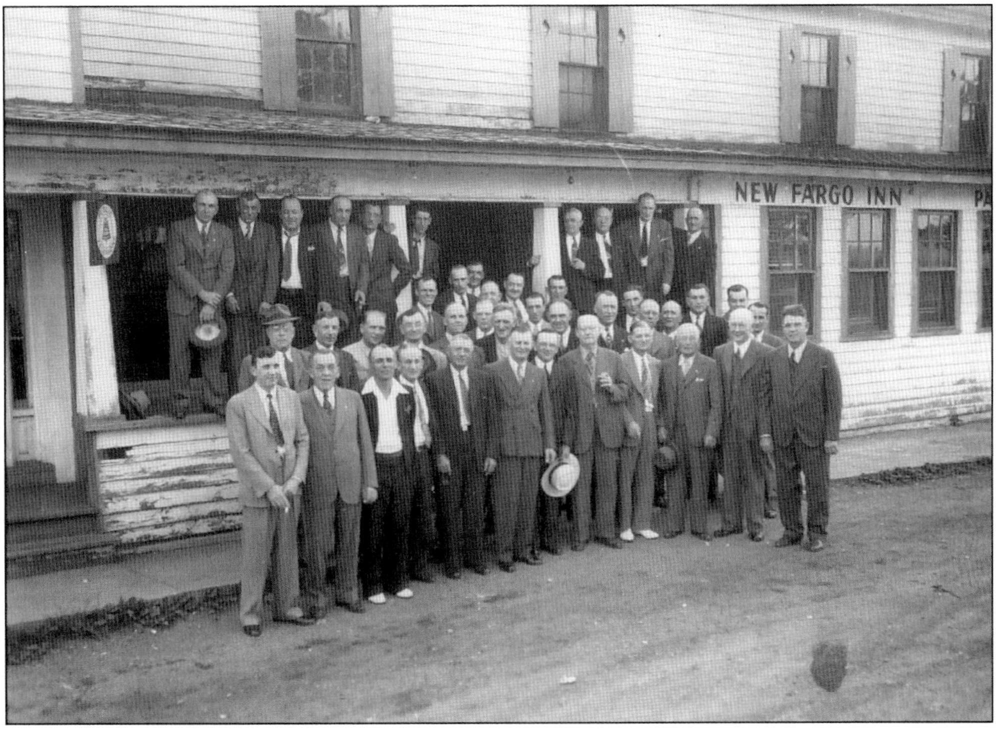

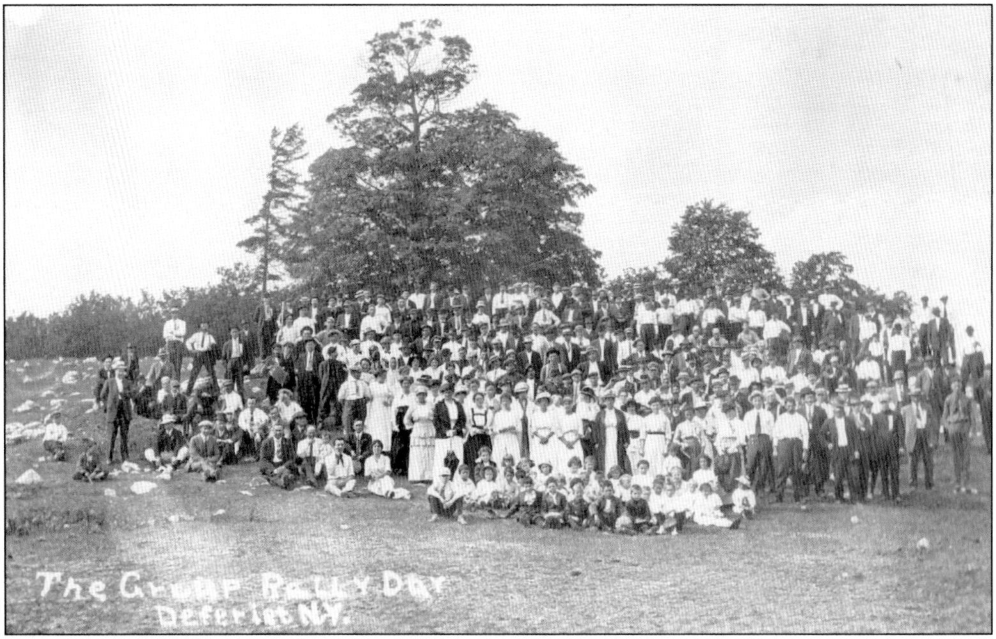

The 1915-to-1917 conflict in Deferiet was of national importance because it was a struggle for the survival of unionism in the paper industry. Strikebreakers protected company property, and scabs replaced workers. It was the intent of the St. Regis Paper Company management to have a nonunion mill.

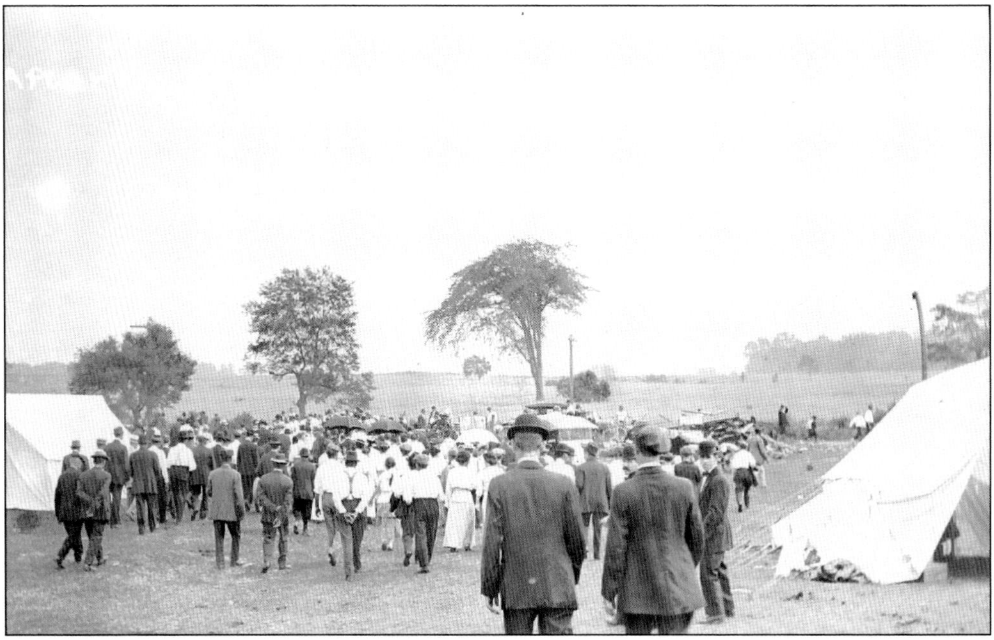

The strikers are walking to the meeting place to hear a speech by J.T. Carey and to give each other support. Notice how well dressed they are.

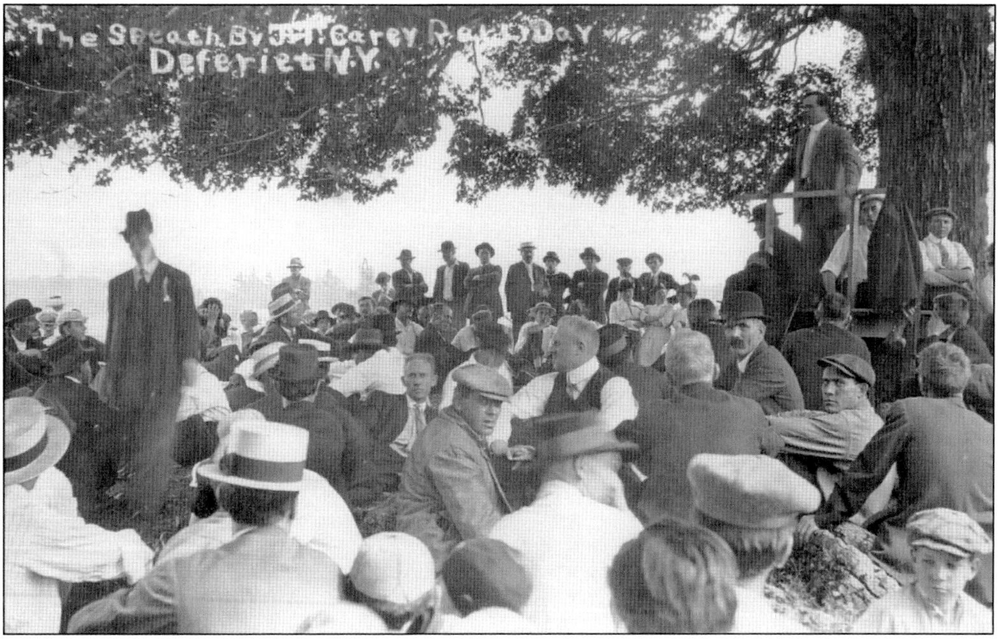

J.T. Carey, president of the International Brotherhood of Pulp and Paper Makers, speaks to the strikers at a rally on May 26, 1915. The location is Camp Tylkoff at the "Meeting Tree." Not only did the workers want an increase in pay, they also wanted the right to unionize.

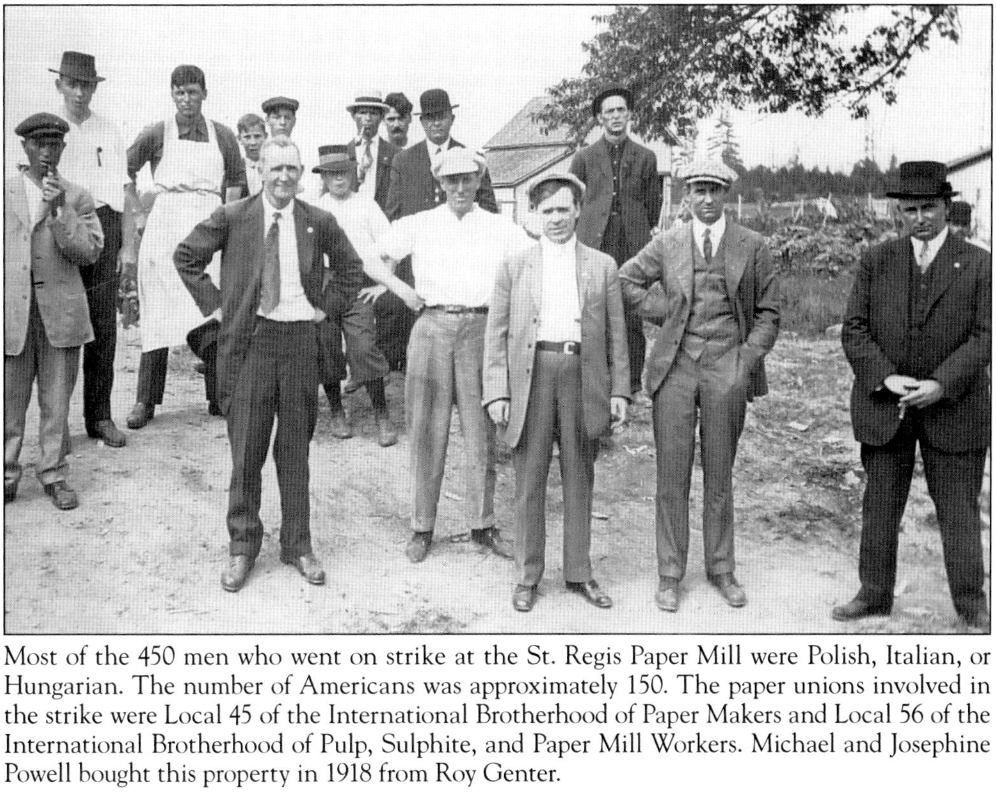

Most of the 450 men who went on strike at the St. Regis Paper Mill were Polish, Italian, or Hungarian. The number of Americans was approximately 150. The paper unions involved in the strike were Local 45 of the International Brotherhood of Paper Makers and Local 56 of the International Brotherhood of Pulp, Sulphite, and Paper Mill Workers. Michael and Josephine Powell bought this property in 1918 from Roy Genter.

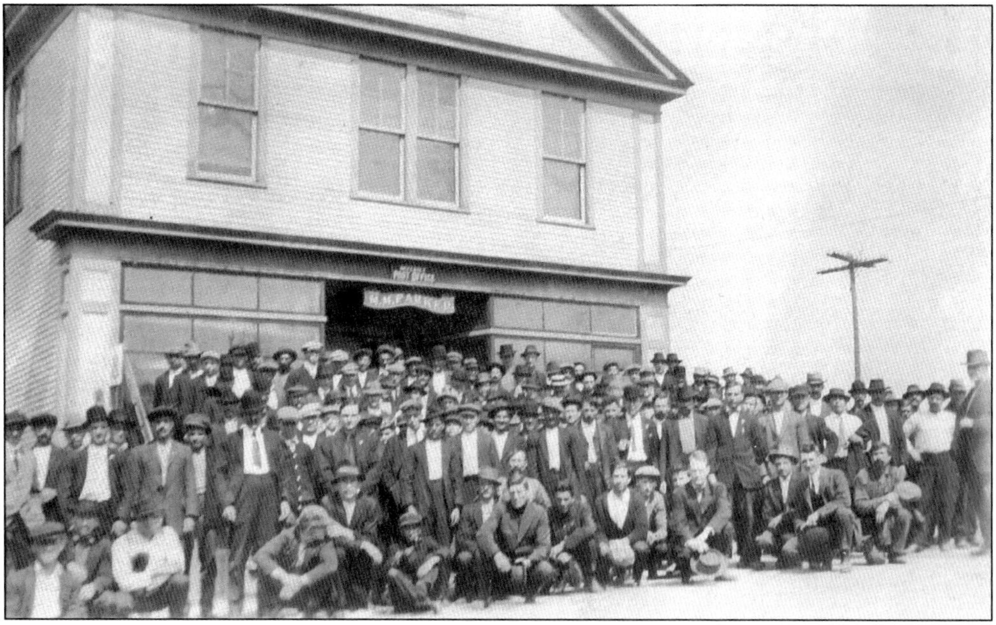

Prior to their eviction from their homes, the strikers met at M.M. Parker's general store. Here, they are posing in front of the store, which also doubled as the Deferiet Post Office. On November 16, 1901, Pres. Theodore Roosevelt appointed Maurice Parker as the first postmaster in Deferiet. In later years, this street was named Parker Avenue in his honor.

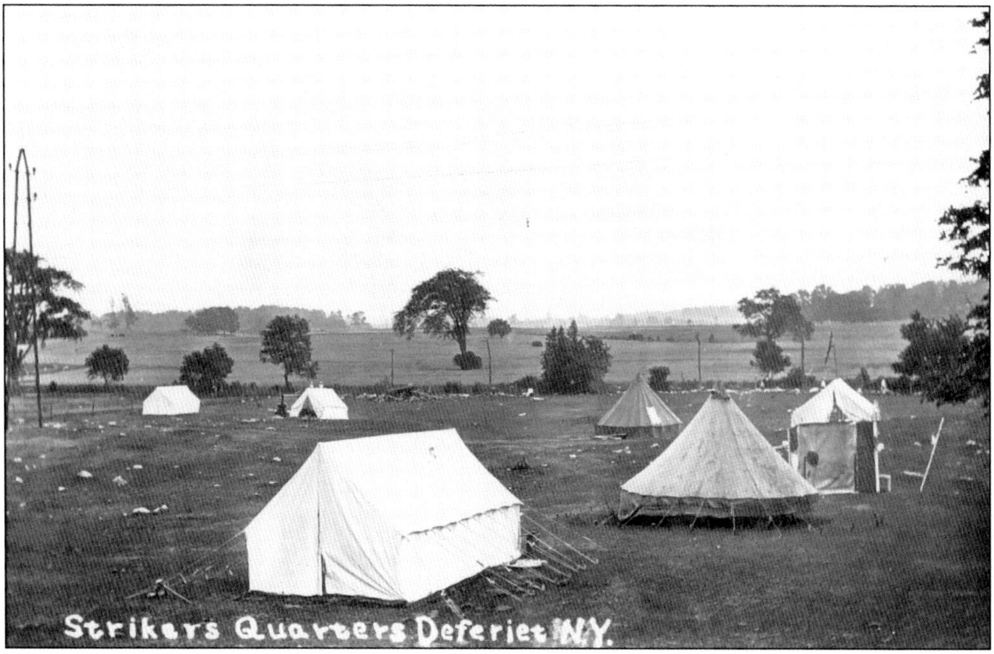

Preparations were made to house strikers and their families at the homes of union sympathizers in the surrounding area. For strikers who did not have accommodations—especially those who boarded in the hotel—tents were made available. "Tent City" was set up on the western side of the Black River across from St. Regis Paper Company at Camp Tylkoff.

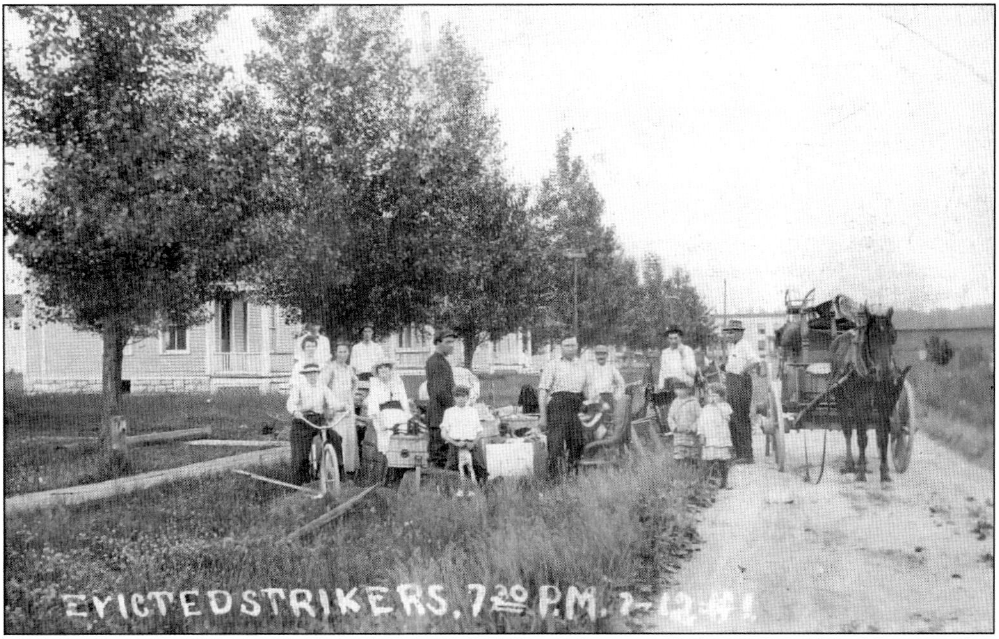

The above photograph, taken at 7:30 p.m. on July 12, 1915, shows a group of strikers who had been evicted from their homes on Anderson Avenue. The Polish Block is in the background. Moments later, the group was photographed looking in the opposite direction toward the general store. These photographs were taken in front of what is now the author's home.

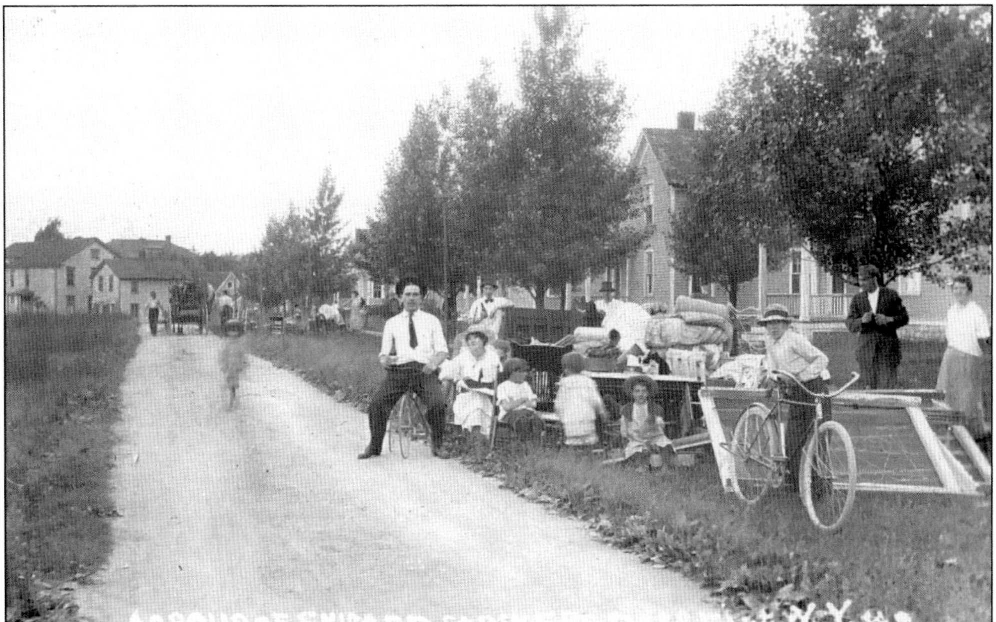

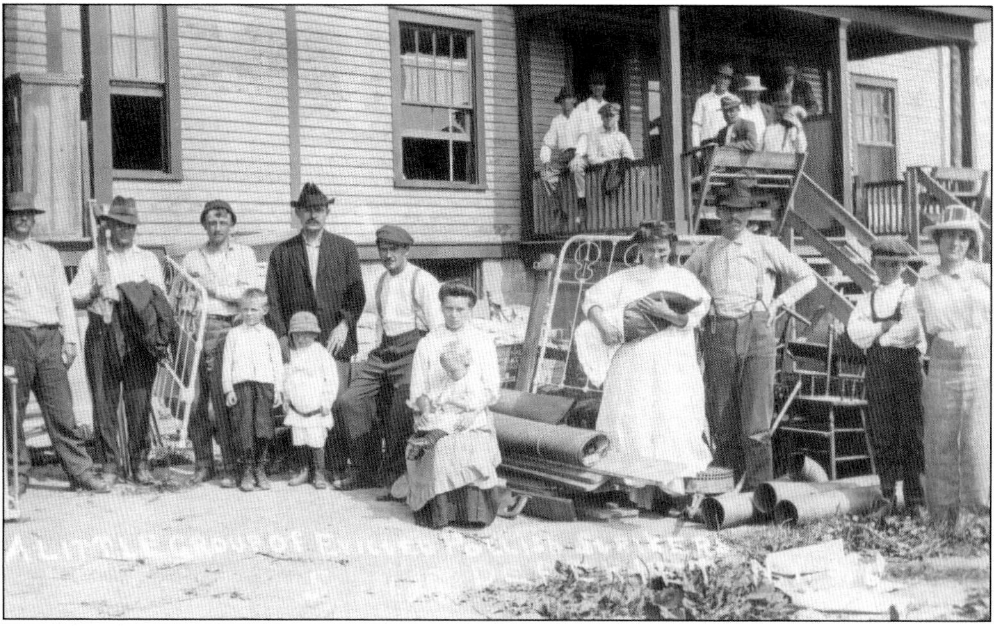

Evicted strikers are pictured with all their possessions in front of their homes at the Italian Block. The strike affected everyone in the family. The woman standing fourth from right is holding a newborn child.

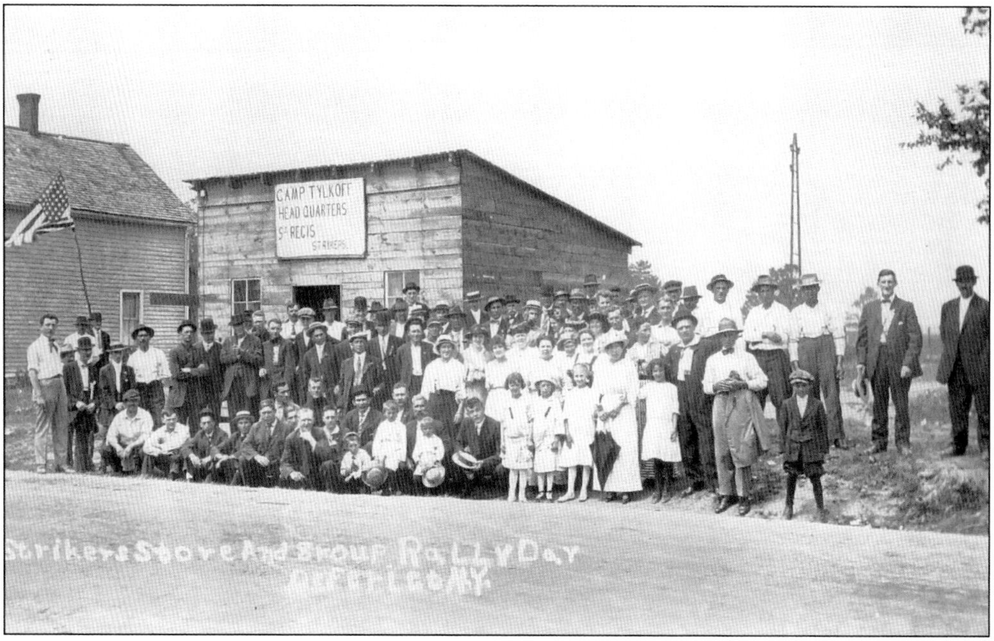

The Union Store at Camp Tylkoff, named for Joseph Tylkoff, organizer of the "foreigners," is the location for this photograph of strikers and their families. Tylkoff is pictured on the far left. The foreigners considered themselves Americans; as one can see, they are flying an American flag in the background. Stephen and Mary Powell built their home on this site in 1954.

The strike was declared settled 10 weeks after it began. Conditions at the mill were normalizing, most workers were given back their jobs, and families returned to their homes. Some of the strikers were bitter, and due to new hostilities at the Deferiet mill, Gov. Charles Whitman ordered Company C of the National Guard stationed at Watertown to take control of the situation on September 3, 1915. In the distance in the photograph below, the headquarters of the militia is set up on the front lawn of the Deferiet School. The Naval Reserves were also called. After two years of struggling, a change in management realized the need for skilled workers to make paper efficiently. The strike was over as reported in the March 19, 1917 edition of *Watertown Daily Times*. (Right, Margaret Murray collection; below, Dorrie Ward Snyder collection.)

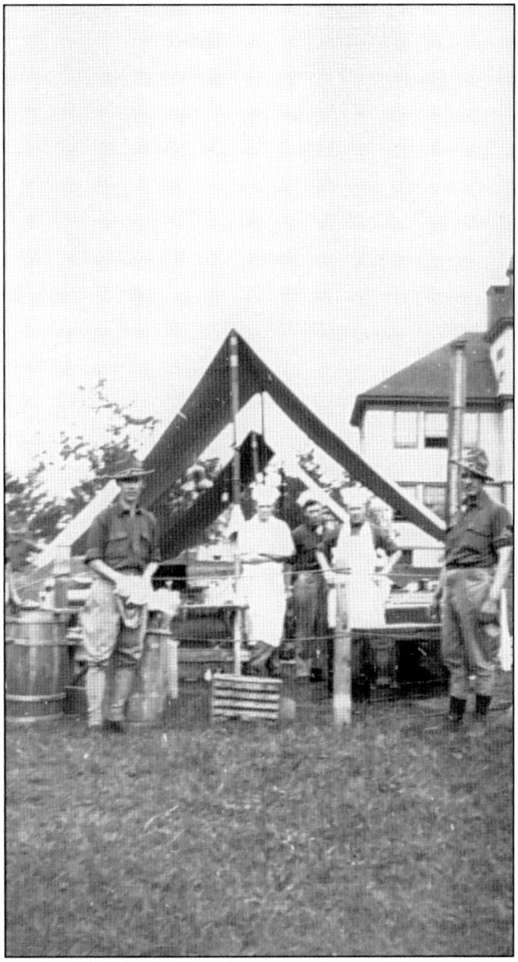

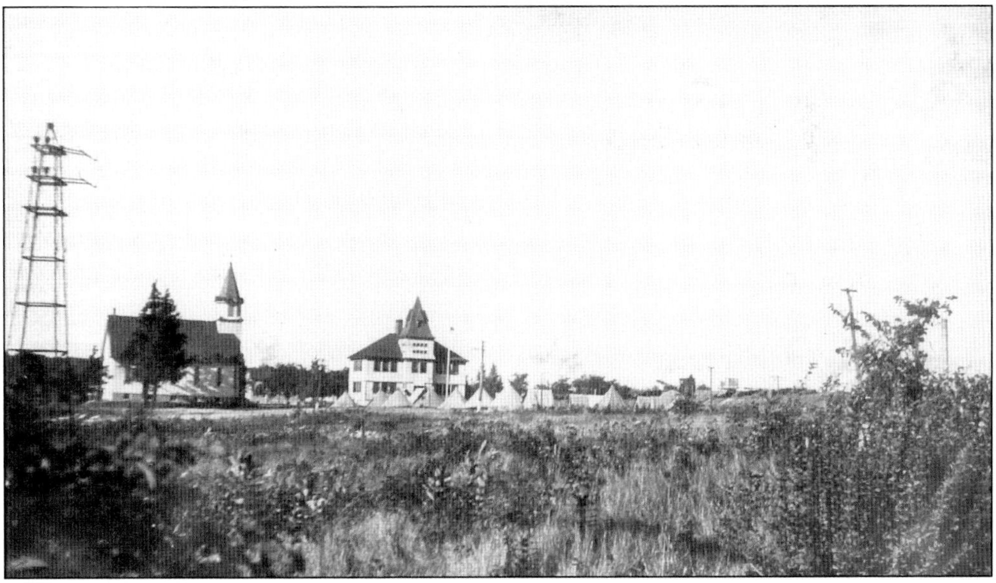

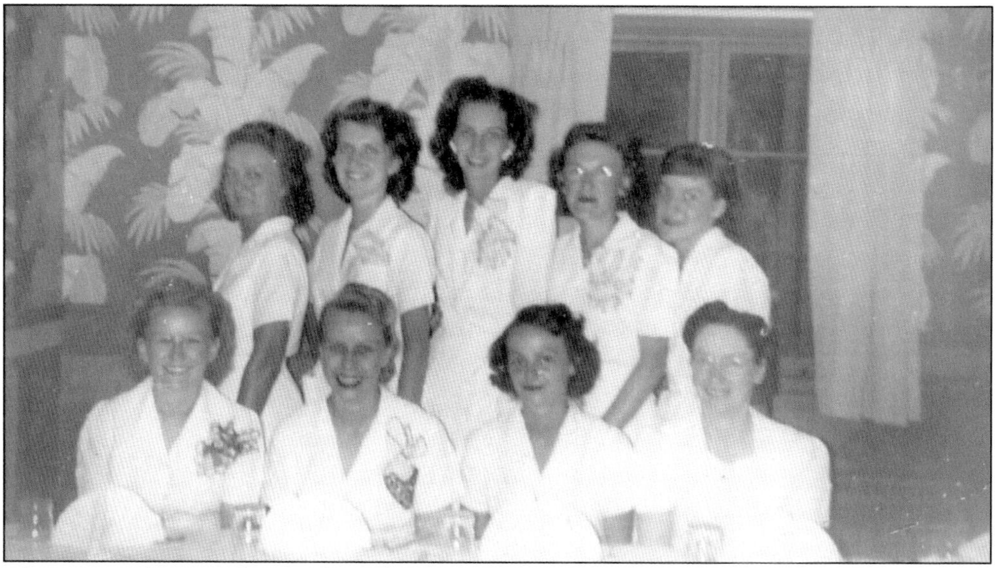

This c. 1948 photograph was taken of waitresses at the St. Regis Inn who were getting ready for a banquet. Each is wearing a white uniform with a handkerchief in the left pocket. Pictured, from left to right, are (first row) Marie Adams Pais, Marie Fifield Tunia, Harriet Porter Sullivan, and Alisha ?, the pastry maker; (second row) unidentified, Patricia Turpin Ricci, Margaret Wager Nabewaniec, Leona Nabywaniec, and Mary Porter Carcasole Kepler. (Edward Nabewaniec collection.)

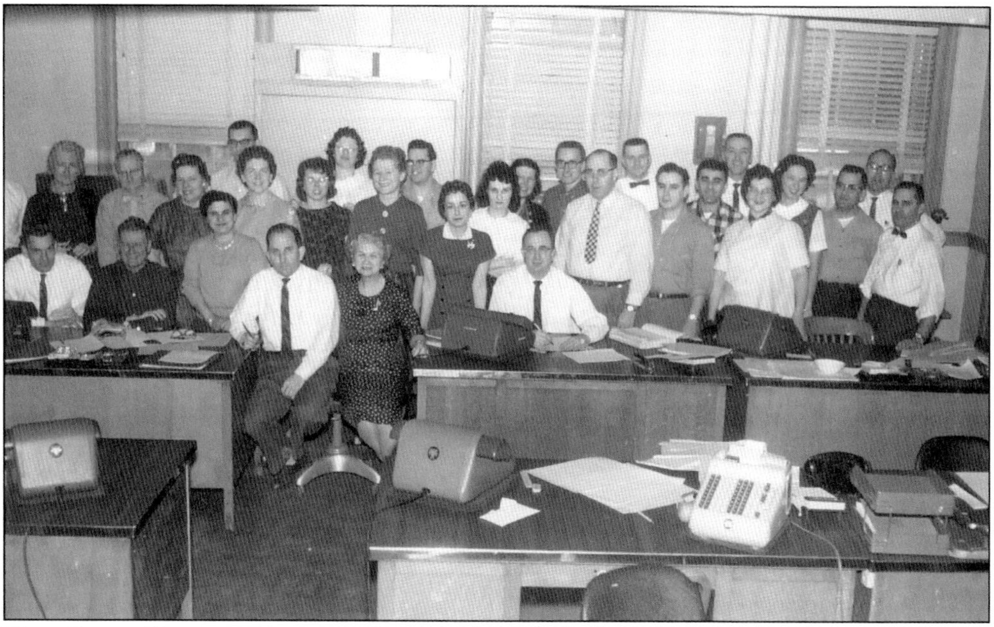

The office staff was as important in running the mill as the papermakers were. The March 1961 office staff includes, from left to right, (sitting) Mario Zando, Glenn Traynor, William Keene, Frances Londraville, and Donald DeLosh; (standing) Katherine Rolfe, Earl LaJuett, Eileen Baker, Flora Abdoo, Roswell Bowman, Norma Mullen, Beryl Huff, Margaret Brotherton, Sharon Wilson, Thomas Brotherton, Patricia Huff, Phyllis Gillen, Georgia Shaw, William Main, Carl Sixberry, Edward Reeves, Robert Ely, Rudy Perry, Harold Cummins, Ruth Theiser Gaebel, ? Holman, Gerry Newman, Paul Richardson, and Donald Kean. (Mullen family collection.)

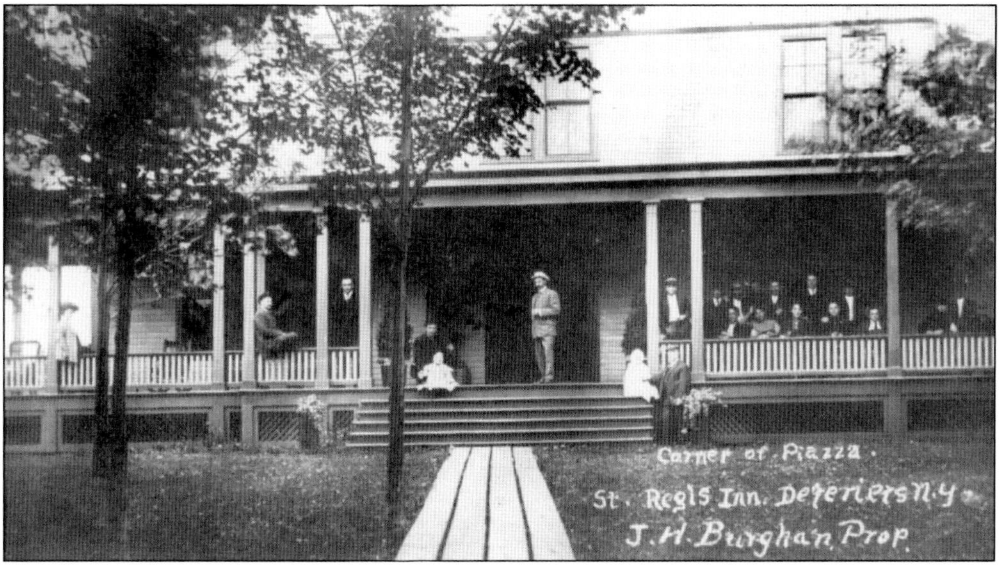

The St. Regis Inn had a broad veranda and was located in a park with a view of the river. It had a reading room with a fireplace, a dining room, billiard room, and barbershop. There were 40 sleeping rooms, and a number of baths and closets. Even though J.H. Burgham was proprietor at the time of this photograph, Fred Fiske ran the hotel when it first opened in 1901.

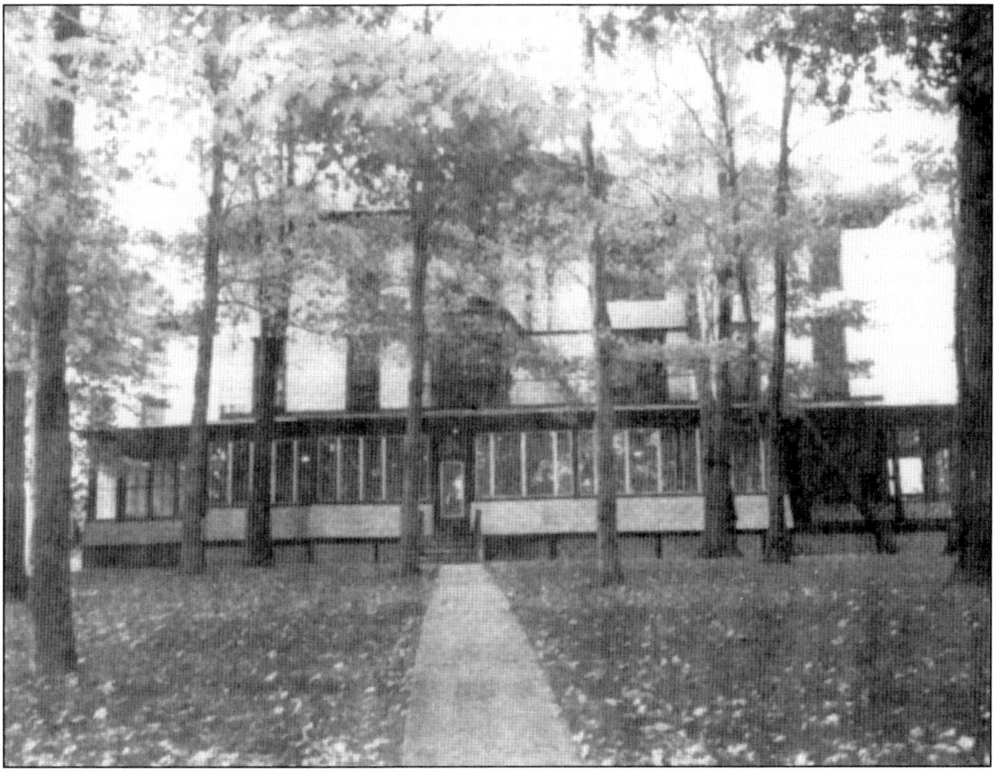

The St. Regis Inn was a Deferiet landmark known for its cuisine and hospitality. The last owner of the lodging before it was torn down in 1965 was Rexford Thomson. The bar was purchased by the Lamantia family and placed in their Sahara Restaurant in Carthage.

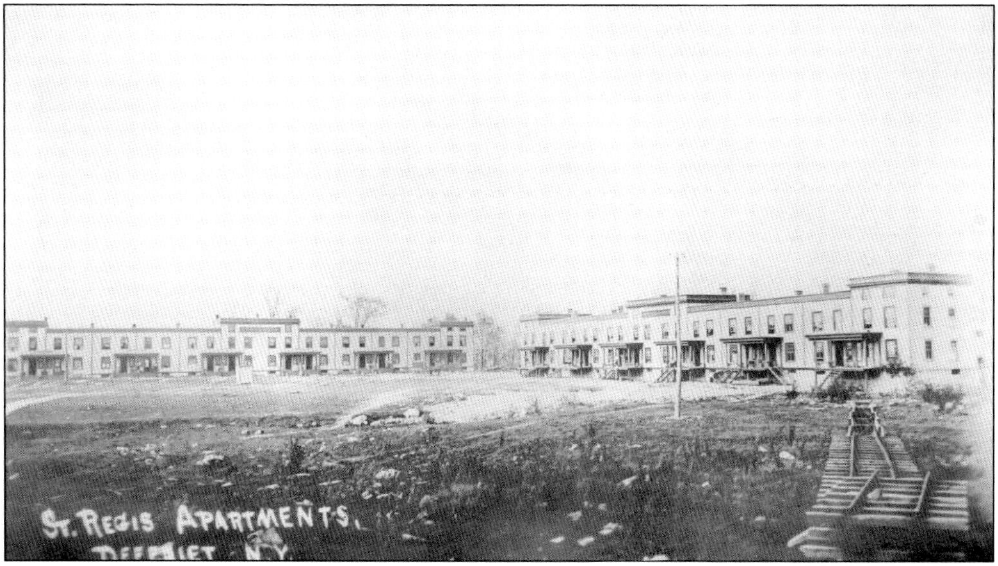

Better known as the Polish Blocks, each of these two-story sections had 12 residences, whose occupants had names like Woycik, Ganeriski (originally Gaworecki), Siedlecki, Yuhas, Tymoczko (Tymczrth), and Italian names, such as Zando (Zandomenego). The common area in front was a gathering place, a baseball diamond, and, in later years, a skating rink. If a laborer did not earn $10, the rent for that week would be nothing.

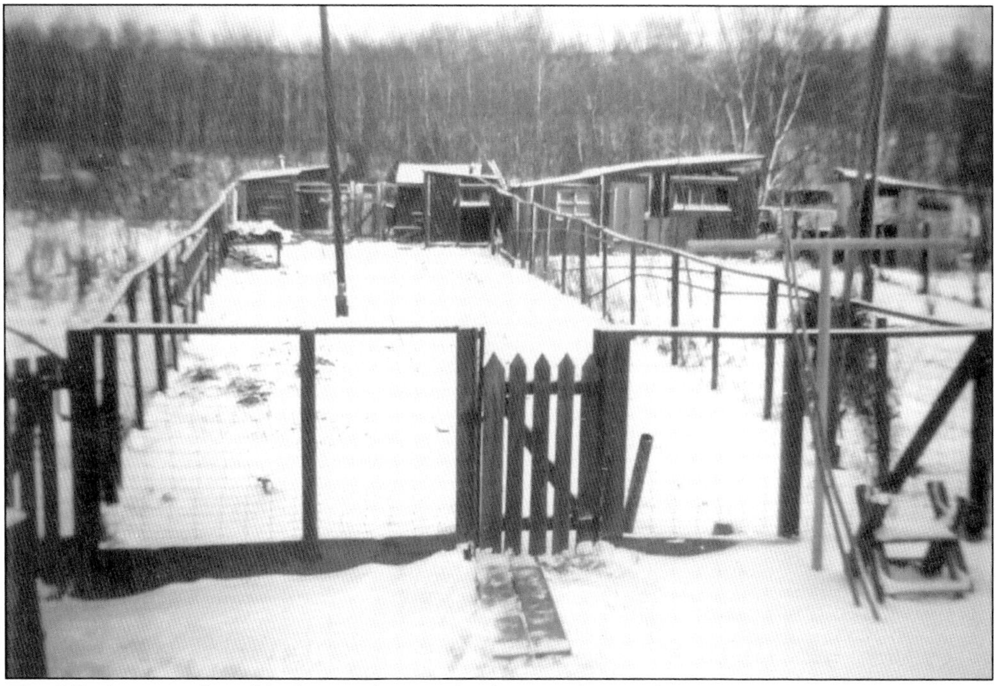

The folks living at these blocks were known for their gardens and wine-making. This winter scene at the new Polish Block shows the gardens belonging to Michael Siedlecki, Andrew Miterko, and Henry Stevens. Some 1,500 bottles of wine were confiscated from three homes in the Italian Block on April 23, 1929, during Prohibition. All of the men were arrested for having illegal beverages. (Michael Miterko collection.)

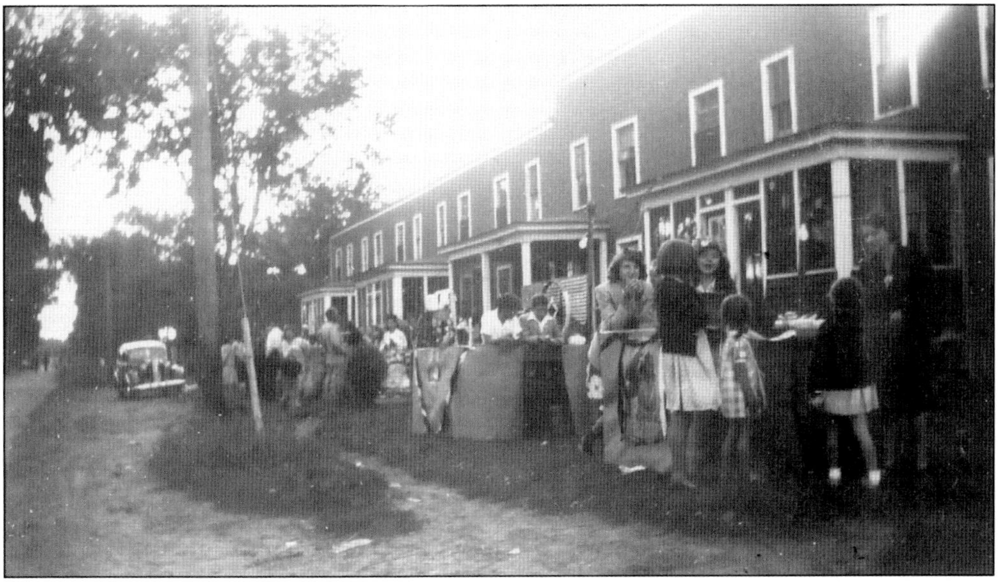

This 1942 photograph shows a lawn social in front of the Italian Block. On the far right, the little girl with the dark sweater is six-year-old Angeline Cassoni. She is talking to her mother, Anna. Italian food, wares, and a fishpond were part of the festivities. In later years, lawn socials were held at the Deferiet Grade School. (Angeline Cassoni Cronk collection.)

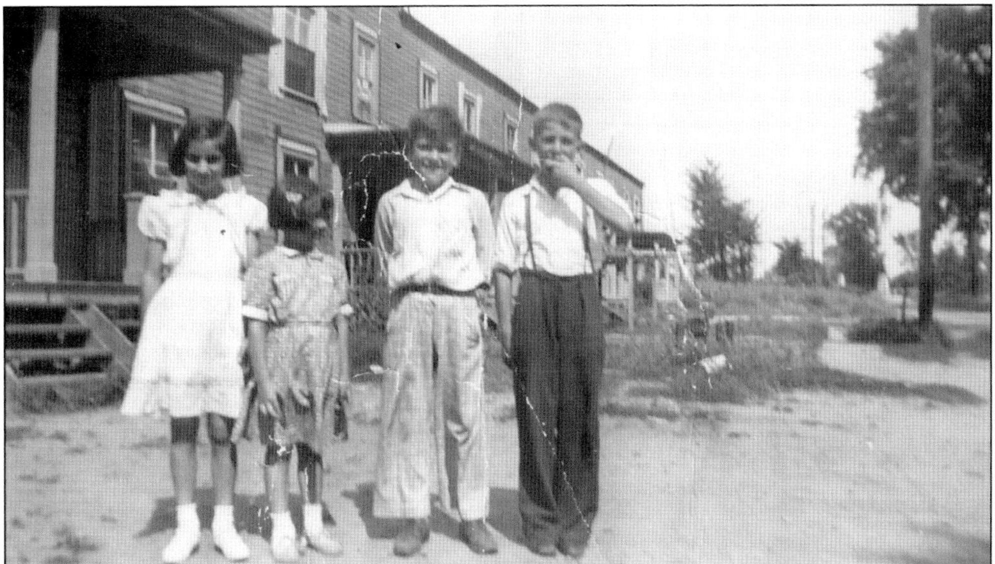

Friends Katherine Gerace Palladino, Teresa Palladino Bossuot, Joseph Carcasole, and James Greci, eating an apple, pose in front of the Italian Block in this 1938 photograph. (Vincent Schneider collection.)

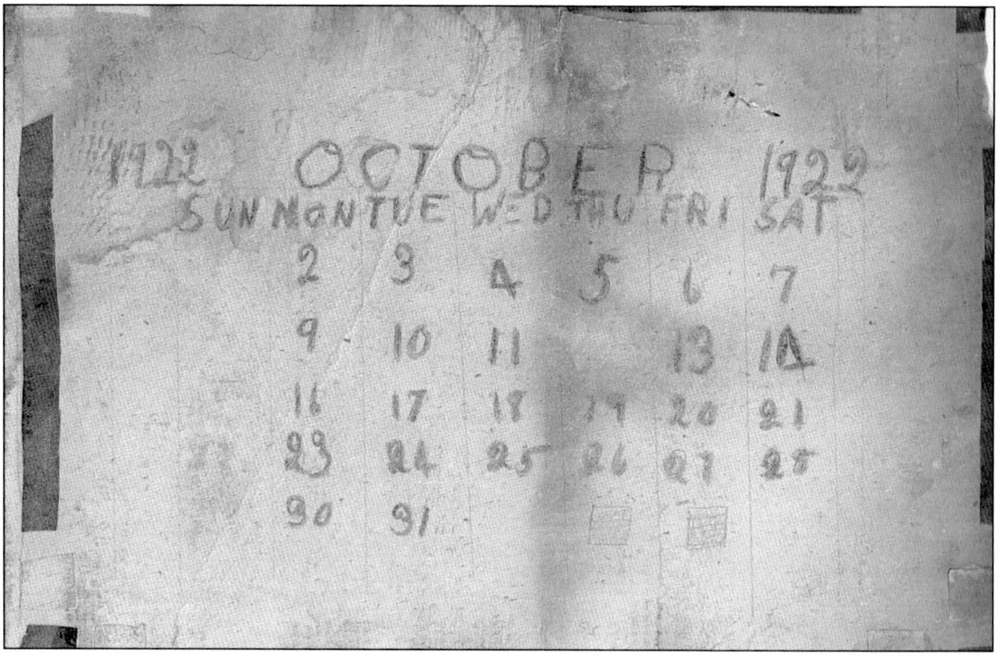

When the Deferiet Grade School was renovated for the St. Regis Court apartments, homework from some students was found in the walls. A teacher wrote on the back of Harold Grosse's work, "Figures are not made very well, practice making figures." Grosse was the father of Doreen Grosse Miterko, Richard, and Jean Grosse Andrus. (Deferiet Archives.)

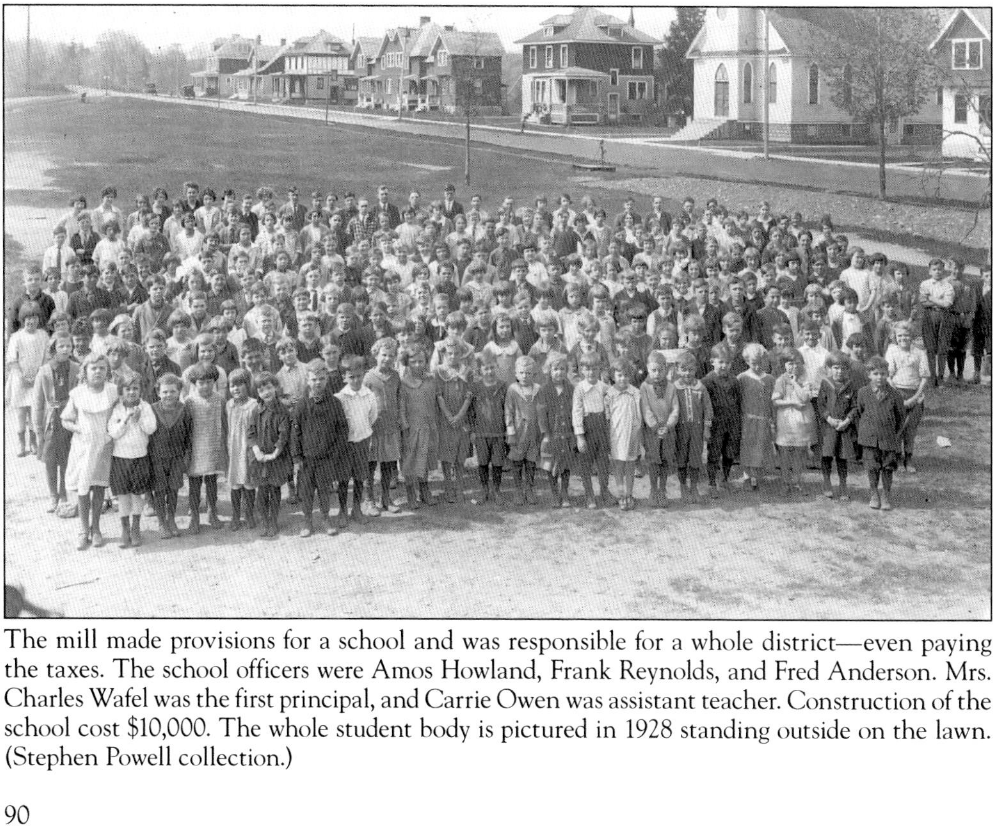

The mill made provisions for a school and was responsible for a whole district—even paying the taxes. The school officers were Amos Howland, Frank Reynolds, and Fred Anderson. Mrs. Charles Wafel was the first principal, and Carrie Owen was assistant teacher. Construction of the school cost $10,000. The whole student body is pictured in 1928 standing outside on the lawn. (Stephen Powell collection.)

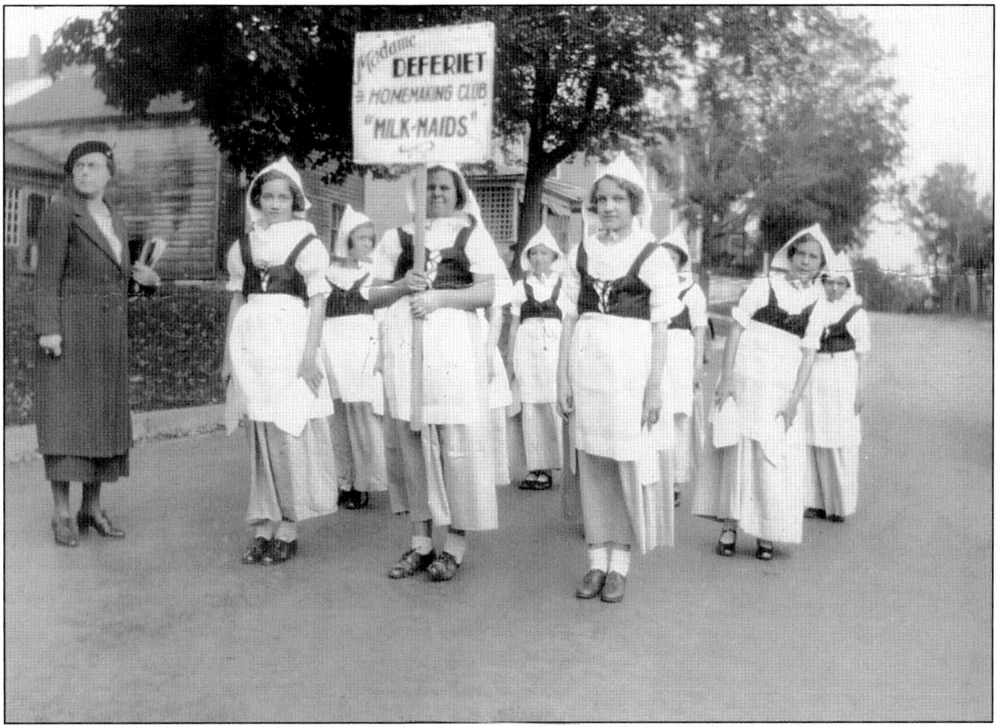

Teacher Grace Sheley is seen with the Madame DeFeriet Homemaking Club assembling to march in a parade in Carthage. Holding the sign is Suzanne Siedlecki Clark, and Ladora Palmer Demers is to the right in the first row. (Margaret Murray collection.)

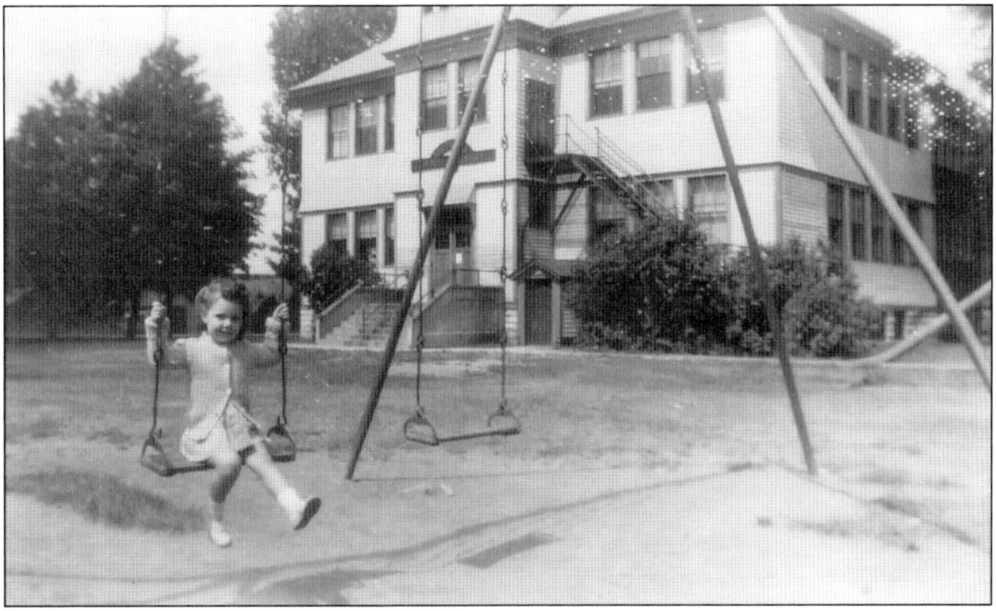

When attendance at the school increased, a brick addition was constructed to the rear of the school around 1921. Instead of wooden steps, cement steps were added, and eventually the swings were moved closer to the steps. In 1942, Eileen O'Brien enjoys swinging on the school lawn. (Dennis Turpin collection.)

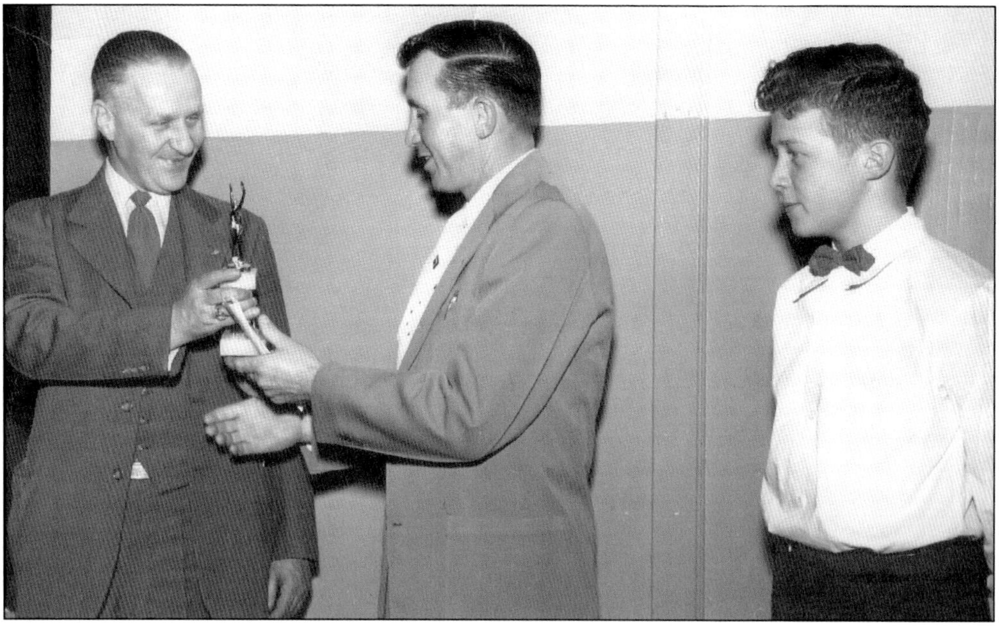

Jefferson County fire coordinator Charles Hayes (left) presents a fire safety trophy, the first in the county, to Deferiet Grade School for clearing the school of 130 students and teachers in 31 seconds as part of a fire prevention program. The trophy is being presented to fire chief Eugene Moody (center) and Charles Morse Jr., president of the eighth grade, who accepted it for the school. (Deferiet Fire Department Archives.)

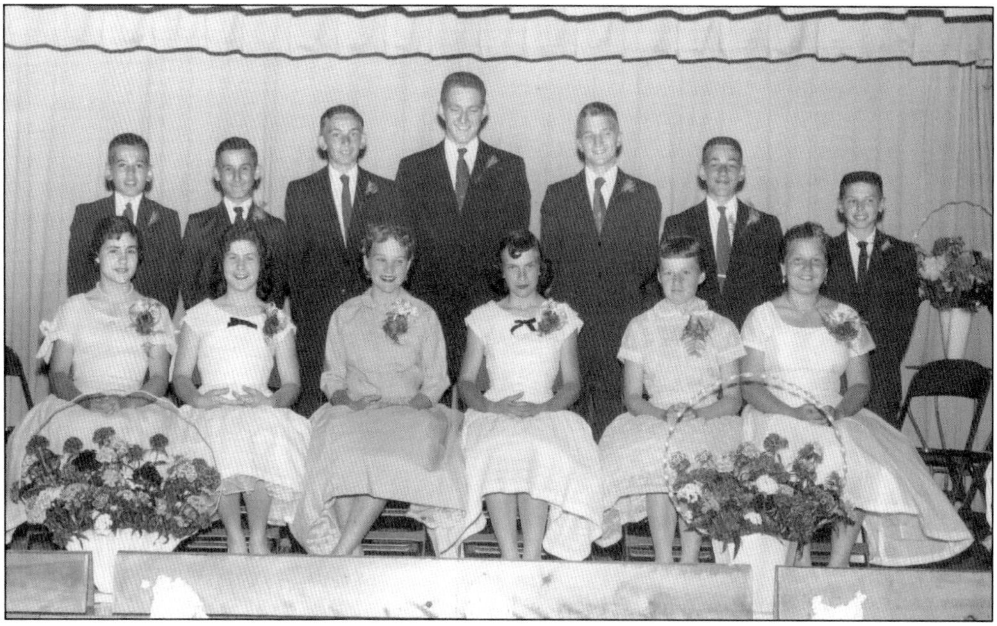

June 20, 1957, was the date of the final eighth-grade commencement at Deferiet Grade School, before centralization of the Carthage District. Pictured, from left to right, are (sitting) June Hall Cross, Nancy Dufresne Miles, Carol Kochubinski Lozo, Judy Miles Rutledge, Sandra Higgins Blondin, and Ann Marie Stanford Eddy; (standing) Ronald Corey, Arthur Shatraw, Edwin Hodkinson, Eugene Saber, Carl Kochubinski, James Martin, and John Hurley Jr.

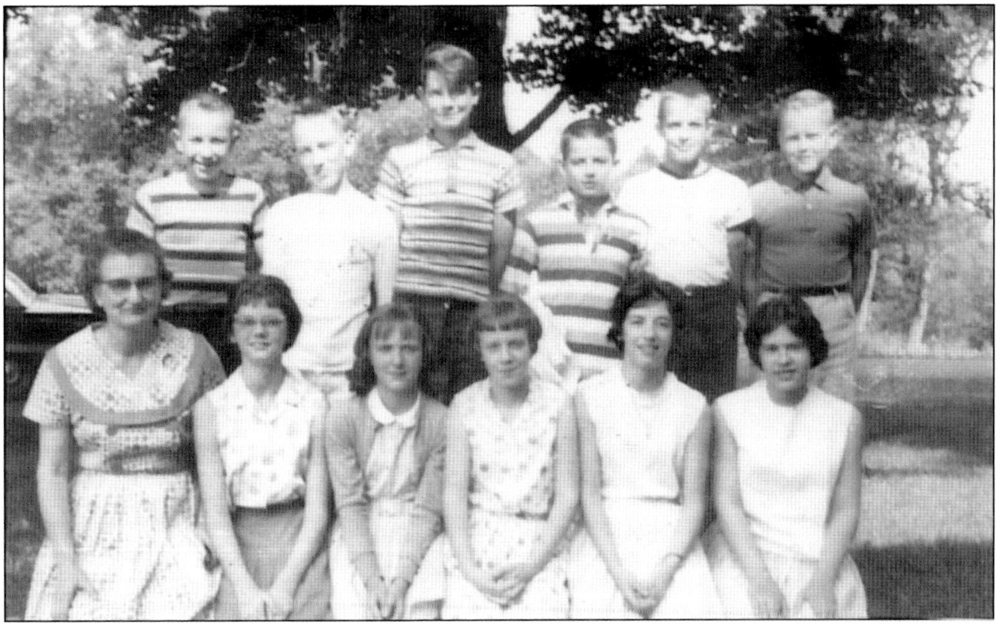

Inez Rowley and her sixth-grade class pose on the front lawn of the Deferiet School in June 1962. Pictured, from left to right, are (first row) Rowley, Elizabeth Hurley Sobol, Sue Bears L'Huillier, Catherine Piche Pierce, Shelley Carcasole Getman, and Paula Piroli; (second row) John Pais, Ralph Libby, Robert Nabewaniec, Michael Powell, Eric Wiley, and Dale Steenburg. Pais went on to be elected mayor of Deferiet in 1984. (Shelley Carcasole Getman collection.)

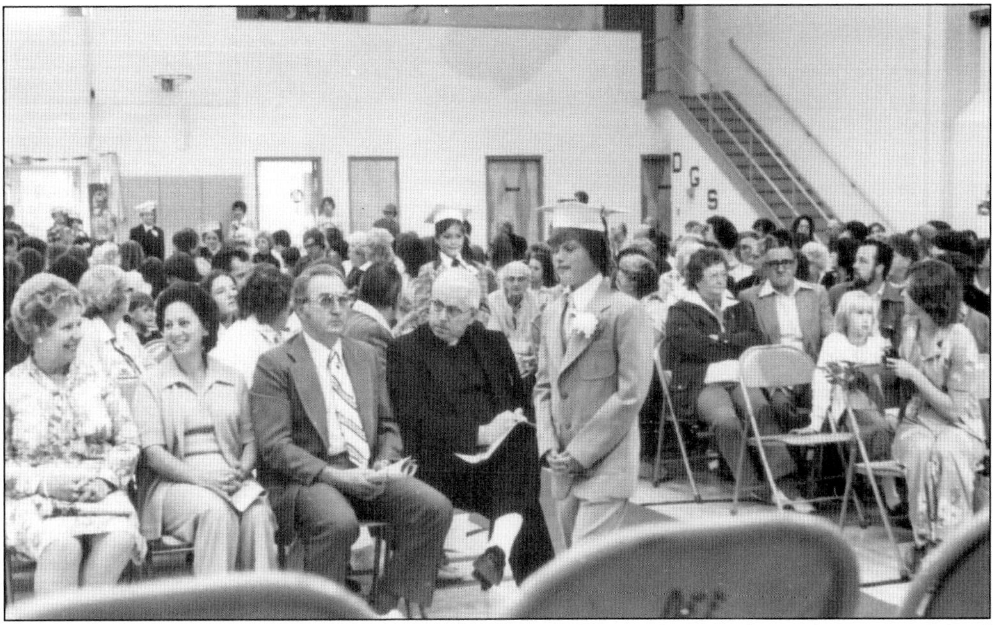

Daniel Nevills leads his fifth-grade class in the final graduation from Deferiet Elementary School before its closing in 1978. Following him are, front to back, Michael Sharp, Irving Cross Jr., and Craig Zando. The rest of the graduates were Carrie Beirman, Roxanne Covell, Eric Hubbard, Kristine LaPierre, Denise Lawton, Kelly McIntyre, Eugene Perrigo, Jackie Powell, Lloyd Putman, Janet Saber, Cathy Stevenson, Robin Thomas, and Brenda Wilder. Sally Hirschey was the teacher.

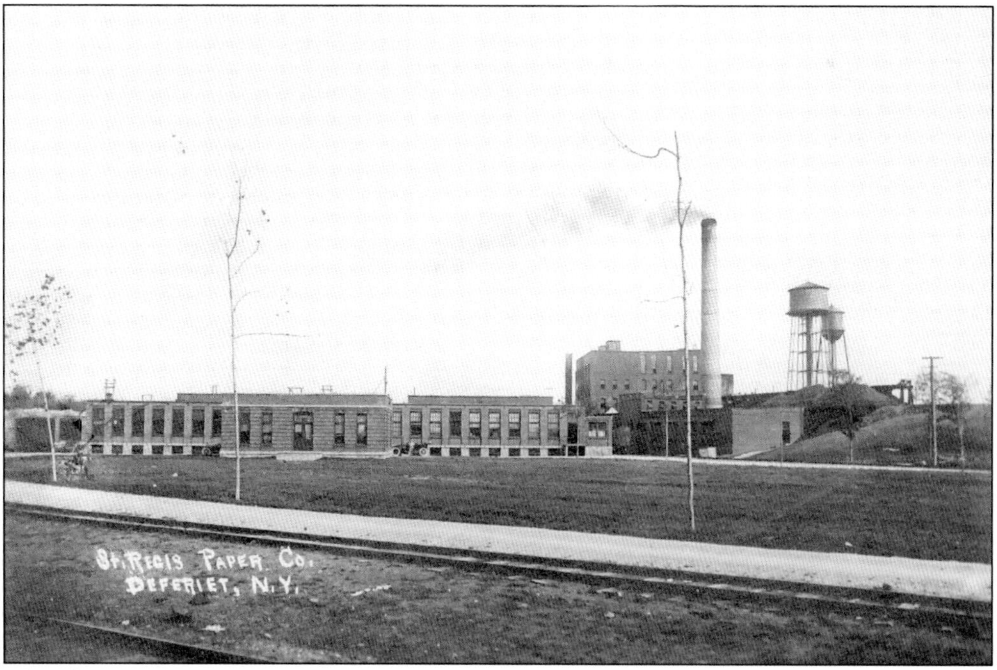

This photograph is of the original mill of the St. Regis Paper Company. The building in front was the time office, and the long building housed the paper machines; No. 1 machine is at the far right. The tall building behind the smokestack is the clay room. The large, round water tower holds the company's firefighting water supply, and the village water tower is in back. (Dorrie Ward Snyder collection.)

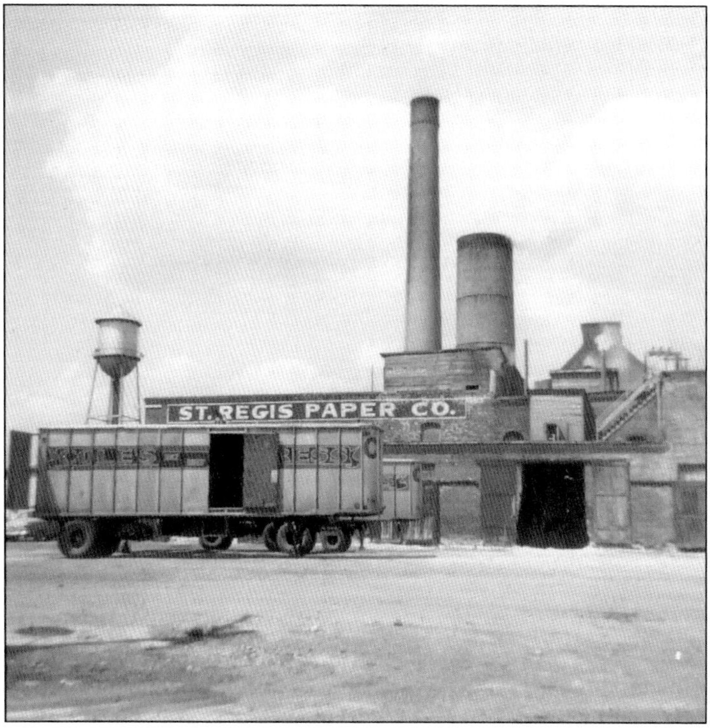

A 1979 issue of *Forbes* magazine ranked St. Regis Paper Company as the nation's third-largest seller of paper products. After paper was produced and taken off the winders, the rolls were transported by rail or tractor trailers to buyers. (Monica Miterko Vincent collection.)

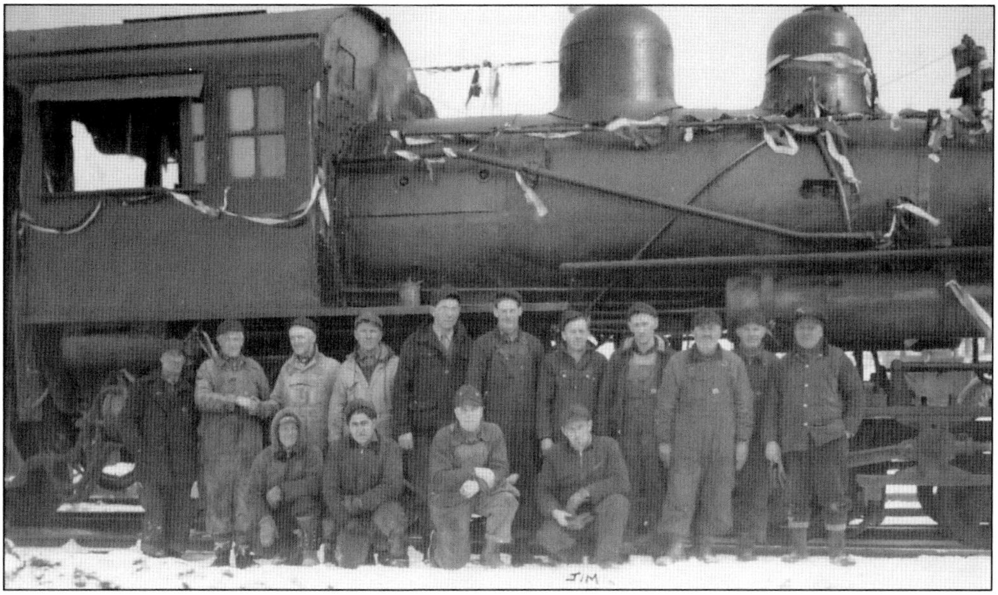

Harold Williams took this 1948 photograph in the yard of St. Regis. Pictured are, from left to right, (kneeling) Tony Garceau, Louie Rambone, Patrick Dillon, and James Cassoni Sr; (standing) Norris Higgins, Clarence Talbot, Ernie Griffin, Francis Bacon, William Talbot, Harry DeLosh, Walter Higgins, Donald Higgins, Angelo Mallizzia, Dewey Wetmore, and Andrew Lapolla. (James Cassoni Jr. collection.)

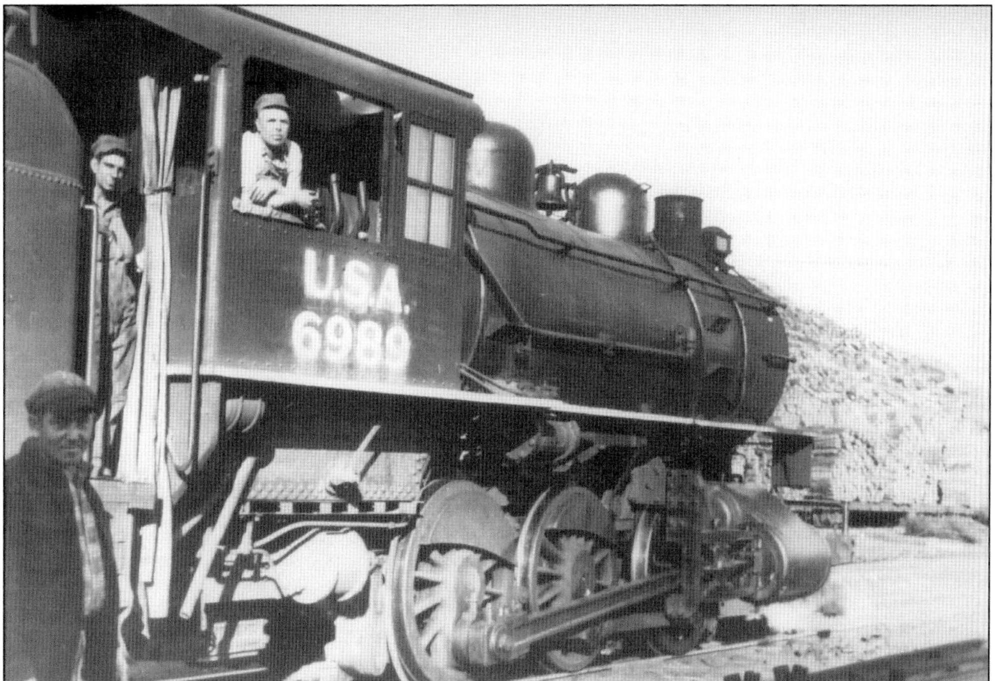

St. Regis locomotive No. 6989 is shown in front of a pile of ground wood in the yard. James Cassoni Sr. is the conductor, Charles Farr is the engineer in the door, and Francis Dillon is the engineer in the window in this late-1946 photograph. (James Cassoni Jr. collection.)

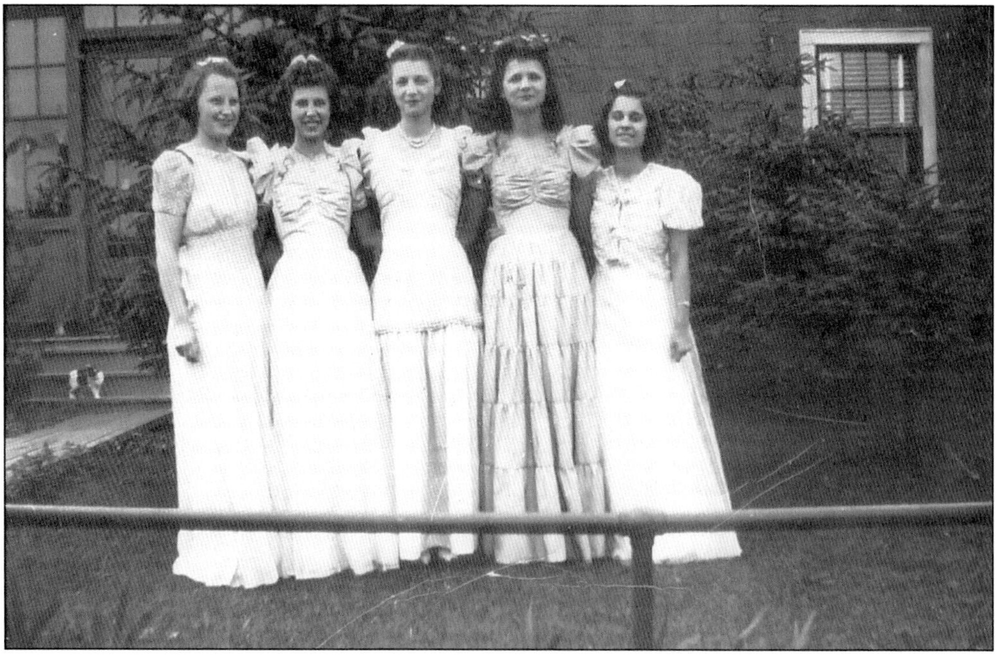

Exquisitely dressed, five Deferiet friends stand in front of the Polish Block before attending the 1940 Carthage High School Alumni Banquet. They are, form left to right, Margaret Pastor Lovejoy, Virginia Hedden Cook, Stella Woycik Rigabar, Albina Ganeriski, and Anna Multian Yuhas. (Stella Rigabar collection.)

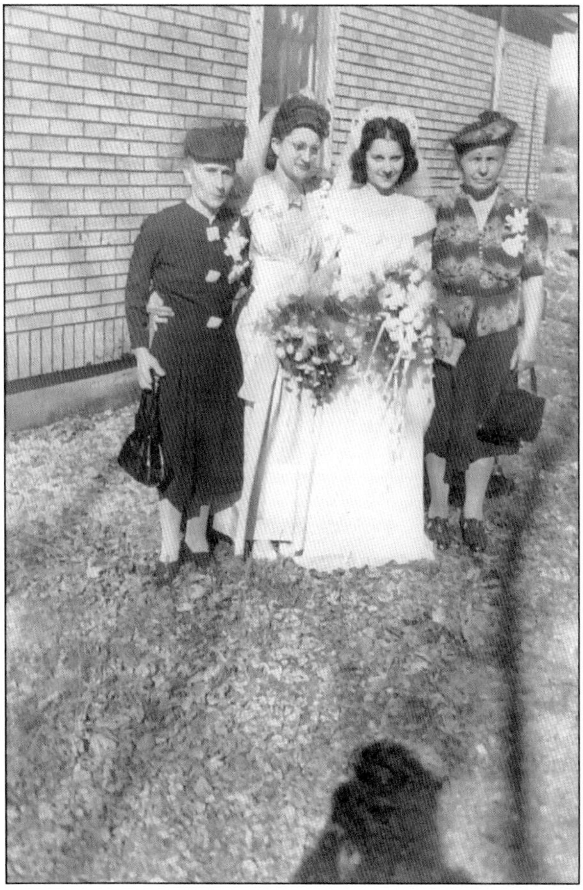

Anna Multian married Stanley Yuhas on October 26, 1946, at St. Rita Catholic Church. Like many Deferiet marriages, it blended two families from different ethnic backgrounds. Pictured are, from left to right, Julia Tymoczko Multian, mother of the bride; Jenny Multian Krall, sister of the bride; Anna; and Katherine Yuhas, mother of the groom. Mrs. Multian emigrated from the Ukraine and Mrs. Yuhas from Czechosolvakia. (Patricia Yuhas Kempney collection.)

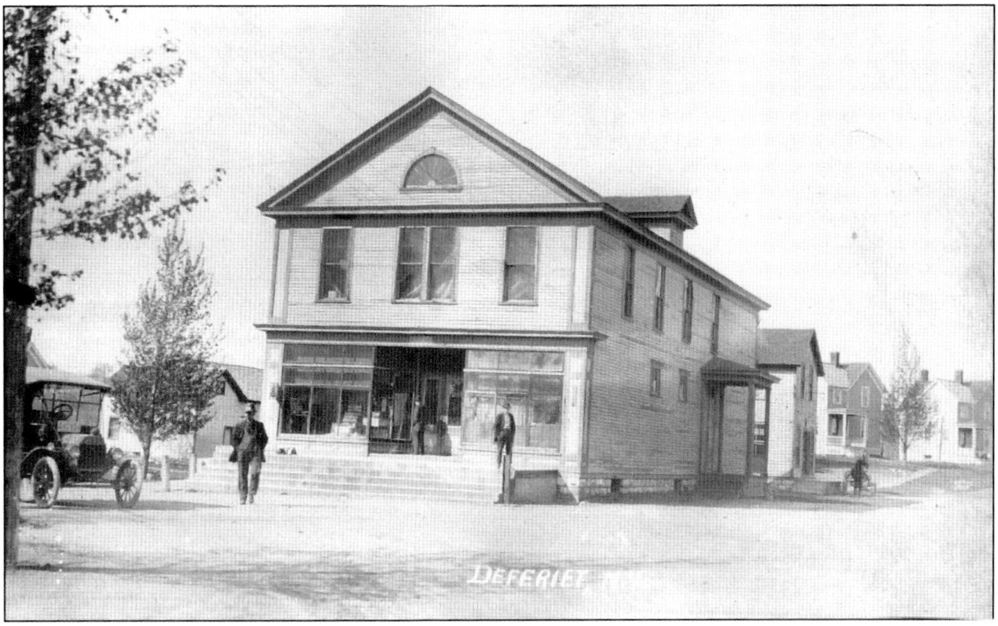

With $25,000 capital, the People's Bank of Deferiet opened on March 31, 1924. The front building is a store, the building in back is a meat market, and the bank was constructed between them; the assembly hall over the store was extended to become a common second floor. Due to lack of patronage, the bank ceased operation in 1927. The post office moved here from the general store after the bank closed.

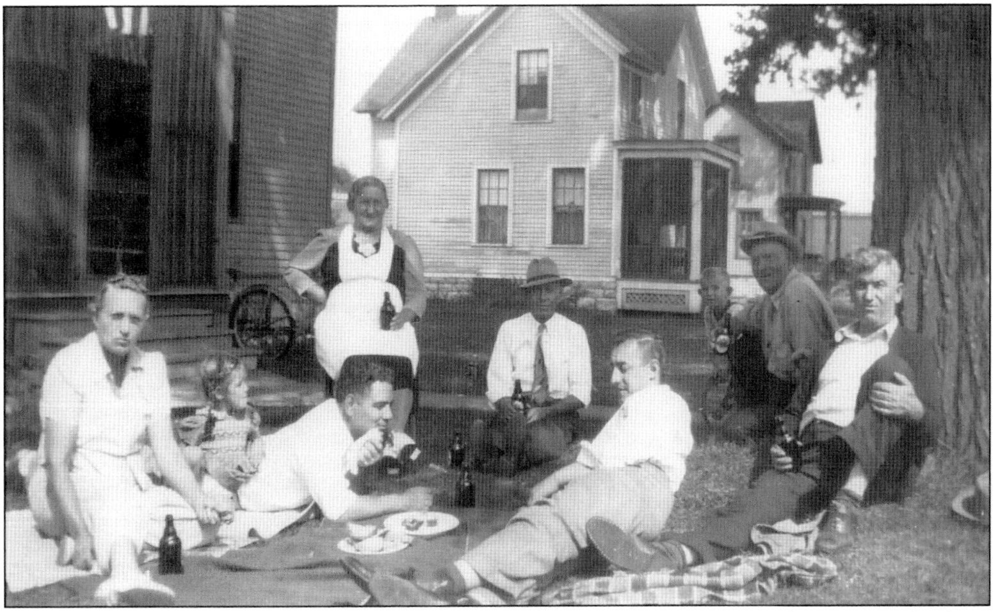
Labor Day 1942 finds this group of relatives enjoying a picnic with cold refreshments on the front lawn of Joseph and Sophia Turpin's house on Anderson Avenue. Pictured are (first row) Veronica Halko Nabywaniec, Carol Martin, Richard Martin, Joseph Turpin, and John Nabywaniec; (second row) Sophia Halko Turpin, Joseph Turpin Sr., Richard Martin Jr., and Peter Halko. (Dennis Turpin collection.)

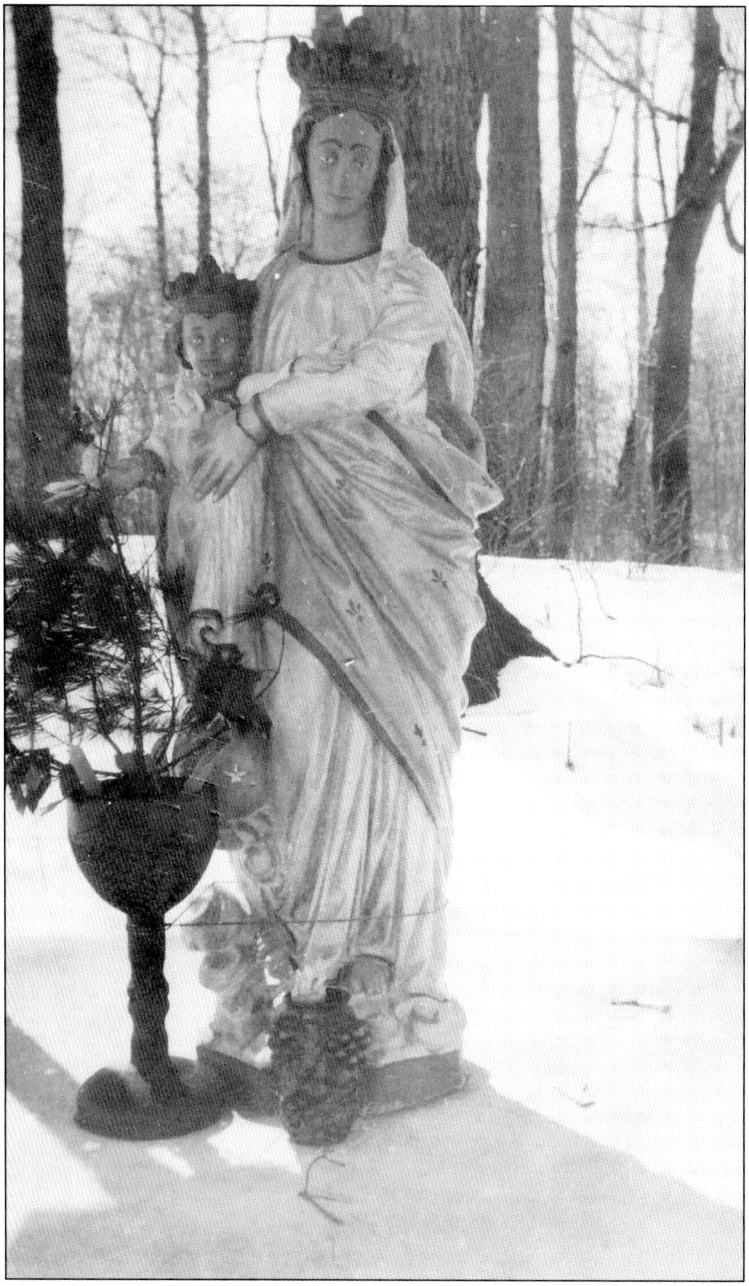

The original "Wayside Shrine," located in the woods near Deferiet, consisted of a wooden box containing a crucifix and a statue of Mary. Ellen and William Keib, a mason during construction of the canal at the St. Regis Paper Company, erected it in 1921 with the hopes that travelers would pray for a safe journey, due to the many accidents near the narrow bridge in that area. It was replaced two years later with a larger statue of the Blessed Mother and Christ Child, which was placed on a concrete base with a wooden canopy. When World War II ended, Afifi Moses, Mrs. Michael Habib, and Mary Ablan fulfilled a promise to improve the shrine because their sons had returned home safely. Moses erected a brown-shingled building with two windows, Habib placed a sidewalk, and Ablan installed the lighting. The shrine was also called "Madonna of Route 3."

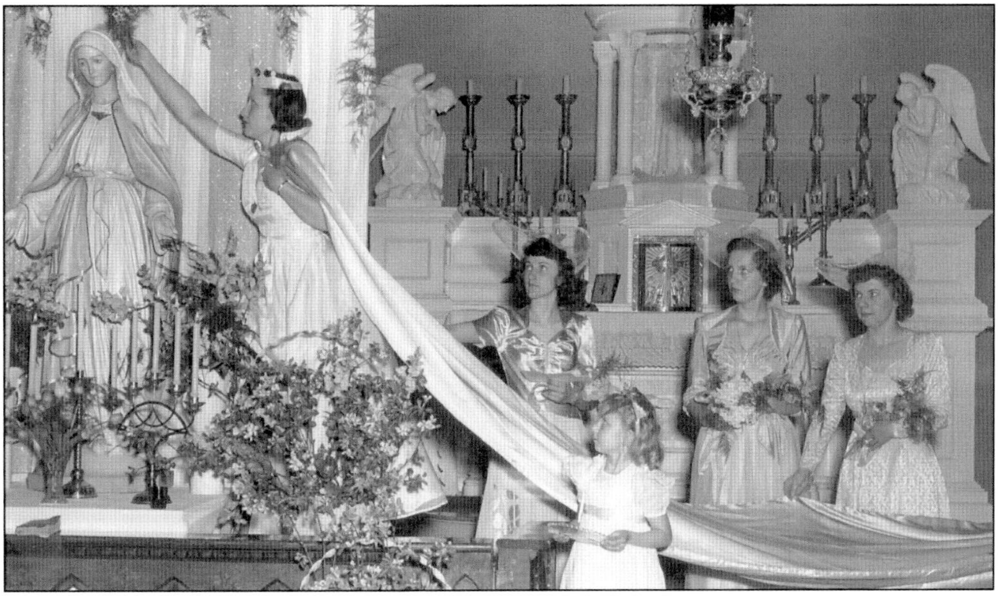

For Catholics, the month of May was chosen to honor the Blessed Mother. Margaret Pastor Lovejoy was chosen queen for the 1947 May crowning ceremony at St. Rita of Cascia Catholic Church. Bernetta Ganeriski Miterko, Helen Zebney, and Eileen Baker are her attendants. The crown bearer is Mary Anne Croitz. (Sr. Mary Anne, SSJ.)

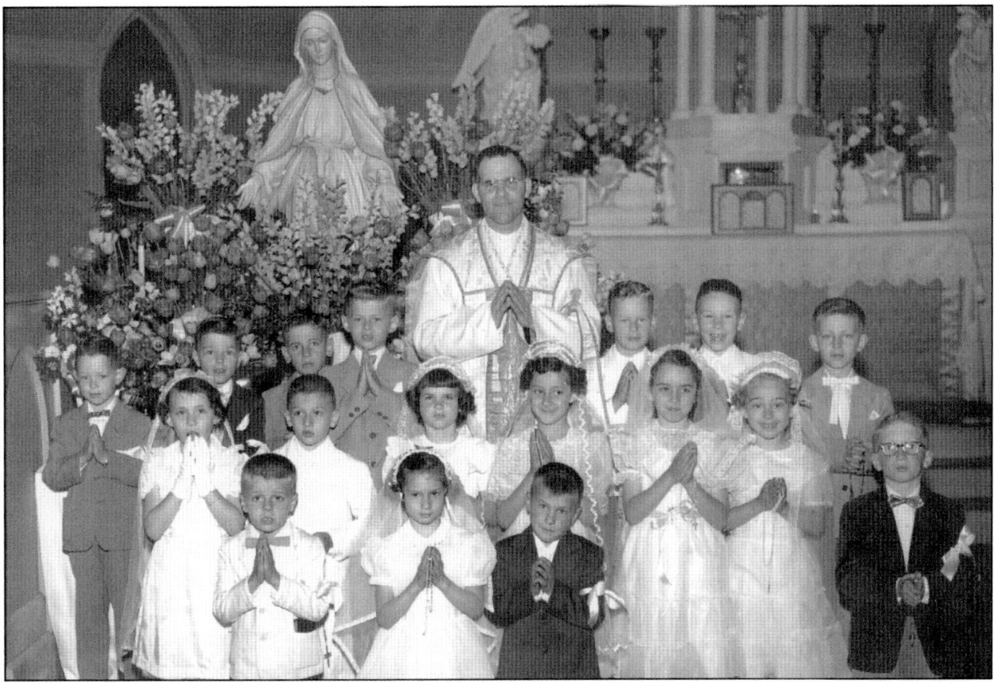

This is the First Communion class at St. Rita Catholic Church on May 16, 1954. Pictured are, from left to right, (first row) Stanley Vars, Janet Zando, and John Croitz; (second row) Sharon Joynt, George Cassoni, Mary Murtaugh Mitchell, Annette Vitrano, Joanne Kosztowski Armstrong, Judy Wells, and Robert Cowan; (third row) James Parmele, James Ginger, Richard Staab, John Miterko, assistant pastor Rev. Howard McCasland, Bruce Steenburg, Robert Hurley, and Richard Piere.

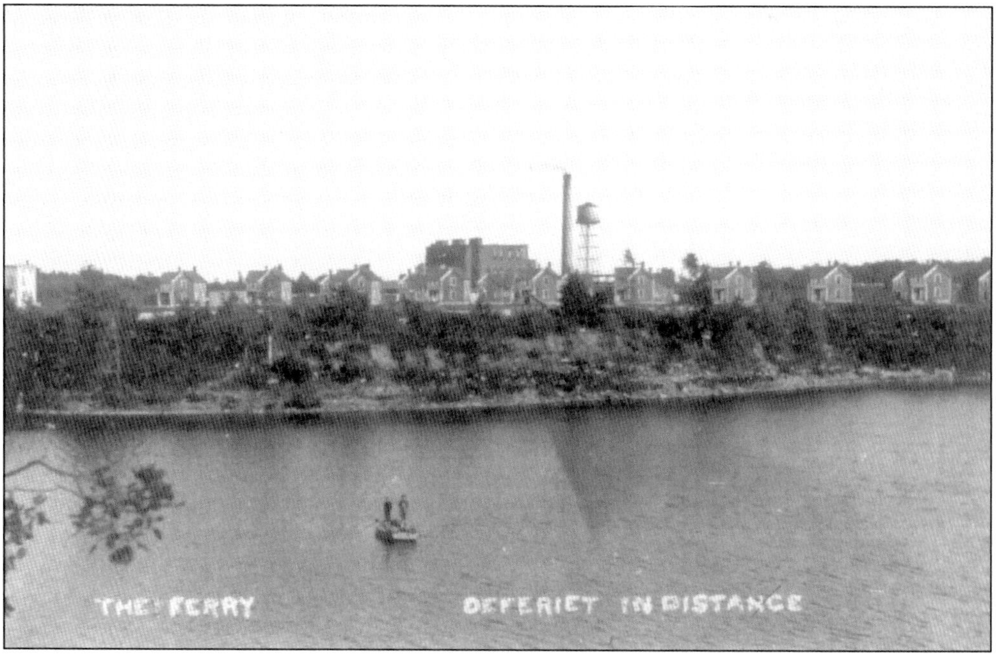

This photograph shows three people crossing on the ferry between the east and west sides of the Black River on a calm day. On the left is the Polish Block next to a front view of the houses on Riverside Drive, originally named River Street.

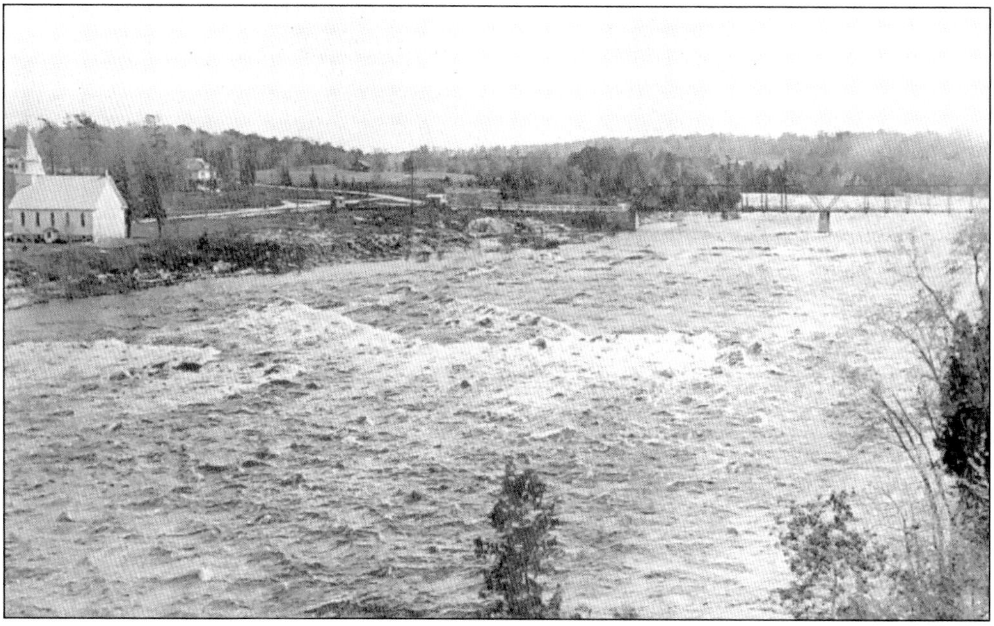

This view looking toward the bridge shows St. Rita of Cascia Catholic Church, which was incorporated on January 11, 1913. St. Regis deeded the land on May 8, 1913. The church trustees were Terence McManus and Michael Adams. In 1958, the first resident pastor assigned to Deferiet was Rev. Francis Ruddy. The Reynolds family home and the superintendent's residence are in the background. (Deferiet Archives.)

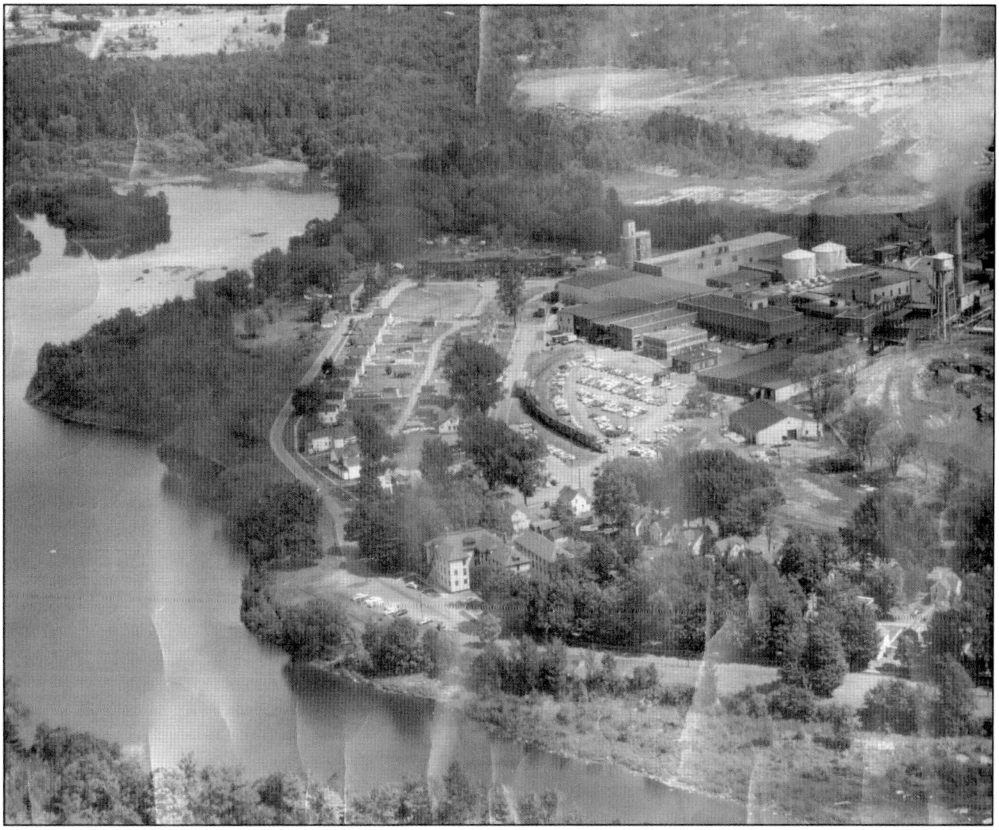

The St. Regis Paper Company in Deferiet was at one time considered a prize in the papermaking industry. Looking toward Munns Corners and Pine Camp (now Fort Drum), this aerial photograph captures the water, the ground-wood area, the Regis Inn, and the Polish Blocks. (Monica Miterko Vincent collection.)

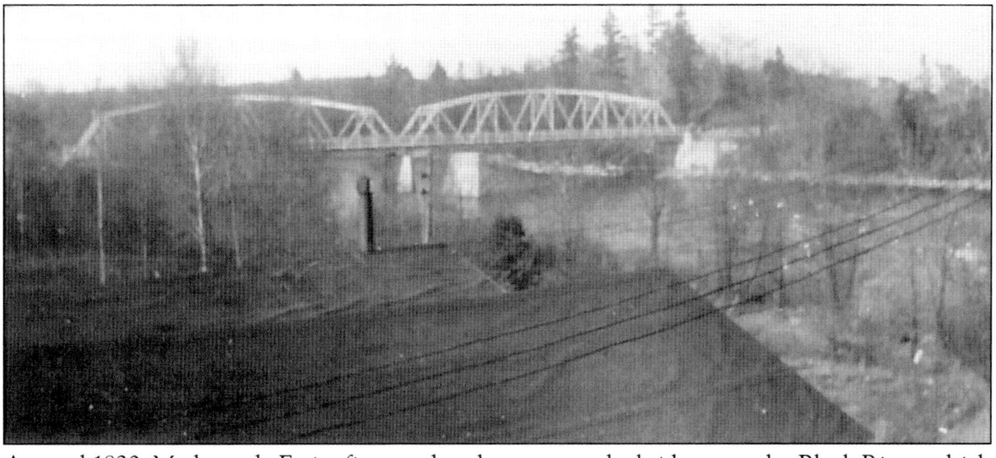

Around 1830, Madame de Feriet financed and constructed a bridge over the Black River, which was so swift that she could only cross it at certain times of the year. She was upset with a Mr. Clark of Great Bend, who could not see an advantage for the bridge. This 1945 image from Riverside Drive looking toward Great Bend shows a view of a newer bridge. (Francis Burke collection.)

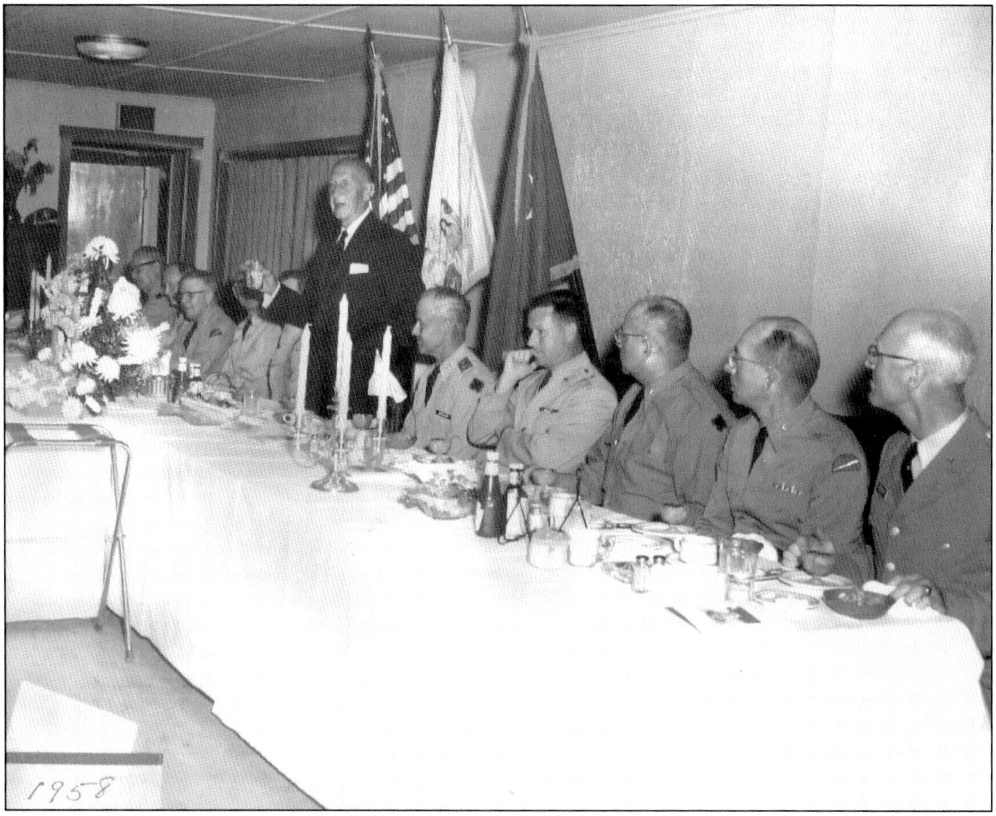

Being two miles from a military base, Deferiet had a close relationship with the troops. The military supported the town's two well-known restaurants—the St. Regis Inn and Johnnie's Inn. This 1958 photograph shows a banquet honoring the military at Johnnie's Inn. A fire destroyed the venue on June 22, 1976. (Sonja Siedlecki Pierce collection.)

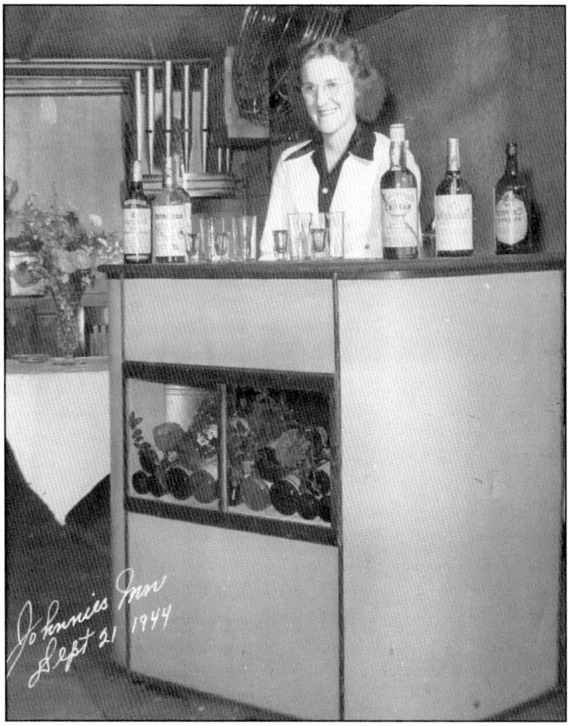

Bartender Leona Nabywaniec prepares the bar for a banquet on September 21, 1944. Notice the large fan in the corner, as there was no air-conditioning in the building in those days. (Sonja Siedlecki Pierce collection.)

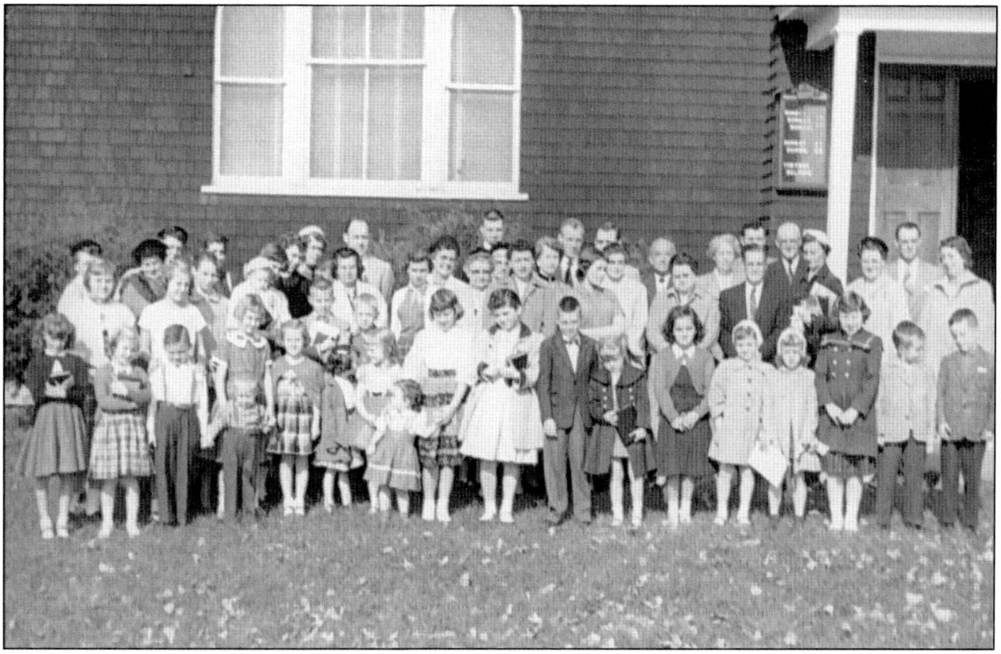

The Union Independent Church was dedicated on March 8, 1914, with Rev. B.J. Davison pastor in charge. The trustees were Frank Reynolds, Ellis Locklin, and James Alexander. It was deeded from St. Regis in 1959. Parishioners stand out front in this undated photograph. With a dark collar on her coat, Dorrie Snyder is below the right window jamb. (Dorrie Ward Snyder collection.)

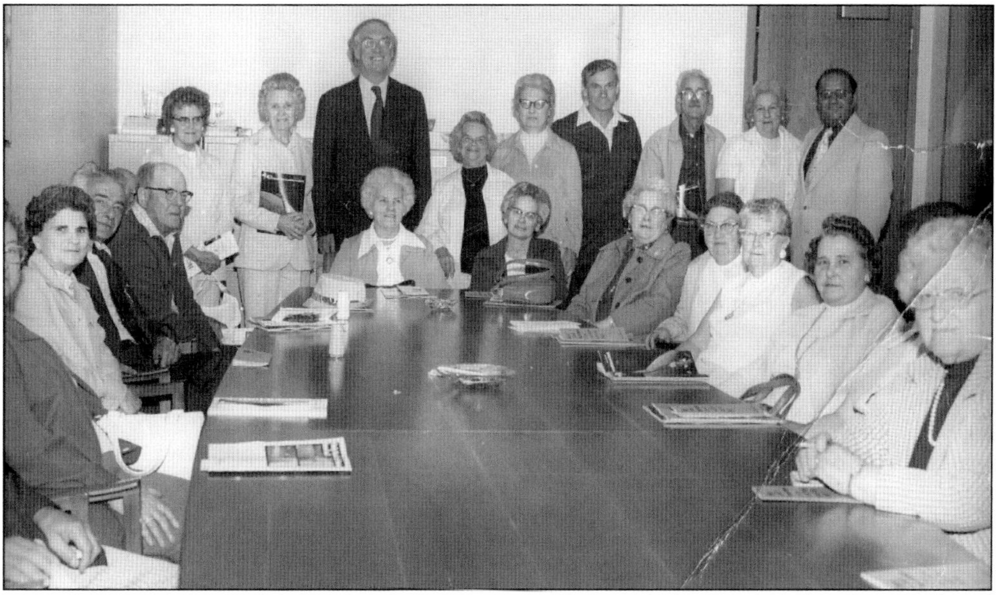

Formed in 1972, the St. Regis Senior Citizens of Deferiet are seen here with their state representatives during a trip to the New York capital, Albany. Pictured, from left to right, are (around the table) Jean Saber, Anna Cassoni, Nicholas Cassoni, Richard Wilsie, unidentified, Olive West, Lois Lancaster, Leona Trim, two unidentified, and Mary Martin; (standing) Francis Phelps, Elizabeth LaJuett, Sen. H. Douglas Barclay, Bernice Brotherton, Marion Zando, Mario Zando, Lester West, Grace Worden, and Assemblyman Robert Nortz. (Senior Citizen Archives.)

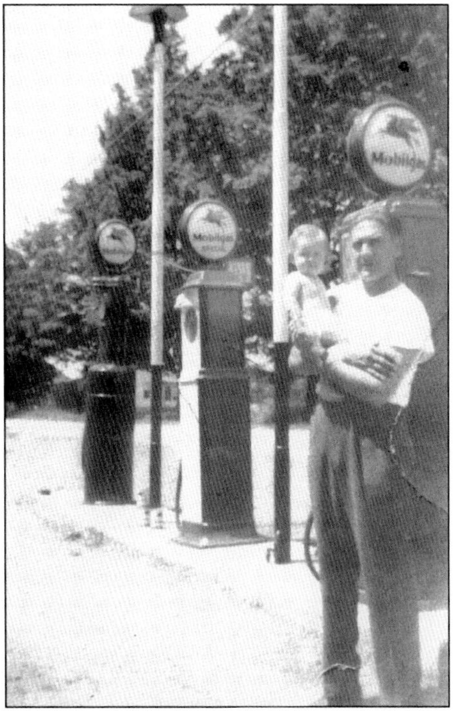

John Bears holds his seven-month-old daughter, Marcia, in this 1947 photograph. He and his wife, Lillian, bought their home, which had been a state police barracks prior to them buying it. Along with running the gas station, they rented out cabins that were on the property located on Route 3. (Marcia Bears Bridge collection.)

This December 21, 1947, photograph shows a group of parishioners from St. Paul's in Black River and St. Rita's in Deferiet packing up food they collected during Thanksgiving to be sent to Europe for support after the end of World War II. Starting clockwise from the back are Eileen McLean Perkins, unknown, Barbara Monnat Burns, Frank Cassoni, Kay Lonsberry, Gino Zando, Eileen Baker, and Edward Pultorak. In 1978, Gino Zando became mayor of Deferiet.

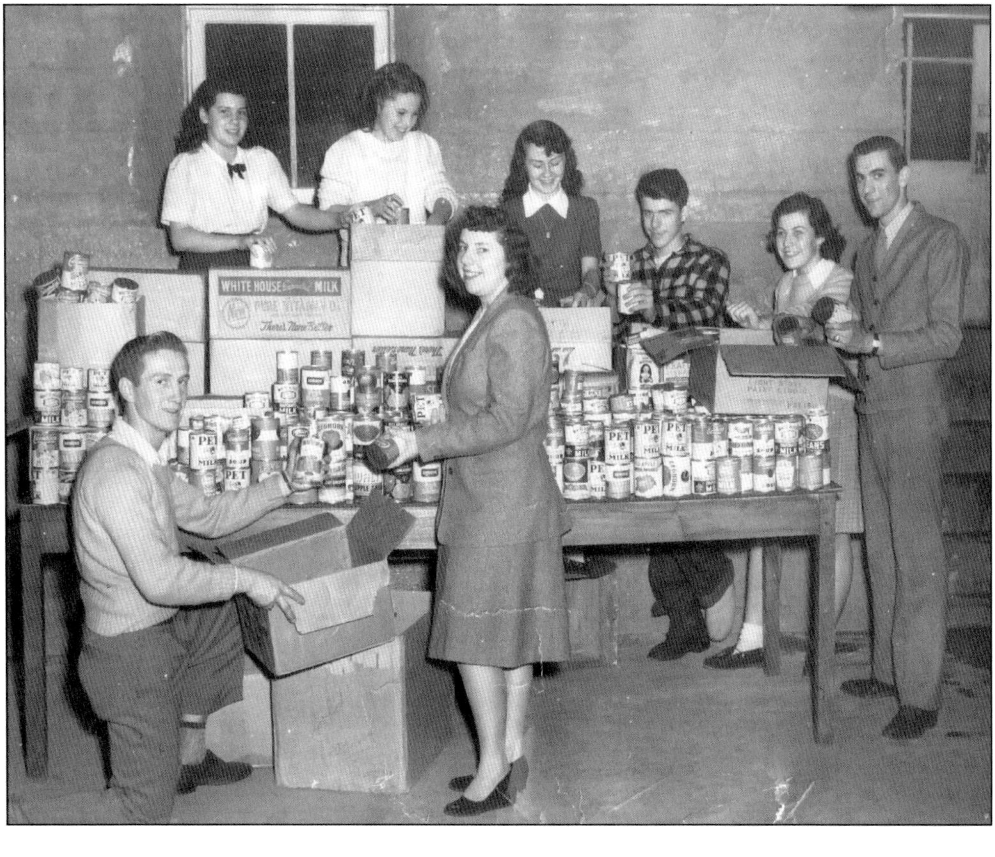

In 1919, a meeting of Polish men was held in Parker's Hall, above this store, to establish a school that would teach them English and encourage them to become citizens; 12 men registered for classes. In this 1939 photograph of the store, Irene Kerekes DeLosh (left) and friends are getting ready to go skating. An unidentified man is standing behind the door. (Mullen Family collection.)

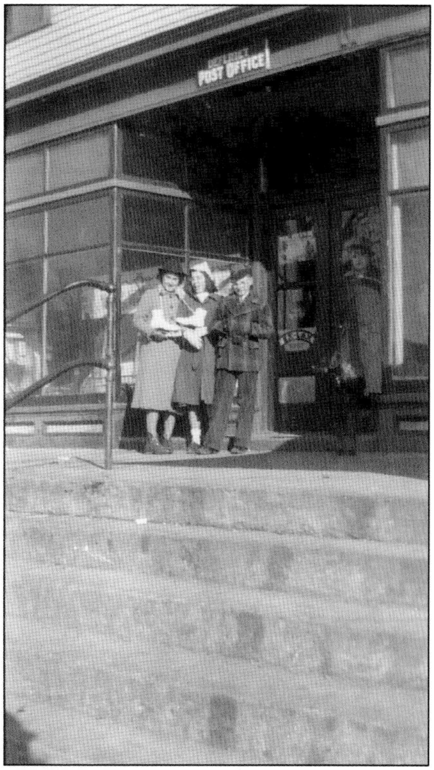

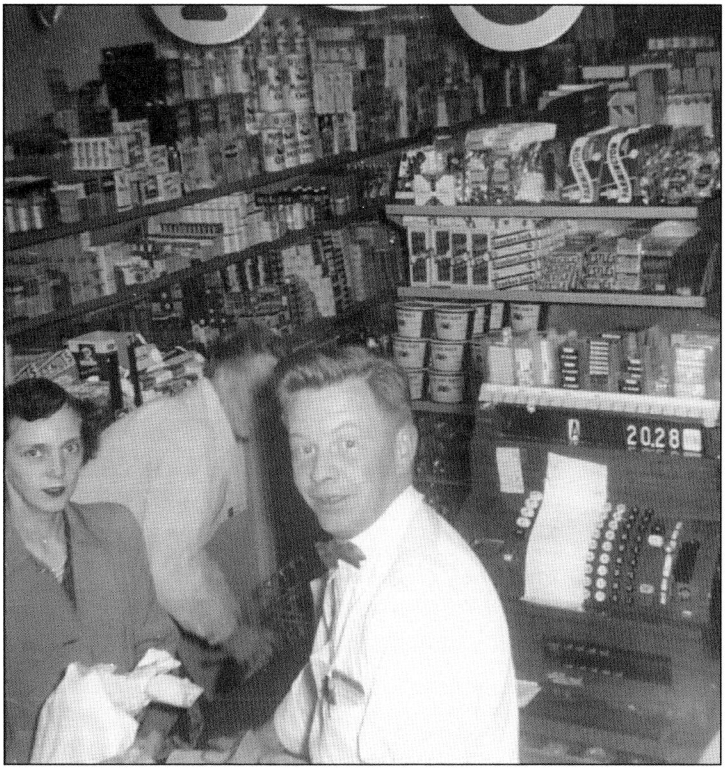

Frederick Piche, proprietor of the Deferiet Foodland, waits on a customer. On April 30, 1962, he became the postmaster in Deferiet and held the position until his retirement. Notice the price of groceries on the cash register. (Thomas Piche collection.)

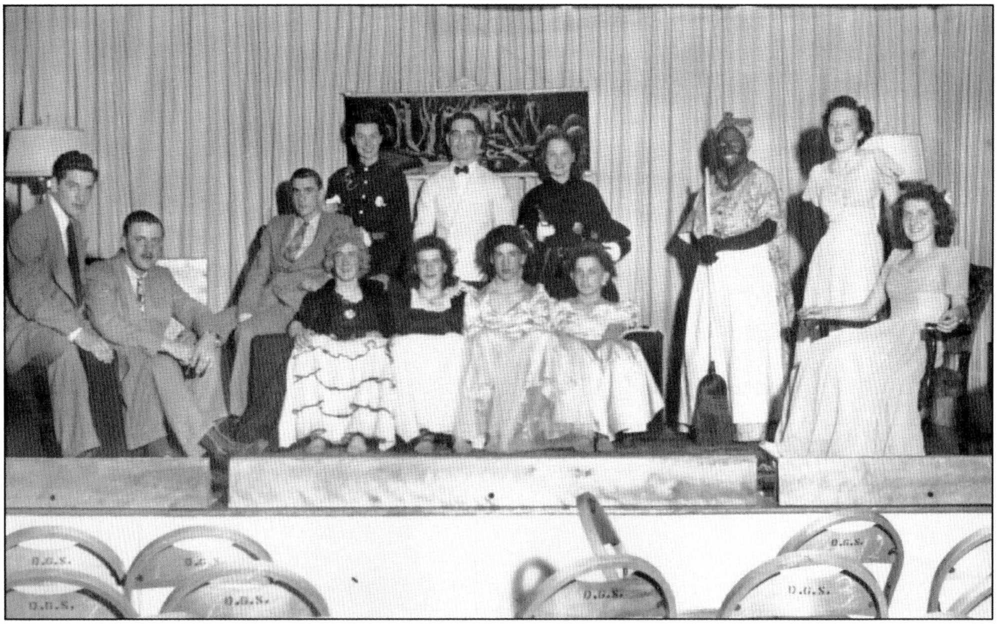

This 1946 photograph shows members of St. Rita's Parish rehearsing for the comedy *Four Beautiful Dolls*, which was presented at Deferiet Grade School. From left to right are Americo Carcasole, Stanley Zaremba, Gino Zando, Regina Yuhas, Dick Martin, Margaret Pastor, Eileen Baker, Betty Baker, and Patricia Turpin; on the couch dressed as females are Edward Pultorak, Frank Cassoni, Samuel Millich, and Donald Melisko. Patricia Turpin did a clarinet solo of Russian folk music.

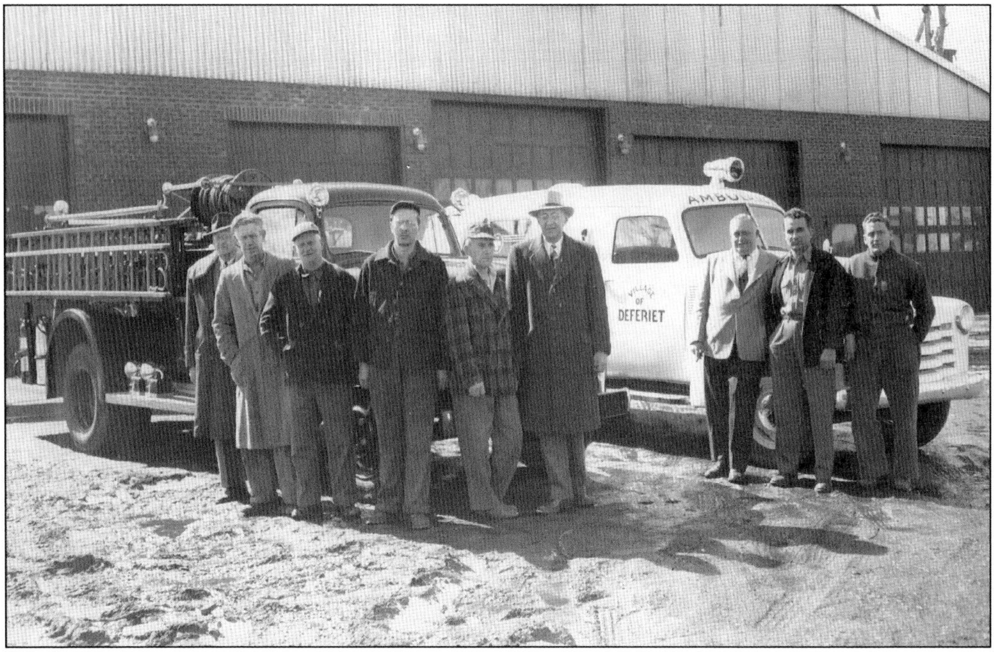

The Village of Deferiet and the candy fund of local unions helped finance an ambulance, to be driven by firemen. Pictured with the new ambulance are, from left to right, Lynn Robinson, unidentified, Fire Chief Gilbert DeLosh, Al Benson, unknown, Clifford Wenzel, mill superintendent Patrick Moran, Joseph Powell, and Donald Rigabar. (Deferiet Fire Department Archives.)

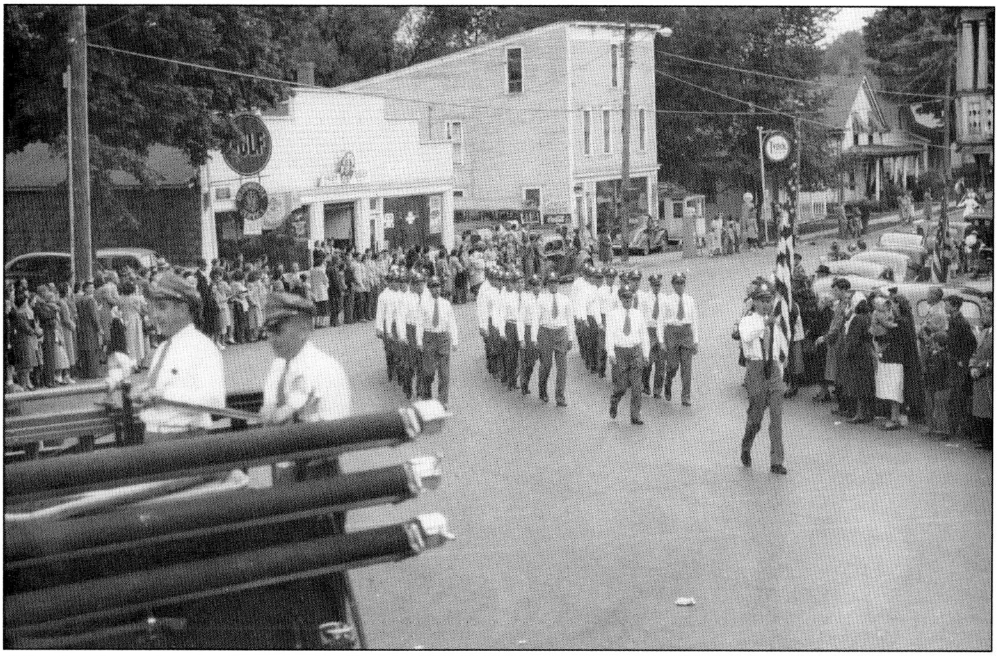

A bucket brigade was the means of fighting fires before the Deferiet Fire Department was organized in 1948 to protect the property of St. Regis Paper Company and the citizens of Deferiet. Gilbert DeLosh was chosen as the first fire chief. This photograph shows the department's first parade appearance, on May 27, 1949, in Philadelphia, New York. (Deferiet Fire Department Archives.)

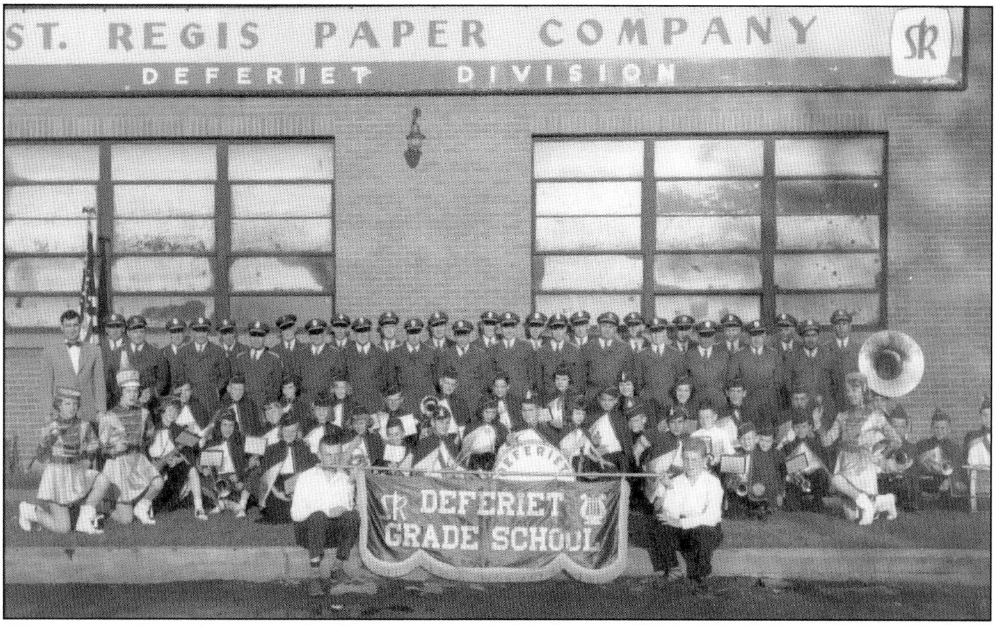

There is nothing that captures the essence of Deferiet more than this early-1950s photograph. The fire department has been the heart and soul of the village because its have been involved in so many aspects of local life. The firemen and the school band wear uniforms of blue and gold, the colors of the St. Regis Paper Company. Their precise military style earned the firemen many marching awards. (Deferiet Firemen Archives.)

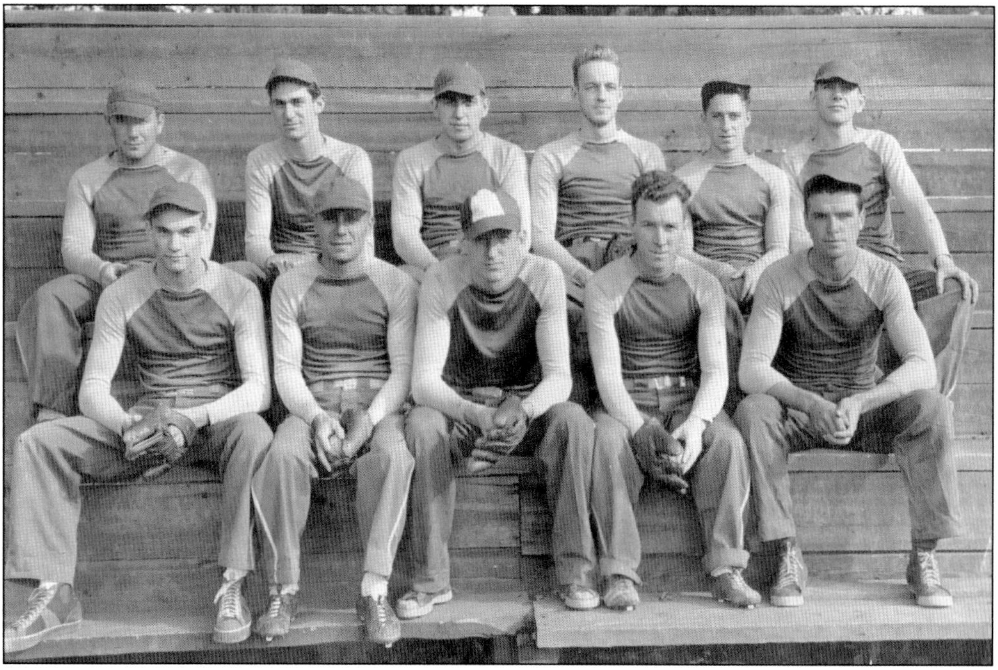

The 1941 St. Regis Inn softball team won the Northern New York Tournament in Carthage, the bi-county league, and played in the New York State tournament in Rochester, where this photograph was taken. Pictured, from left to right, are (first row) Mario Zando, Stephen Krall, John Miterko, Ivan Hedden, and Steve Blasek; (second row) Italo Ventiquattro, Louis Zando, Julius Siedlecki, Byron Steenburg, Tom Piroli, and Alexander Siedlecki. Absent was Edward Jaworski. (CRT.)

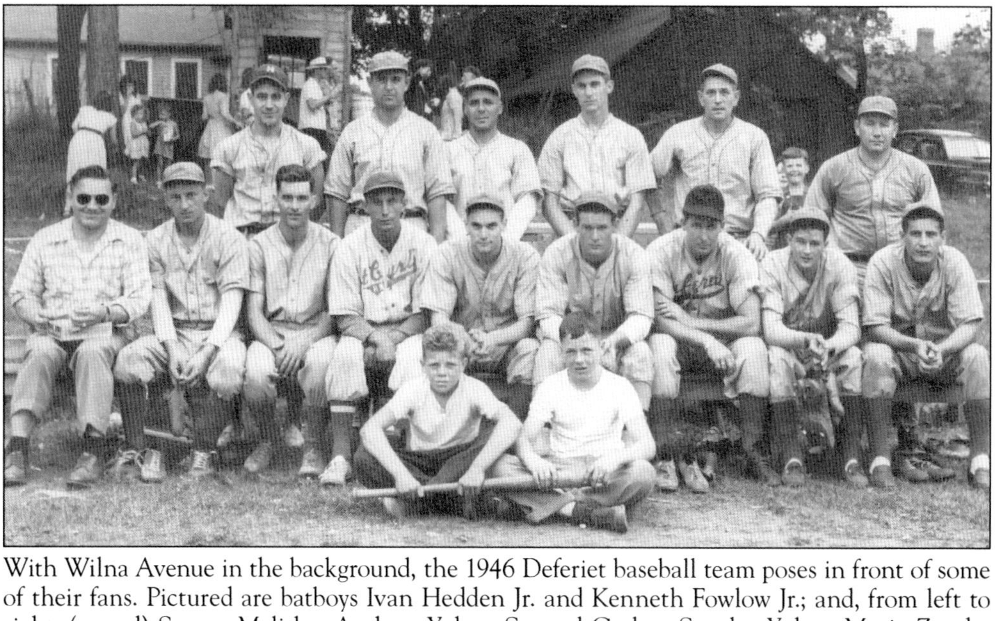

With Wilna Avenue in the background, the 1946 Deferiet baseball team poses in front of some of their fans. Pictured are batboys Ivan Hedden Jr. and Kenneth Fowlow Jr.; and, from left to right, (seated) Steven Melisko, Andrew Yuhas, Samuel Gerber, Stanley Yuhas, Mario Zando, Harry DeLosh, Thomas Ward, Gilbert DeLosh, and Stanley Siedlecki; (standing) Edward Turpin, Kenneth Fowlow, manager, Stephen Krall, Louis Zando, Mert Horne, and Italo Ventiquattro.

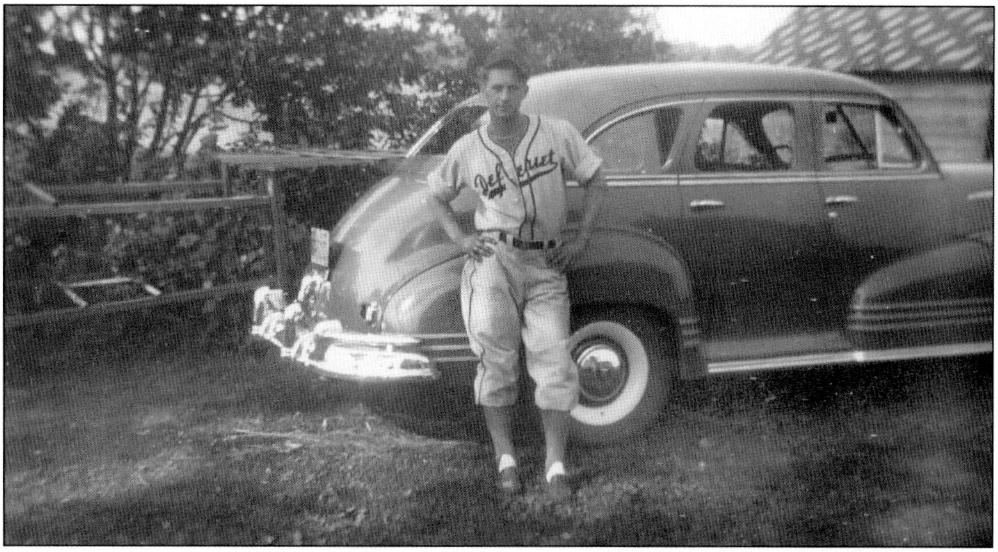

Chester Mullen poses with this 1947 Pontiac belonging to his father, Joseph. The St. Regis Company first organized baseball teams for laborers in 1905. Since then, baseball and lacrosse have become synonymous with Deferiet. Bennett Gaebel, Kyle Gaebel, Zackery Mulvaney, and Paul M. Zando have played on NCAA Division III national championship teams in college lacrosse at Cortland State; Ben and Paul in 2006, and Kyle and Zackery in 2009. (Edward Mullen collection.)

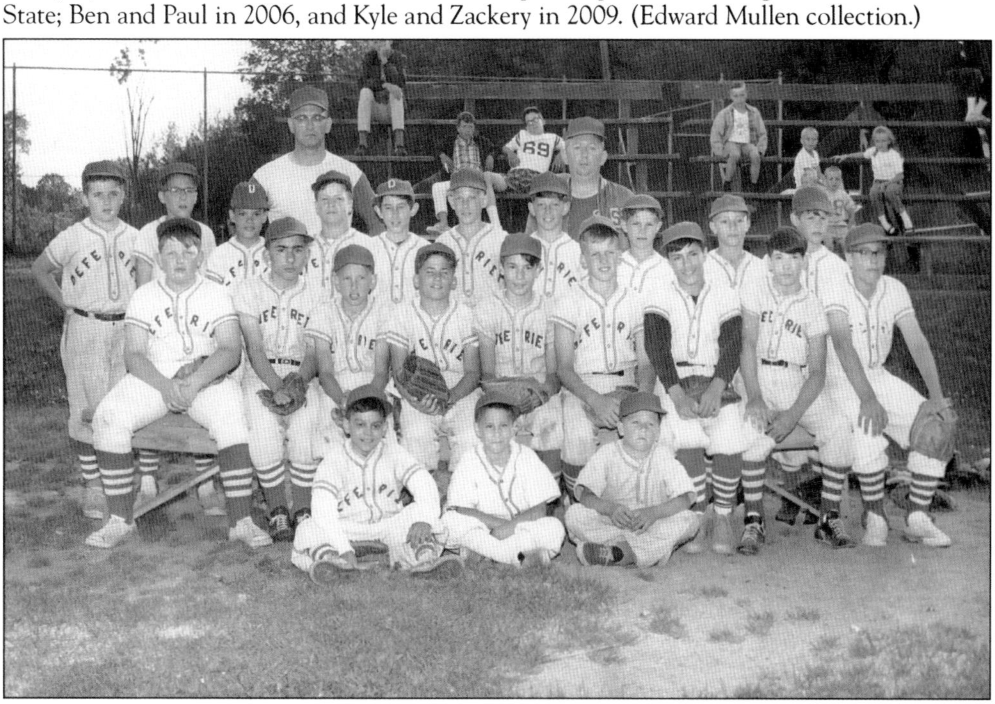

Pictured are the runners-up in the Black River Valley Peewee Baseball League in 1967. They are, from left to right, (first row) James Yuhas, Kirk Ventiquattro, James Weaver; (second row) William Fowlow, Vincent Schneider, Kevin Killian, Kevin Wood, Joseph Zando, Michael Millich, David Bowman, Michael Carcasole, and Thomas Ventiquattro; (third row) John West, Dominic Ventiquattro, Robert Bowman, coach Samuel Millich, Timothy Lewis, Marc Huley, Dale Weaver, Gary Miterko, coach Leland Weaver, Ronald Foster, Norman Gagnon, and Kim Foster.

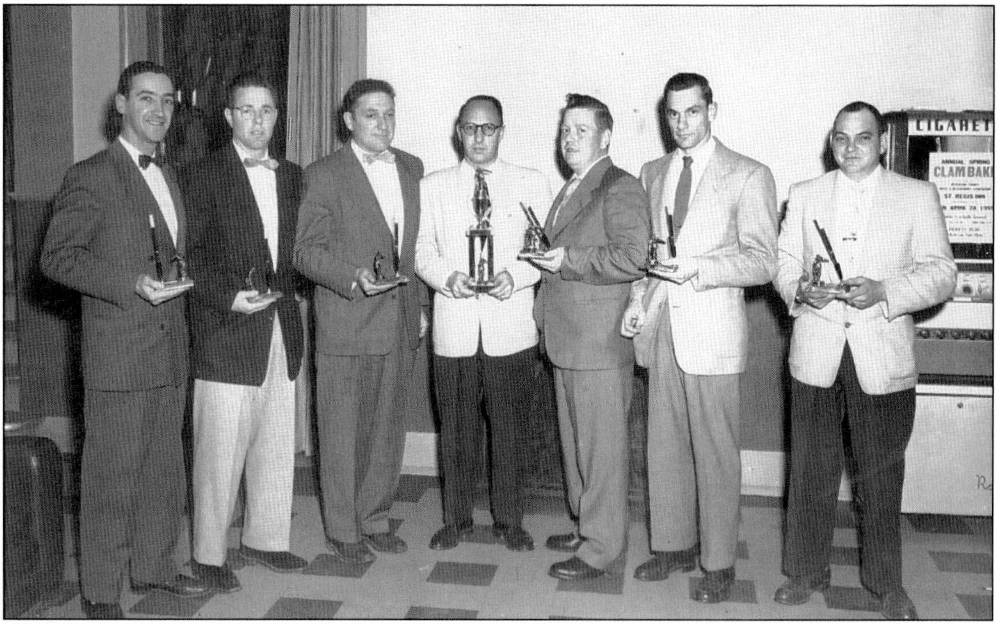

In 1939, an annex was added to the left side of the St. Regis Inn to accommodate a bowling alley. When the hotel was torn down, Andrew Yuhas moved the alleys to his new establishment, the Whistle Stop on Route 3. Bowlers on this 1955 men's team are, from left to right, Harold Cummins, James Wakefield, John Bears, Walter Dinberg, sponsor, unidentified, Mario Zando, and Wallace Scott.

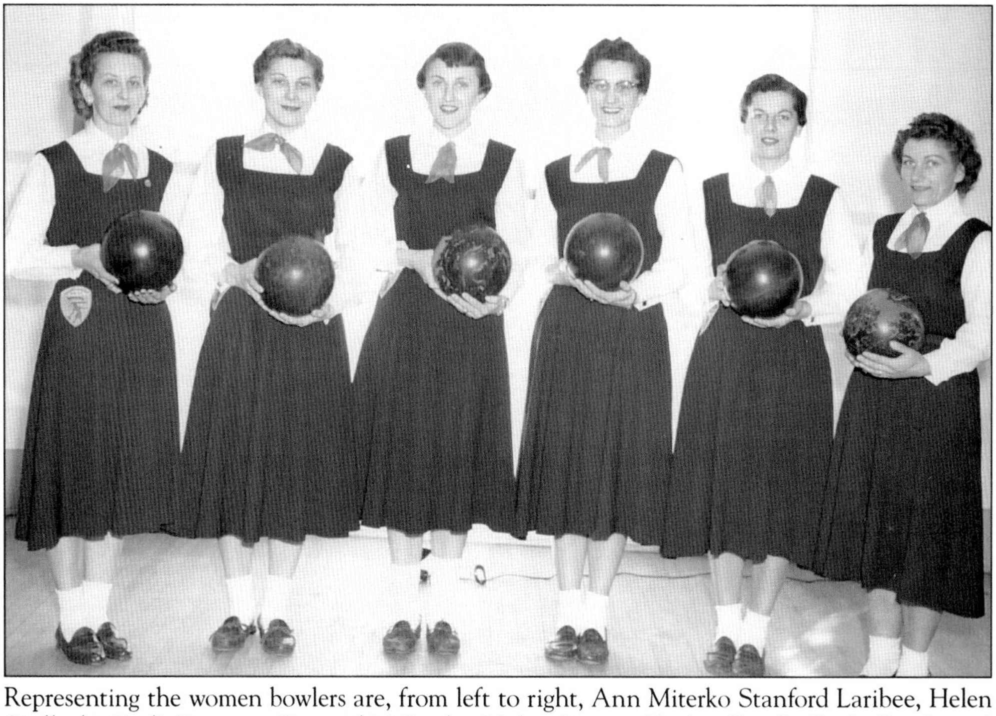

Representing the women bowlers are, from left to right, Ann Miterko Stanford Laribee, Helen Siedlecki Piroli, Bernetta Ganeriski Miterko, Helen Sarama Kepler, Sue Siedlecki Staab, and Agnes Melisko Mattingly. (Richard Staab collection.)

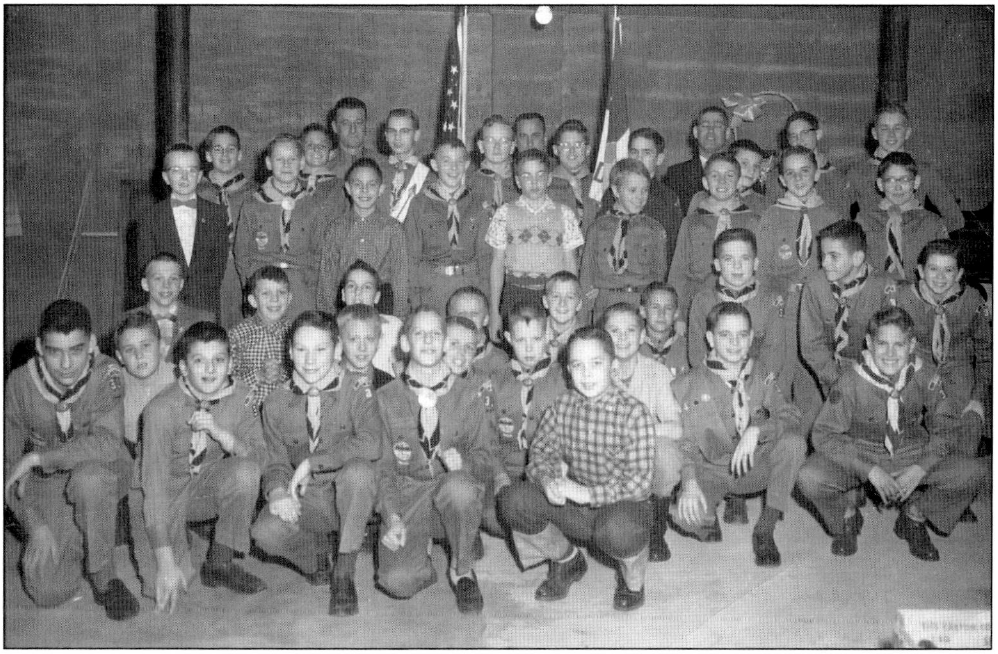

Deferiet Fire Department sponsored a Cub Scout Pack in 1951. Members were David Turpin, Fred Hall, Stephen Krall, David West, Robert Bertrand, James Martin, Eugene Saber, James Lancaster, Michael Plazza, John MacVean, William Grosse, Charles Morse Jr., and Peter Zando. This 1956 photograph is of the Deferiet Boy Scout Troop 31. (Edward Nabewaniec collection.)

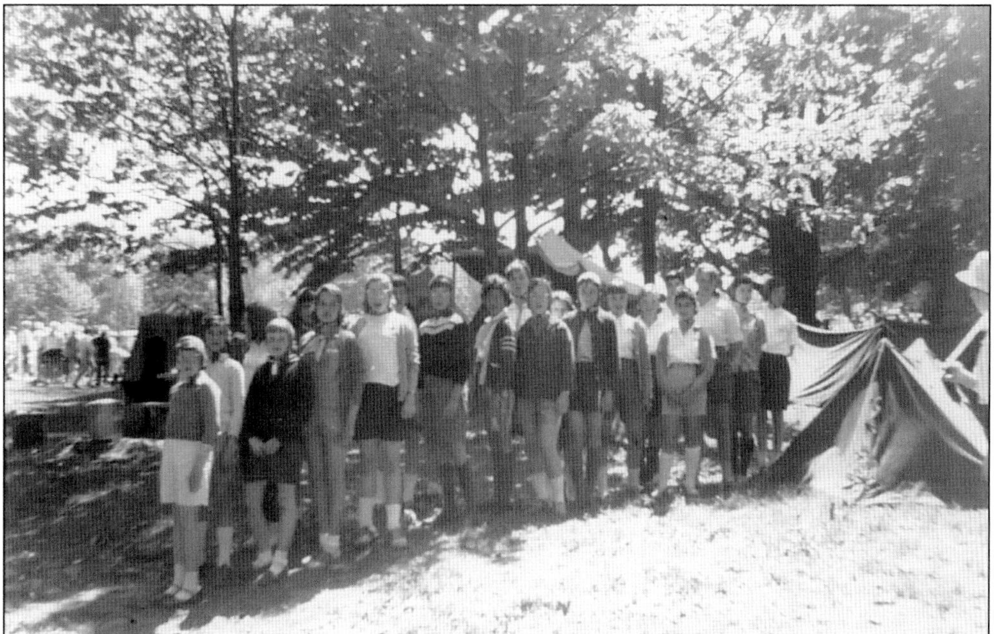

In 1957, Girl Scout Troop 66 was formed under the leadership of Suzanne Wiley and Genevieve Murtaugh. The Deferiet Girl Scouts hosted a day camp for the surrounding area troops with 100 girls attending at Pine Grove Park. Suzanne Wiley can be seen just to the right in the photograph.

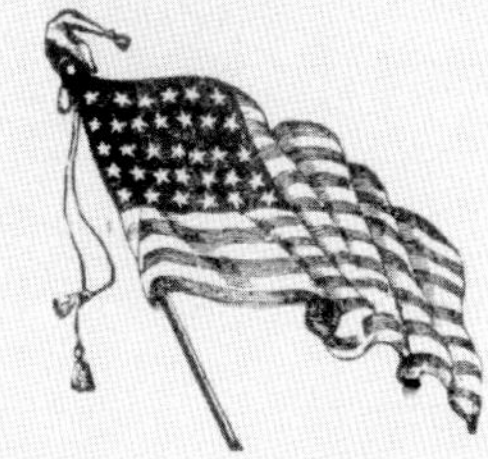

History of the Captured German Cannon of Deferiet, N. Y.

THIS German Cannon you have just seen is what is known in military circles as a seventy-seven milimeter field piece. This type of death dealing fighting apparatus has a range of four miles and is conceded to be the most effective of all arms used in the great World War.

This particular piece was captured at the offensive of the Argonne Forest. Less than one year ago it was dealing out its deadly work on our brave boys. How well they stood up against its work is shown in part, by the seventeen bullet holes and shrapnel marks that show on the cannon. They stand as mute testimony of the accuracy of aim and the bravery of our heroes.

This captured German Cannon has been awarded by the U. S. Government to the people of Deferiet for patriotism displayed in the late Victory Loan.

It and one other non-banking community near New York city were the only ones awarded a cannon in the State of New York.

Deferiet's allotment in the Victory Loan was $16,500.

How well the call was answered is shown by the results. Out of a Rand-McNally population of eight hundred it gave 565 subscriptions, totaling 301800 or eighteen times its quota.

Unveiled at a Labor Day ceremony on September 1, 1919, Deferiet's captured German cannon is described here. It has a long and celebrated history, which is shared in the next few images. Thirty-six men from Deferiet served in the Great War.

This German cannon captured in World War I was given to Deferiet in 1919 for the town's patriotism and allotment for the Victory loan. The 1909 Krupp 77-millimeter field gun was placed at the entrance to the village. In 1940, a rainstorm caused a derailment of coal cars, which damaged the cannon. Two years later, St. Regis Paper Company and the American Legion Bassett-Baxter Post donated it to the scrap metal drive to help the World War II effort. Taking part in a ceremony before the cannon was handed over were C. Tabbot, Pete Hart, Lyman Beeman, Walter Barker, Edward Mushtare, William Bush, Dan Reynolds, William Talbot, James Burton, Frank Callahan, past county commander of the Legion, L. West, Jackson Palmer, Elmer Bailey and Gerald Johnson, commander of the Legion. (Right, Francis Burke collection; below, Jean Yousey collection.)

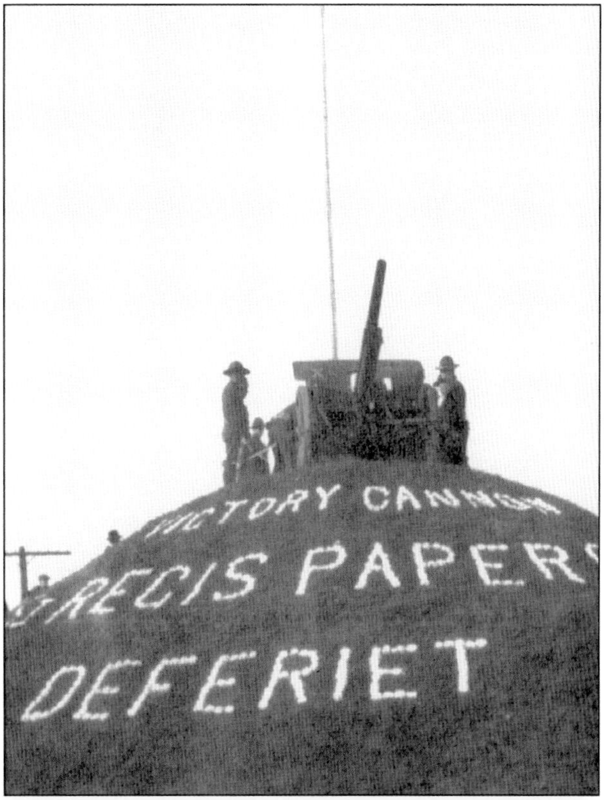

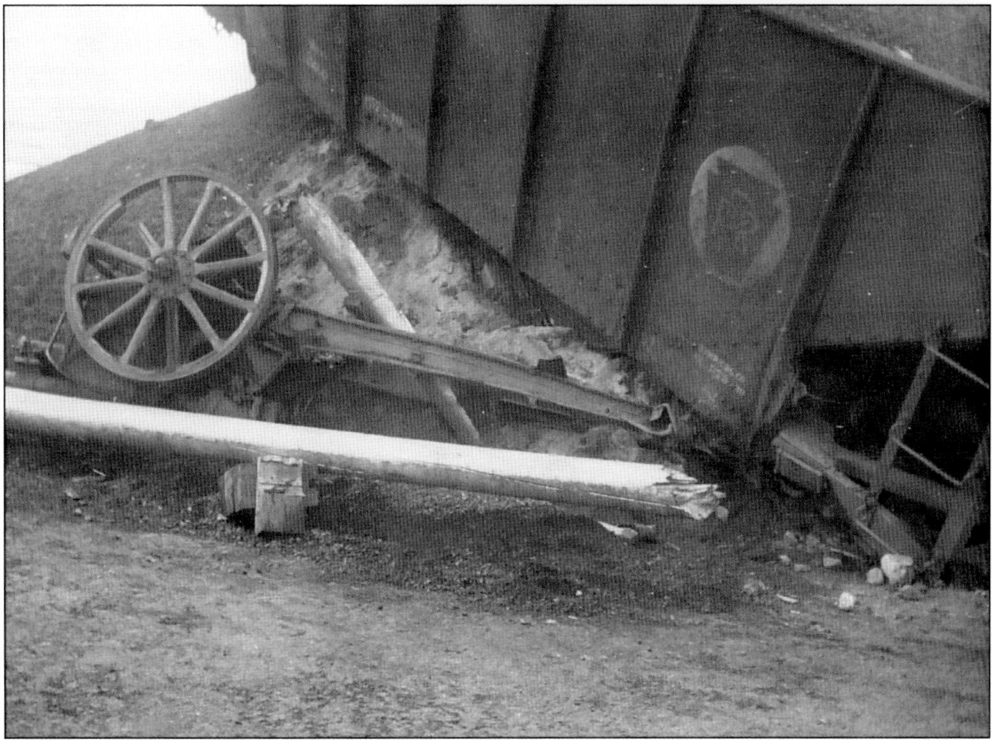

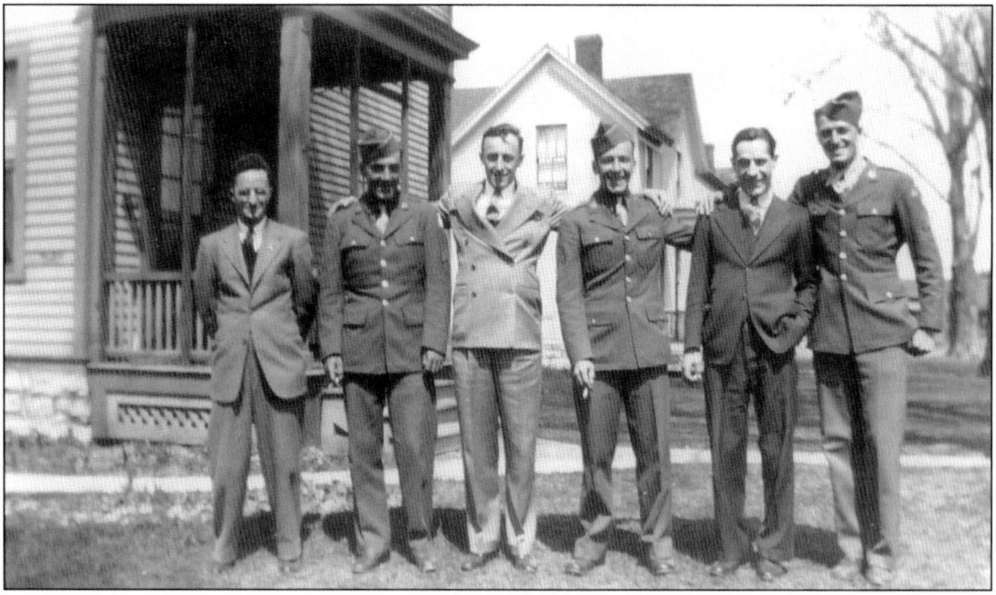

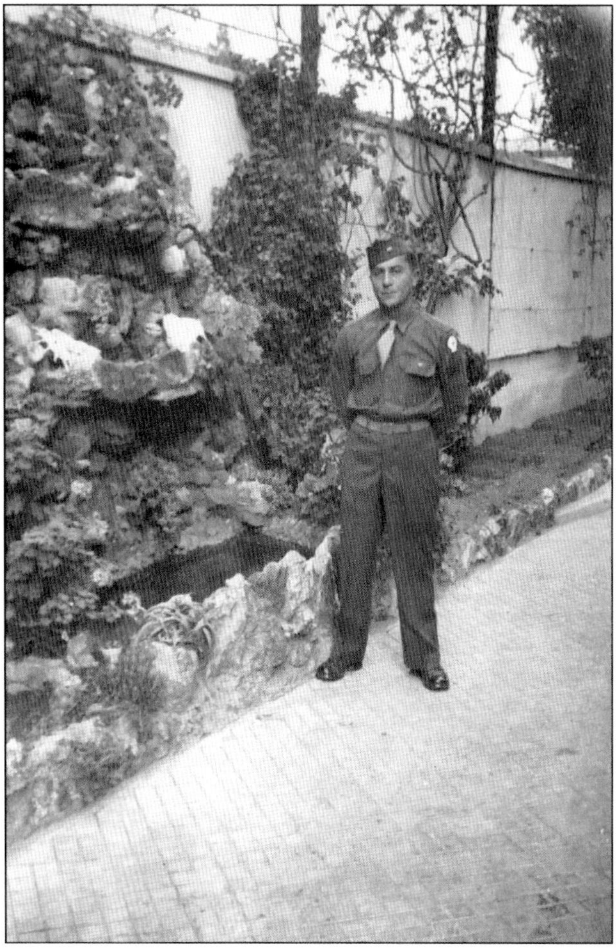

Pictured in 1941 are, from left to right, Paul Snyder, Carlton Hunter, Joseph Turpin, Edward Nabywaniec, Edward Turpin and Aloysius Nabewaniec. Even though the Nabywaniecs are brothers, their names are spelled differently due to mistakes on their birth certificates. (Dennis Turpin collection.)

Mario Pais, pictured in Italy during World War II, and Joe Piroli, stationed in Egypt, were interpreters during interrogations of Italian prisoners because they could speak Italian. For a small community, a large number of residents—six—graduated from service academies. Those who attended the US Naval Academy were Willard Backus, Paul J. Zando, Christopher Dingman, Ian Dingman, and Rene Martin. Lee Dingman graduated from the US Military Academy at West Point. (Marie Adams Pais collection.)

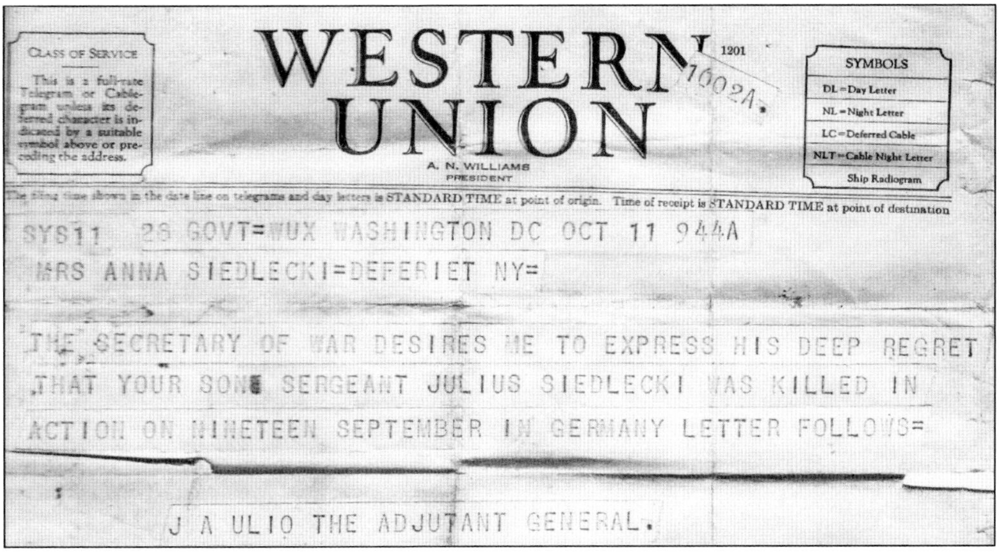
CLASS OF SERVICE

This is a full-rate Telegram or Cablegram unless its deferred character is indicated by a suitable symbol above or preceding the address.

WESTERN UNION

1201

1002A.

A. N. WILLIAMS
PRESIDENT

SYMBOLS

DL = Day Letter

NL = Night Letter

LC = Deferred Cable

NLT = Cable Night Letter

Ship Radiogram

The filing time shown in the date line on telegrams and day letters is STANDARD TIME at point of origin. Time of receipt is STANDARD TIME at point of destination

SYS11 26 GOVT=WUX WASHINGTON DC OCT 11 944A

MRS ANNA SIEDLECKI=DEFERIET NY=

THE SECRETARY OF WAR DESIRES ME TO EXPRESS HIS DEEP REGRET THAT YOUR SON SERGEANT JULIUS SIEDLECKI WAS KILLED IN ACTION ON NINETEEN SEPTEMBER IN GERMANY LETTER FOLLOWS=

J A ULIO THE ADJUTANT GENERAL.

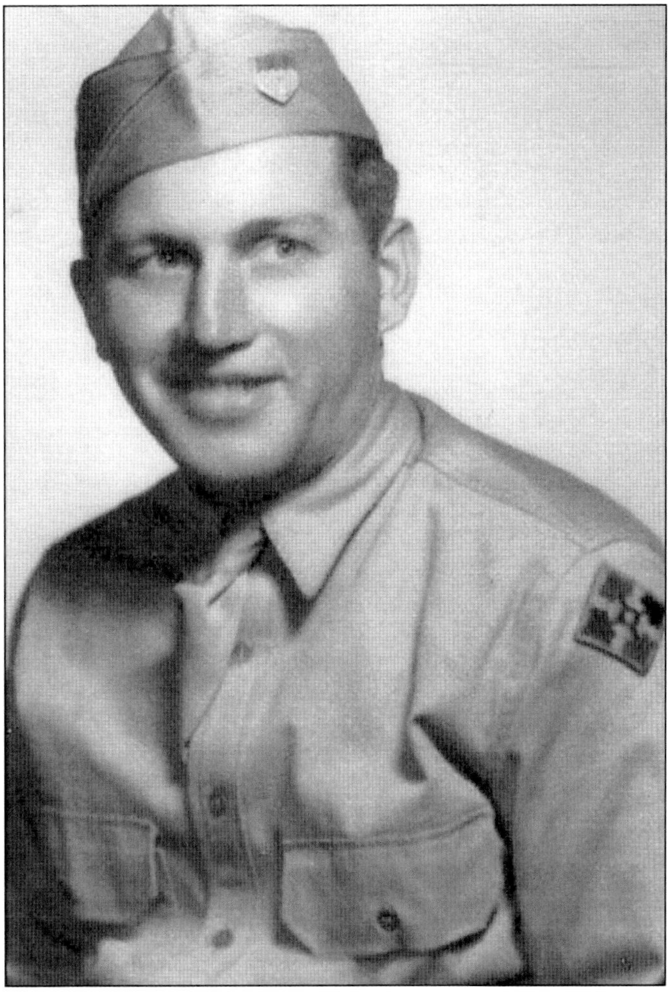

Julius Siedlecki (right) was chosen to represent all of the Deferiet military who have served the country from World War I to the present day. He lost his life in Germany and is buried, along with Vernon Stanford, at Henri-Chapelle American Cemetery in Belgium. During World War II, Deferiet sent an extremely high number—157 men and women out of approximately 850 people—to serve in the war. Above is the telegram Anna Siedlecki received from the War Department. Local Gold Star Servicemen include (World War I) Elias Getman, Lenard Ripton, and Thomas Wilton; (World War II) John Czoper, Carl Meyer, Maurice Petrie, John Powell, Kenneth Salzbrun, Joseph Schreck, Alexander Siedlecki (brother to Julius), Julius Siedlecki, Vernon Stanford, and Maurice Ward. (Richard Staab collection.)

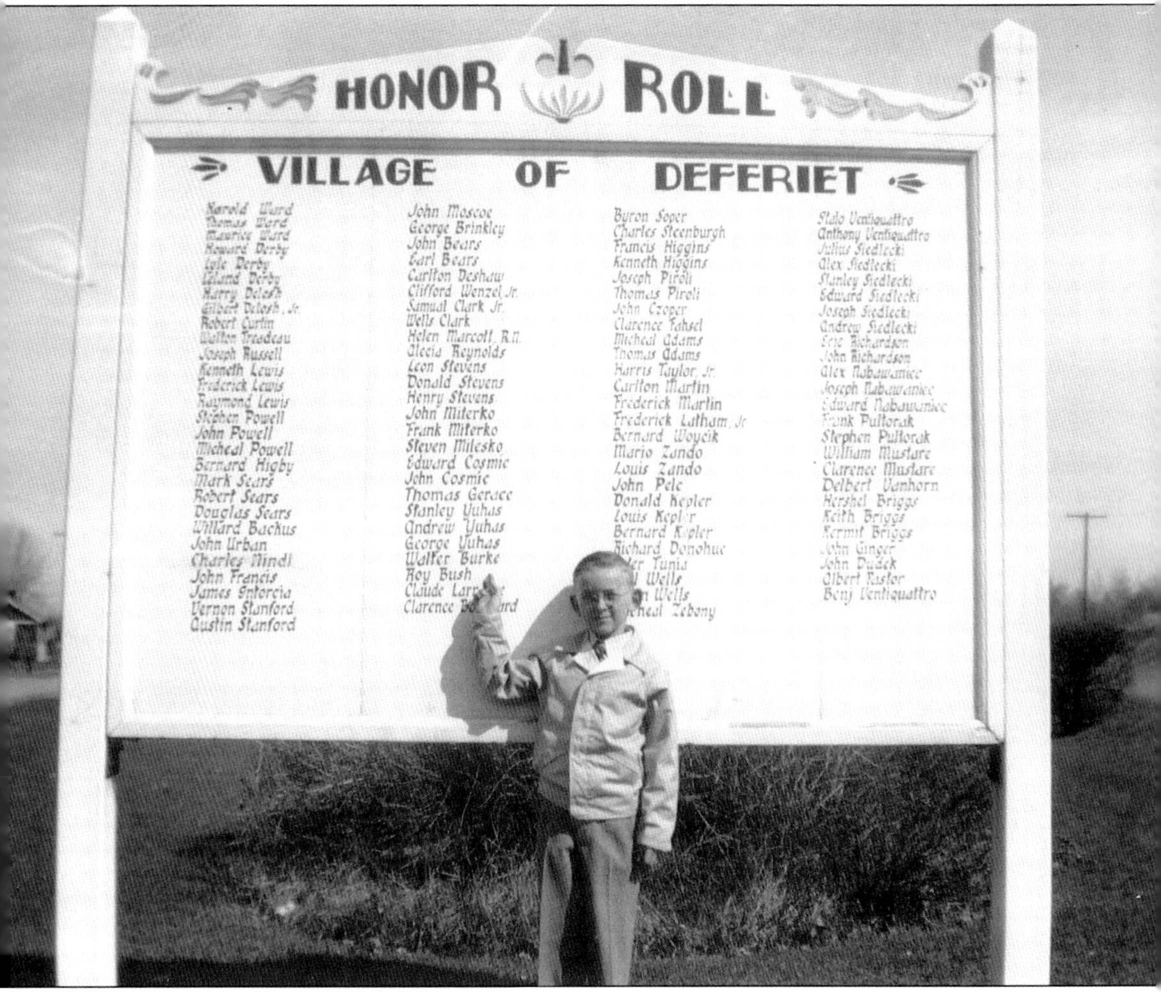

In this 1943 photograph Francis Burke points to his brother's name on the Village of Deferiet Honor Roll of servicemen, all of whom had already been called to duty during World War II. The board stood at the entrance of the village—like the cannon from World War I that preceded it and the yellow-ribbon garden that salutes present-day servicemen. Jenika de Feriet had a vision for a community to be built on the underdeveloped land. Sherman and Anderson had a vision for a prosperous industry. Immigrants who left their homelands and constructed the mill and settled here had a vision for a better life. The men whose names are seen on the honor roll had a vision to keep their nation free. A grateful village thanks all servicemen, from World War I to the 10th Mountain Division soldiers stationed at Fort Drum and living in Deferiet today. (Francis Burke collection.)

Four

Stone Houses
The Limestone Heritage

As Noadiah Hubbard followed the course of the Black River north in 1798, he could hardly be unaware of the limestone backbone of the land through which he traveled. He had become familiar with this hard stone when he supervised the building of canal locks in Little Falls, New York, and it would become his material of choice when constructing numerous houses, businesses, and public buildings in his new home, Champion. Several names of stonemasons have come down through the years, including Asa Eggleston, of Champion, and Wilson Pennock, who lived near Great Bend.

While the limestone in Champion came from several quarries toward Carthage, the majority of the stone in Great Bend was from the Woolworth Farm just outside of the village on County Route 47, near the site of the 2012 home of Stella Wells. One of the most impressive of the stone buildings in Great Bend itself is the Jefferson Hotel, originally a stop on the stage route that ran through the region. Several of the original buildings have disappeared over the years, but an amazing number still survive. Many were built as farmhouses, others as businesses, and a few as schools or churches. One reason so many have survived is the fact that they are largely fireproof and have resisted the ravages of time better than many wooden structures.

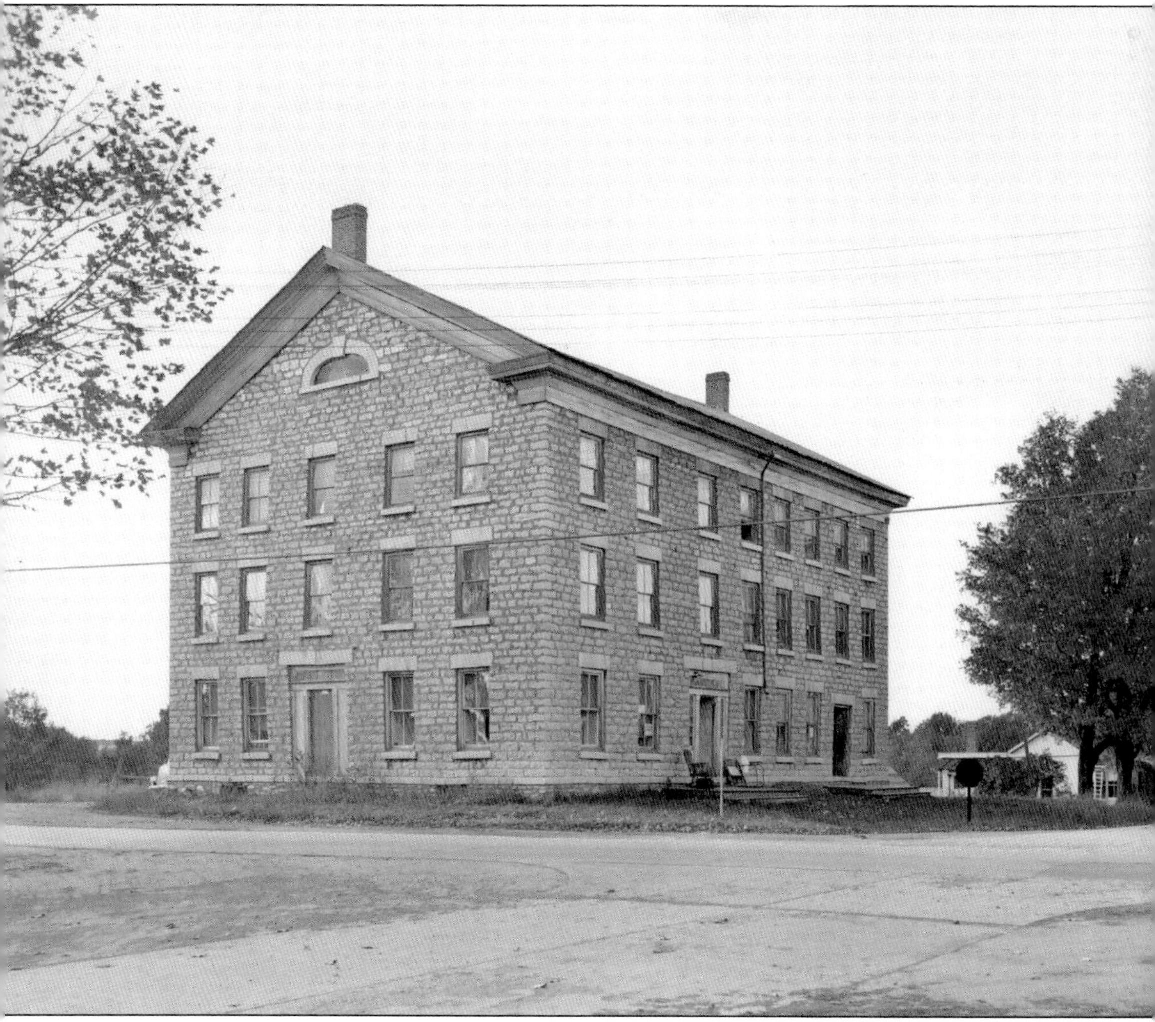

The Jefferson House in Great Bend is a former stagecoach tavern. The three-story Georgian Colonial structure was built in 1842 by Jewett Clarke, a contractor on the Black River Canal. It is substantially put together, and there are several interesting stories told about its construction and history. When the rafters were being set in place, they suddenly gave way, and three men precipitated into the cellar. Amazingly, none was seriously hurt. Also, several years later, a Mr. Clarke drowned in the nearby Black River. There are unsubstantiated tales of tunnels leading to caves along the Black River, and the idea that this may have been part of the Underground Railroad has circulated periodically. If the caves and tunnels do exist, it is more likely they were used for smuggling. Originally, the top floor was a ballroom with a fine spring floor that was the site of many popular balls both before and after the Civil War. For many years, the structure was used as a tenement house, and currently has a number of small apartments occupied by Fort Drum personnel.

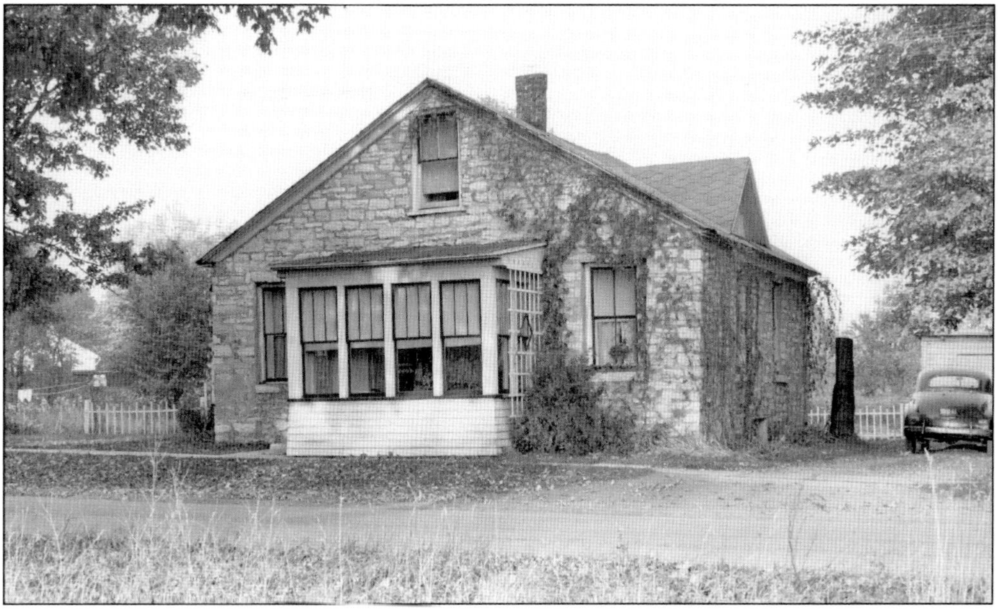

Great Bend District No. 9, built before 1860, was the school at which Frank W. Woolworth (of five-and-ten fame) and his brother Charles S. received their early educations. In 1874, a frame building was constructed across the street for the "new school," and the little schoolhouse was converted into a dwelling. Up until the present time, it has had a number of owners, and is currently occupied.

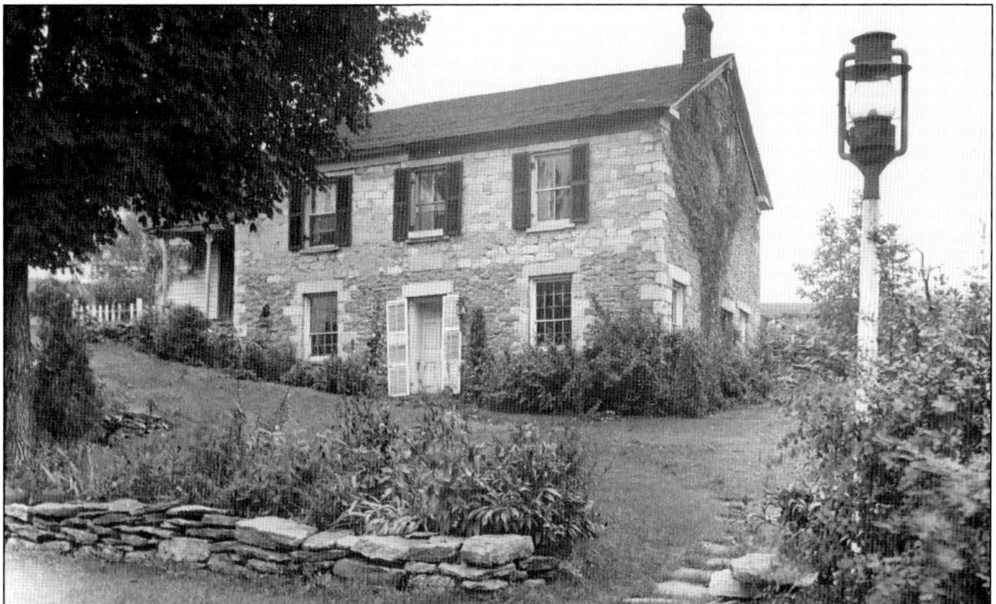

In February 1828, Asa Gates bought the land from Noadiah Hubbard and built this house for his bride, Mira. Engraved in the lintel over the front door is "A.G. 1828." The entry on the ground level leads to the original kitchen, which is complete with a cooking hearth, crane, and beehive oven. From the beginning, every deed of the property has transferred the right to use the freshwater spring.

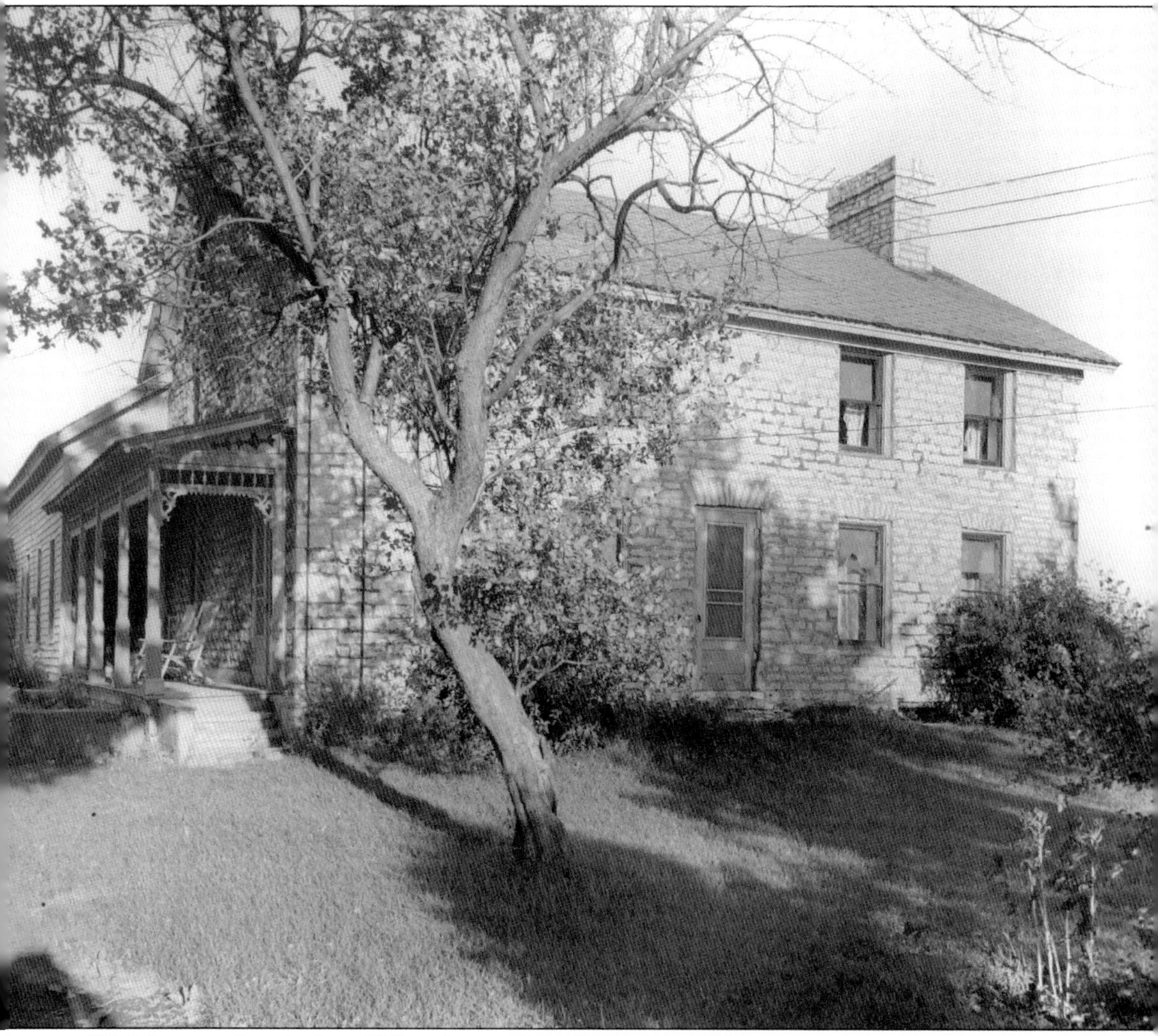

With his own hands, Rev. Wilson Pennock built the fine old limestone mansion that is located about a mile from Great Bend on the road that runs to Champion. The date of construction is said to have been around 1825. The property is next to the old Henry Peck farm, which also has a fine old native limestone house, currently owned by John Peck. This farm is owned and operated by John C. Peck and his wife, who moved into the home in 1970. As the house had been vacant for some 10 years, extensive renovations were done. Two rooms were combined to make the present living room with its limestone fireplace and hand-hewn beams. The kitchen underwent major renovations including new cabinetry, but the original cabinets are in an adjoining section of the house, where they are used for storage. The cellar shows the remarkable remains of the superstructure of the main fireplace and ash-pit and supports for the first and second floor fireplaces. Wooden additions to the house were done at two later dates; each section has a separate entrance.

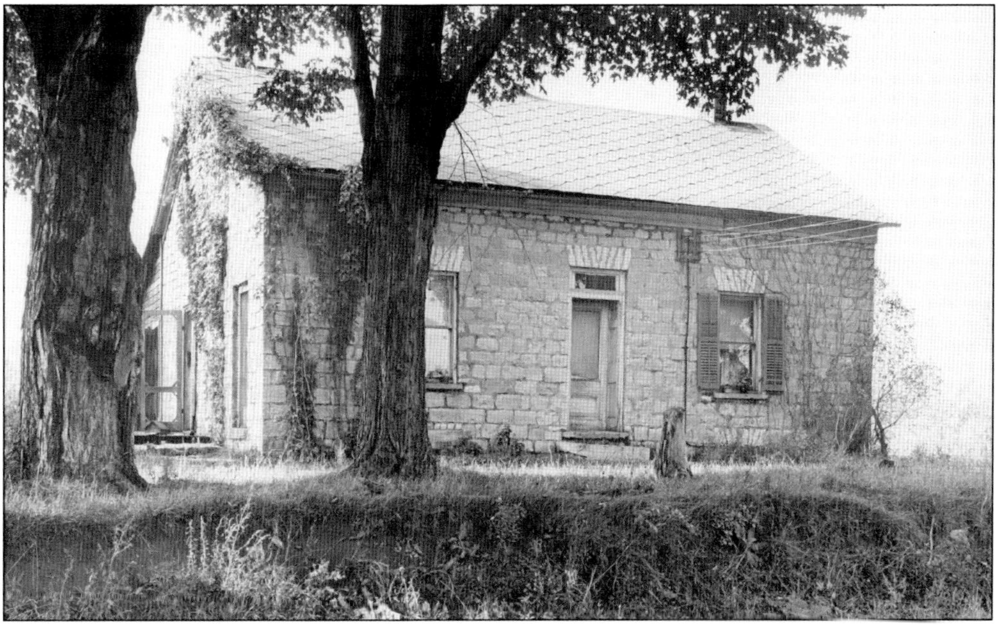

Osee Wilmot was among those who settled the town of Champion before 1812. Today, his little stone house can be seen on the north side of Route 126 between Champion village and West Carthage. At one time, it had a long wooden wing on the west end and a white picket fence. The house, built of native limestone, is at least 170 years old, but the records fail to tell whether Wilmot was the builder or whether he purchased the home from someone else.

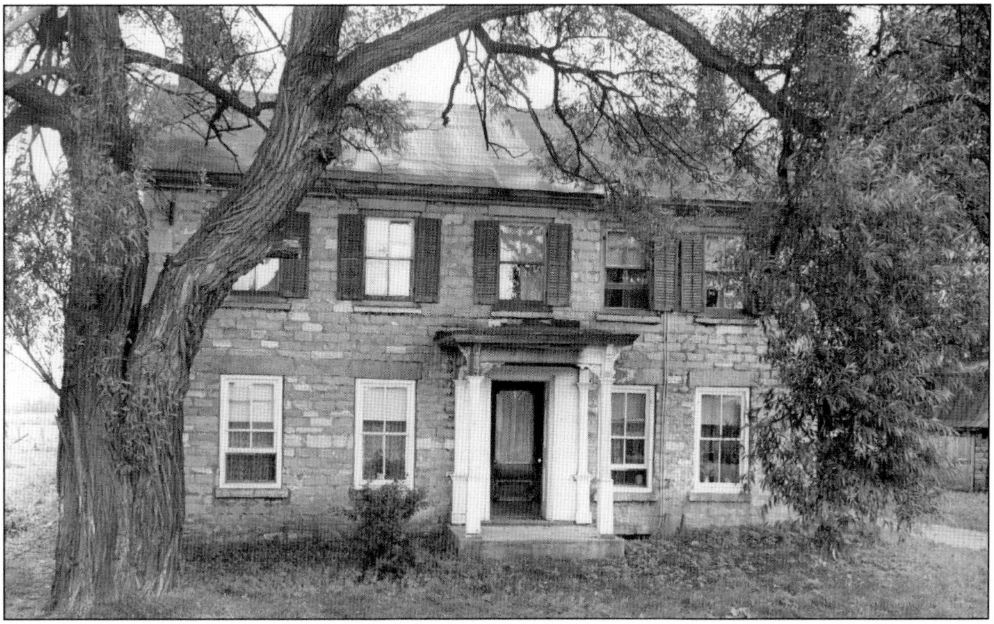

The Adam Bowhall (or Bohall) house, about five miles out on the Martin Street Road in the town of Champion, has a most picturesque setting. Although the front porch is a more recent addition, Adam Bowhall, one of Jefferson County's earliest settlers, arrived before 1815 and probably constructed the house out of native limestone. Records show he bought 147.25 acres of land there from Storrs and Champion on March 8, 1811.

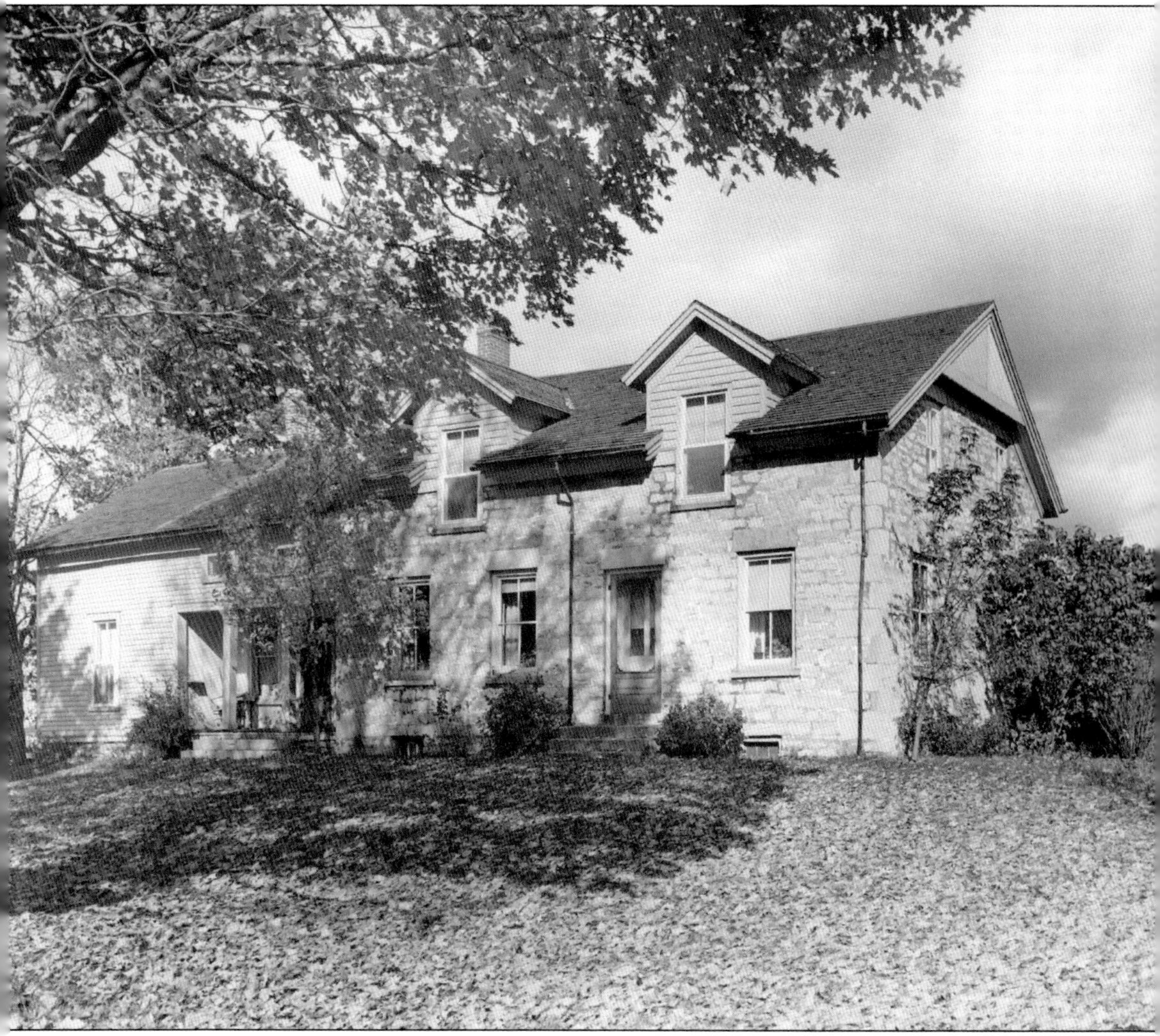

One of the earliest Jefferson County settlers was Joseph Peck, who was a native of New Haven, Connecticut. He was also a member of the governor's foot guards and a Revolutionary soldier with four years of service who fought at the battle of Lexington as an artillery officer. He settled in the town of Champion in 1803, and two years later relocated to a log cabin on the site of the stone house pictured here, which is a short distance from Great Bend on the Champion Road. This home, always owned by the Peck family, was erected about 1827 from stone quarried from a ledge on the nearby farm of the parents of Frank W. Woolworth, the chain store magnate. When it was thought there was enough stone, construction began, but the supply ran out when the walls were two feet above ground and more limestone had to be quarried. The dormers were added about 1920 and provided almost the only natural light on the second floor. A fireplace in the "bicentennial room" was built of limestone from the farm in 1976; the overmantle consists of hand-hewn beams from the old horse barn.

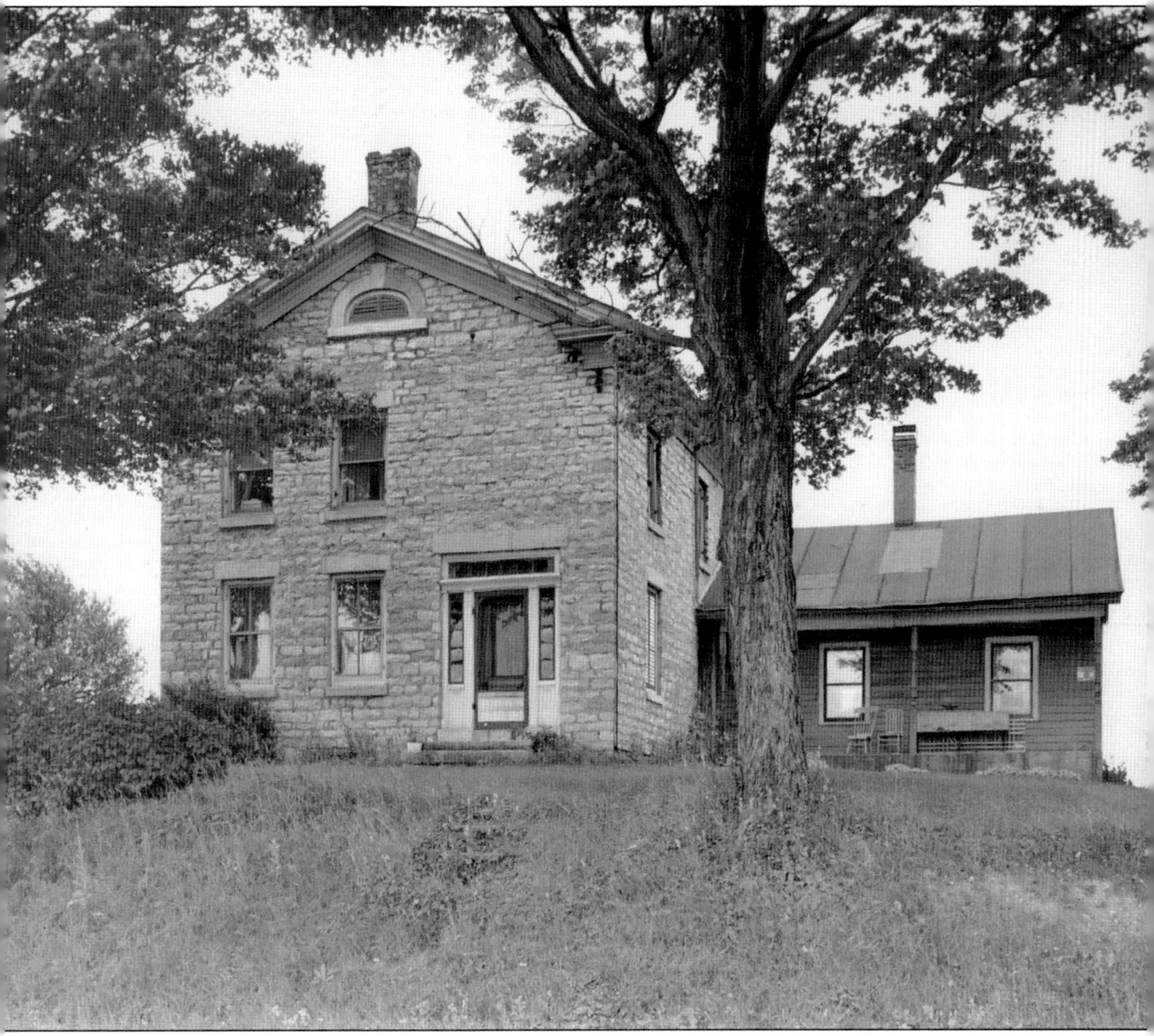

A stone set in the peak of the rear gable of the larger part of this house states that it was built in 1842. Tradition has it that the residence, situated not far from Great Bend on the west side of Martin Street Road, was built by William Griswold. In any case, it remained in Griswold hands long enough for the name to become synonymous with the home. A Greek Revival structure, it has its original transoms and front door. There is a cistern in the cellar along with the supports for the original fireplace. There are two wooden additions. The first was probably an enclosed summer kitchen. The hand-hewn beams with pegs, exposed stone from the original exterior wall, and the original stone threshold are visible today. The second addition is the current kitchen, with sawn beams spiked together.

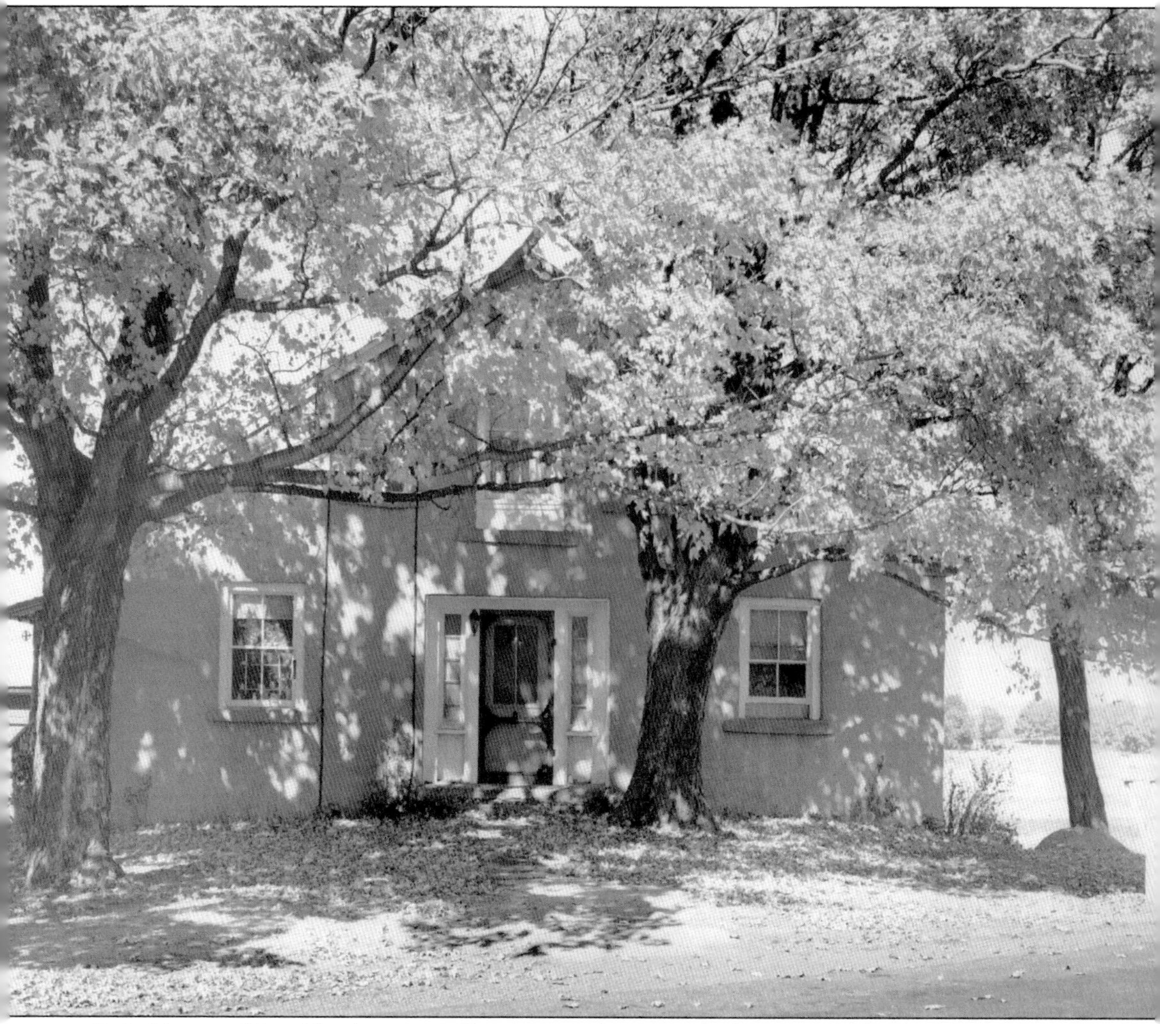

Probably one of the oldest houses in Champion is the quaint little cottage built of native limestone that was long owned and occupied by Roy C. Hubbard, great-grandson of Joel Hubbard, who was a brother of Capt. Noadiah Hubbard and one of the two first settlers of the county. It is on the left hand side of the road that leads to West Carthage at the junction of Route 26 and Line School Road. The house, which was given a coat of stucco in 1950, may have been erected earlier than the Hiram Hubbard house. The year of its construction is not known, but was likely around 1810. While the name of its first owner is difficult to trace from the county records, there is some internal evidence that this may have originally been a Noadiah distillery. It also has the rounded front steps found in many of Hubbard constructions.

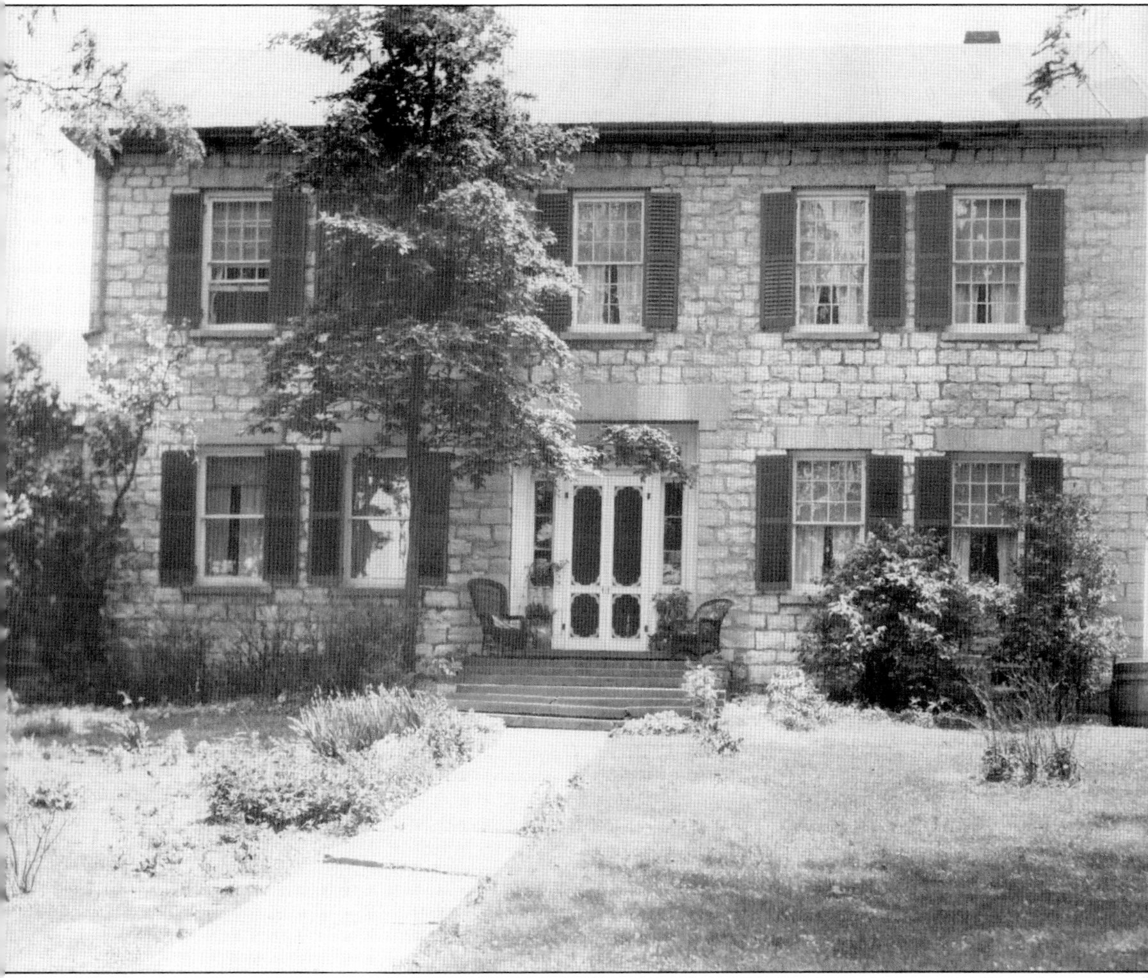

Built from 1831 to 1832 in Champion hamlet, this excellent old stone mansion was the third residence of Noadiah Hubbard. When Capt. Hubbard first established himself in the area, he occupied a log cabin. Later, he erected a frame house, which still stands and is in use a few hundred feet from the residence in this photograph. The current owners have lived here for about five years, and have thoroughly enjoyed this historic home. They have one functional fireplace in the dining room, but have relocated its twin to the present study. This one was not only closed up, but the area was also boxed in. The kitchen has the original exposed beams, a fireplace, which is currently occupied by a cast iron stove for increased efficiency, and the original beehive oven. The rear of the oven is visible in the attached garage.

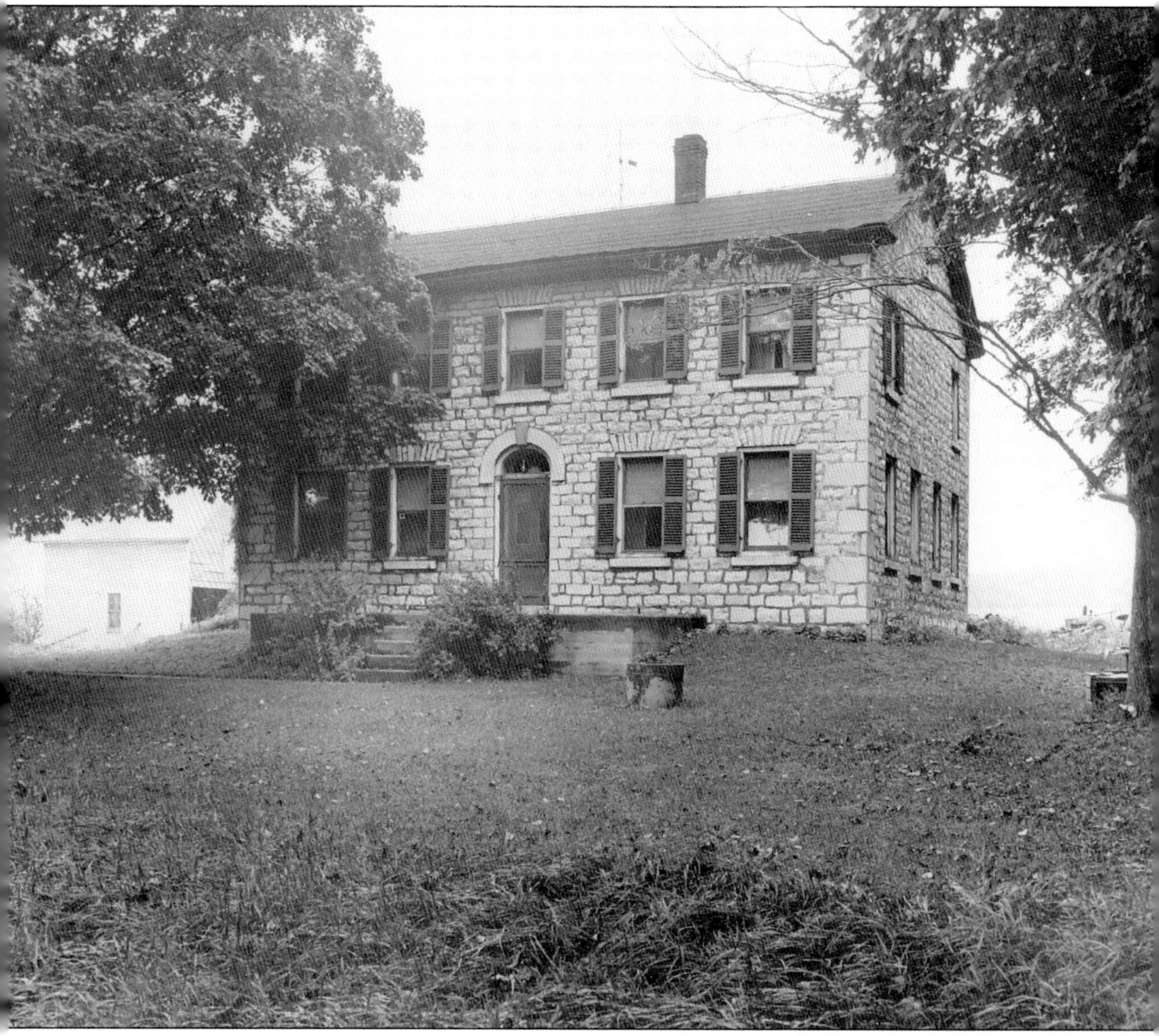

A beautiful Georgian house built of native limestone sits at the rear of a fine grove of large maple trees well back from the south side of the Watertown–West Carthage Road, a short distance from Champion village. A magnificent vista across the Black River Valley to Carthage is open to the occupants of this mansion. Apparently built for William Dorwin in 1823, the house and farm eventually came into the possession of William Pierce Freeman, a grandnephew of William Dorwin, and consequentially it became more commonly known as the Freeman place. There is a tradition that the mansion excited the envy of Noadiah Hubbard, Jefferson county's earliest settler, resulting in Hubbard building his mansion in Champion village in 1831 a mere two feet wider.

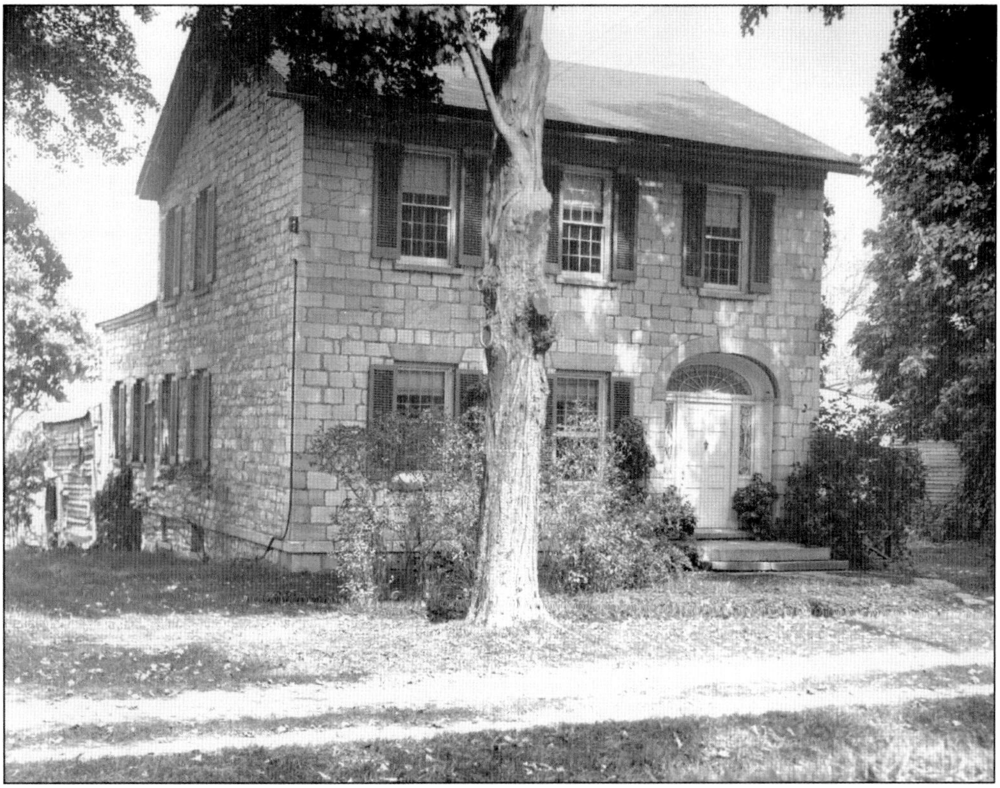

In 1820, Noadiah built this stone house across the road from his frame home. It is a stately Federal house constructed of local limestone. Local stonemason Asa Eggleston is mentioned as being in charge of many of Noadiah's stone buildings. Noadiah's daughter, Parnell, writes of her father's preference for stone construction. Local bluestone used for houses was quarried about three miles from Champion, on the way to Carthage. According to Parnell and others, her father constructed a cider mill, a potash factory, the meetinghouse, the distillery, the stone schoolhouse, and several homes and barns of stone. In 1833, this house went to Hiram, Noadiah's eldest son. Below, tea is taken in the front parlor with two Hubbard women, Francis Van Ripper and M. Hubbard Mott. This building is currently being rehabilitated by 4 River Valleys Historical Society.

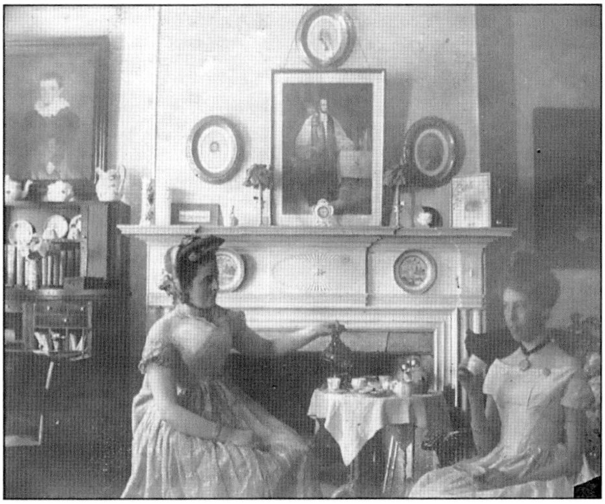

Discover Thousands of Local History Books Featuring Millions of Vintage Images

Arcadia Publishing, the leading local history publisher in the United States, is committed to making history accessible and meaningful through publishing books that celebrate and preserve the heritage of America's people and places.

Find more books like this at
www.arcadiapublishing.com

Search for your hometown history, your old stomping grounds, and even your favorite sports team.

Consistent with our mission to preserve history on a local level, this book was printed in South Carolina on American-made paper and manufactured entirely in the United States. Products carrying the accredited Forest Stewardship Council (FSC) label are printed on 100 percent FSC-certified paper.

MADE IN THE USA